Songs of the Lunatic

Songs of the Lunatic
An Invented Memoir

Ignacio Medrano-Carbó

ISBN: 978-1-78324-313-6

Cover photo: Sergio Carbó

This is a work of fiction. Unless otherwise indicated, all the names, characters, businesses, places, events and incidents in this book are either the product of the author's imagination or used in a fictitious manner. Any resemblance to actual persons, living or dead, or actual events is purely coincidental.

Whilst every effort has been made to ensure that the information contained within this book is correct at the time of going to press, the author and publisher can take no responsibility for the errors or omissions contained within.

Ye, who in some pretty little boat,
Eager to listen, have been following
Behind my ship, that singing sails along,

Turn back to look again upon your shores;
Do not put out to sea, lest peradventure
In losing me, you might yourselves be lost.

THE DIVINE COMEDY
Paradiso: Canto II

...dende el vientre de mi madre
vine a este mundo a cantar

Martin Fierro, Jose Hernandez

'We must die because we have known them' Die
of their smiles unsayable flower. Die
of their delicate hands. Die
of women.

Rilke

For Aleli Carbó
hasta a hoy, en tu eterna ausencia tus ricos campos me florecen

A Circumstance in Nineteen Ballads

The Age of Reason

In the spring of 1958, I was seven years old and living in Havana. According to the Roman Catholic Church, this is the point where, recognizing right from wrong, your soul is accountable for your actions, which could result in condemnation to the *Main Ovens* to endure sundry and unbearable torments for E-T-E-R-N-I-T-Y. In short, the age you can start sinning. The age of reason. I didn't want to let them down.

I was with Tere, another seven-year-old, in an ample room with shelves and shelves of toys. Incidentally, bringing this girl into my toy closet was not intended to reduce her solely to an object of *divertimento*, but simply a matter of privacy.

I already had discovered the orgasm, though not yet linked it to stroking my wiener, or much less to intercourse, which I had no idea existed or caused my existence.

Sometimes, while my mother prepared to bathe me, I'd spring a woody in anticipation. Naturally, it embarrassed me, so I would swing away, trying to hide it. When I began showering by myself, I once let the shower stream fall on my tiny hard-on, focusing on a very strong sensation, which ended in what I would call a *cosquillita* in Spanish, or a tickle-*ette*. A few months later, I found a *Playboy* magazine in one of the desk drawers of my grandfather's study. I immediately took it to the bathroom and, for some reason, lowered my pants to browse through it.

No, I didn't spank the monkey—as I mentioned before, I didn't know what that was—but somehow, instinct dictated that I lower my pants while studying this particular book. The same protocol was not followed the first time I opened my geography or arithmetic workbook, for instance. I remember those voluptuous American centerfolds, which were nearly half my size when unfolded, with their golden hair, immaculate skin, and ample breasts—the focal point in pre-pubic hair *Playboy*. And though they made an impression, I never became a *titman* or developed a blond preference. *Titman* sounded like a hermaphroditic superhero for the new millennia.

So, there I sat on the toilet in my grandfather's bathroom in our fine, custom-designed house a stone's throw from Villanueva University's baseball diamond, with a tiny zirconian hard-on, looking at the centerfold of *recia Americana* with not a clue of what to do with my peepee. But even less aware of the not too distant future—forever fleeing my home and country for hers with a vast number of my countrymen.

Teresita was the daughter of one of my mother's best friends. Her dad was *manco*; his left hand was missing. I was fascinated by how effortlessly he would tap the bottom of a cigarette pack with his stump, pop one to his lips, then upon returning the pack to his *guayabera* side pocket, produce and spark a Zippo on the way to the cigarette tip. Inhaling once to light it, he resumed the conversation on the smoky exhale, never looking down once nor missing a word. Entrancing wizardry, pure and simple.

"Eso es gangsterismo."

He told my father he disagreed with the Castro sympathizers who had allegedly kidnapped Fangio, the Argentine racecar driver, that year in Havana to make a political statement against Batista.

Tere and I would always stray from our families' chat and end up alone, mostly under my bed. There, I showed her where my index finger had been deformed by a savage scar.

2

"Y cómo te pasó eso?"

I told her how once, I boasted to my nanny's daughter that I could crush a light bulb in my hand, hoping she would ask me to stop before I hurt myself. Her daughter laughed after my many attempts at squeezing had failed. I then crushed it against the table. Her daughter screamed at the sight of blood. My nanny ran to the table and found me bleeding profusely with two severed tendons. After rushing me to a clinic, my dad restrained me on his lap and secured my hand against a tabletop as the doctor sewed me up without anesthesia and I wailed in agony. The doc ended up not being such a good tailor, so as a result, I would never again be able to bend the last phalange of my index. I showed Tere.

"Tu eres un lunatico."

I had no idea what that meant. "Lunatic?"

She told me how once, driving past a park off El Malecon near the dark blue sea of the Bay of Havana, a man with long silver hair and beard, dressed in a black suit, hat, and cape, had approached their car and given her aunt some flowers through the passenger window. Her aunt, a stunning woman with an ardent gaze, had offered him some money. He tried to refuse several times, improvising poems about how his having witnessed her beauty and generosity already was his eternal and immeasurable fortune. When, at the beauty's insistence, he finally accepted, Tere saw him bow and wave through the back window until her mother made a left turn two blocks up.

Her aunt had said, *"El pobre, es un lunatico total."*

When Tere asked about the word, her mother had explained it came from the word *Luna*, moon, which was said to affect even normal people, never mind the emotionally delicate.

So Tere had christened me that very day under my bed with the Latin word for the planet's one and only moon. *Luna*.

"I know who that man with the flowers is. *El Caballero de Paris*. I saw him from my car once."

I had actually been a bit frightened of the black-caped figure, although *El Caballero* was harmless. But I wasn't about to tell Tere I had been scared after she christened me with the same word her dazzling aunt

3

had used to denote that formidable vagrant. Hearsay claimed he was the son of a noble family who, after suffering a tragic romance, was reduced to mental frailty, indigence, and the impulse to give flowers and poems. "El Caballero," possibly the first flower child.

Tere and I would stay for hours under my bed, fascinated with each other's stories. I told her I liked her beaded Native American Indian belt and that I had beaded Indian moccasins, the same ones worn when I had slashed my index. Consequently, the left moccasin still had a drop of blood.

"Can I see it, Luna?"

We stepped in my toy closet. I reached for my moccasins, kept next to a plastic Tonto and Lone Ranger set that could be mounted and dismounted from their horses. When dismounted, however, Tonto and the Lone Ranger remained bowlegged and mostly lay on their face or back. A solid argument for that saying from the Golden Age of Cavalry: a man without a horse is not a man.

I gave Tere the bloodstained moccasin.

"*Te dolio mucho?*" (Did it hurt much?)

"No."

"*Dejame verlo?*" (Let me see it.)

I showed her my finger again. This time, she grazed the scar lightly with her finger while musing deeply with her honey-colored eyes, perhaps recreating my unharnessed pursuit of folly but not a bit intimidated by the little maniac himself. My heart pounded tiny craters into my chest. I was a little hesitant with the request I was about to utter but felt very natural with her.

"*Dejame ver el tuyo?*" (Let me see yours.)

She looked up, slightly altering her gentle gaze in bewilderment. She had no scar, no blood.

"*Cual?*" (Which?)

I pointed to her peepee. She didn't hesitate.

"*Enséñame el tuyo primero.*" (Show me yours first.)

I pulled my pants down. No hard-on now, buckaroos, way too nervous. She looked, glanced up at me, and smiled, satisfied with my side

4

of the bargain. She then dropped hers, revealing her little hairless plum. I reached with my finger; it was lightly moist. It held no erotic interest *per se;* it had been purely exploratory, although now, we had shared something which was understood to be frowned upon by adults. Now, we had a secret.

Above us, Tonto and the Lone Ranger stared straight ahead in what appeared to be silent condemnation. They wanted no part of this conspiracy. It wouldn't take eternal hellfire to reduce *them* to a puddle of inedible toffee. Teresita and I went on the swings in the backyard and swung into a sun shower. She sang a Cuban song, which up to then I had never heard, to Saint Isidore to make the rain go away.

"San Isidro el Labrador quita el Agua y pon el Sol…"

I countered with the absurdist, *"Tin-Marin-de-dos-Pingües-Cucara-Macara-Titere-fue,"* a vastly more colorful version of the American, "eenie meeny miney mo," without the racial overtones.

The rain did not subside. On the contrary, the squall came down with a vengeance.

"It's your fault, Luna. You probably made San Isidro mad with your *disparates.*"

Some of the raindrops hurt our eyes as we collided with them. We closed our lids and kept swinging and laughing and tasting the sweet rainwater until our parents came for us with umbrellas.

After Judgment Day, as I burn in Hell for my innumerable blasphemies, heresies, and sensual attachments, I'll close my eyes, and a Cuban afternoon rain will cool my face. And for a blessed second that will last forever, Teresita's breezy laughter will somewhat dull my demon's probing trident.

Training Wheels

I didn't like him. Yesterday, he had bullied some chocolate milk from a scrawny *mulatico* named Leo at recess time. But I can't justify my dislike for Yoyi solely on that move. From day one, he irked me, even had he been the Godchild and not a slob.

His food-stained shirt more times than not stuck out of the back of his pants, revealing a thick handle and the classic "plumber crack" any time he bent over. His family chauffeur and nanny would come to pick him up after school at a small fenced-in playground where we would all wait for our parents or chauffeurs. Since I had a chauffeur, too, I couldn't now in good conscience discredit him from the Bolshevik angle. And frankly, in retrospect, I mostly feel pity for him and disappointment at my narrow-sightedness.

At that playground, he would plant his sluggish gluteus on a ride resembling an oversized lazy Susan with handrails, freeloading while the rest of the kids pushed to spin the metal disc. Any requests that he help push were met with the silent treatment or a, "*No me da la gana.*" Because of his size, you either pushed if you wanted to ride or went to the swings instead.

When he didn't want to leave the playground—which due to his weight and stabbed-pig squeals made a power grab embarrassing and difficult for his chauffeur and nanny—they would go to a nearby *bodega* and recruit back-up: a quart of *Guarina* chocolate ice cream. When the nanny stuck the ice cream container out of the '58 Cadillac's back window, Yoyi jumped off whichever ride he was on, sometimes forgetting his books, and rushed into the car. Once captured, he was taken home to gorge on the frozen lactate.

I'd always had a problem with *niños bitongo*, Cuban for mommy's boys. When I was five, a doctor and his wife visited my parents and left their boy to play in our rather roomy backyard. Somehow, the world wouldn't have been big enough for this guy and me. We got into a scuffle, ending in a ripped ear and cutting the doctor's visit short. His wife looked at me like I was a mass murderer and hugged her screaming child, and though I kept saying, *"Fue sin querer,"* that I really didn't mean it—which was true—the mother kept repeating my *"fue **sin** querer"* with sarcastic inflections. Then, showing the small tear on the upper lobe to my mother, *"Mira lo que le ha echo a mi pobrecito,"* look what he's done to my poor little one. The party ended in an *auto da fe*—three or four lashes with a belt from my dad and sent to my room. Next time I saw the kid at Miramar Yacht Club, he sported two stitches, and his nanny quickly whisked him out of my line of sight.

As requested by our *pre-primaria* teacher, we all brought a box of crayons to class one morning. *Pre-primaria* was pre-school. We were given maps of Cuba and instructed to color the six provinces. Castro, who at that time was just setting up shop in the mountains with a small band of *rebeldes*, has since divided the island into a dozen or more provinces. A *Comandante's* day just never ends.

But at that time, there were only six, so with a box of eight crayons, you had enough for the provinces, the sea around the island, and even one left over, which I used to draw a hog snapper—an eccentric looking fish—riding a tricycle out of Havana Harbour toward Hemingway's beloved Gulfstream. Maybe a premonition of *el exilio* and the abortive invasion of a porcine namesake.

The fish on the tricycle was not as outlandish as it would first appear. One of the provinces in Cuba was named Santa Clara…Saint Claire, my maternal grandmother's name, and she had given me a tricycle just Christmas past. She had always provided me a hierarchy of wheeled vehicles until her sudden death in the back seat of a '59 Lincoln, when a piece of chrome metal framing the window detached from impact and perforated her neck.

Had I drawn the fish a year later, say the first grade, I would have drawn him riding a bicycle, minus the training wheels, to immortalize a dream that came to pass. I dreamt I could ride my bicycle minus the training wheels. The morning after, I told Mama Clara and asked if I could try it. She requested our chauffeur, KiKi, remove the training wheels, even though it meant I would be late for school. Grandma was one of the few adults who understood the magic of the moment in regard to kids. I got on the bike and rode it just like it had felt in the dream, like I had ridden it all my life without training wheels. Now *that* was drugs. I glided, perfectly balanced, endorphins marinating my pre-pubescent cortex.

At this point in time, however, I had only received the tricycle and was honoring Mama Clara by making it an integral part of my map of Cuba, when in walks our orbicular, ice-cream-slurping little regent, Yoyi, with an obscene set of at least fifty *Mirado* colored pencils in a clear plastic sheath under his arm. Naturally, it caught every child's eye in the room. Yoyi disappeared momentarily, and the coloring set trapped within his fat little fingers appeared to glide slowly across the room like an exotic bird. There were enough greens to color every variation of plant life, including mosses and algae, in every rainforest since the beginning of time. The same went for every other color. It was God's own coloring set. And even if it had only been fifty No.2 graphite pencils, fifty of *anything* was a big number for a six-year-old to own.

He sat in his desk, produced a double-holed red plastic sharpener, and was intent on sharpening every pencil. Yoyi was halfway through his oranges, with his desk looking like the aftermath of a ticker tape parade, when the teacher instructed him to sharpen only "those that you are going to use."

I was working on my tricycle wheels, but my crayons were too blunt to define the spokes. So, I asked Yoyi if I could borrow his pencil sharpener.

"No, *Mono ve, Mono hace*." (Monkey see, monkey do)

Just wait until recess time, I thought. But an ally was needed. I knew I was no match for his corpulence. Or maybe I'd do a suicide mission, whatever it took. To grin and bear it was not an option. It was only the first week of school, so I hadn't made any friends yet. But there was that kid, Leo, the one whose chocolate milk Yoyi had seized only a few days ago. He wore horn rims with greasy lenses and had a case of halitosis that could lift the varnish off a desktop in one viscous sheet.

Sometimes, help is not packaged just how we would like.

I told him what went down and asked if he would back me up in case Yoyi got the best of me, as in suffocating below him on the ground. In that case, Leo could box his ears or something. You know, run interference.

"*Okay, vamo 'a-dah'le al Gohdo.*" (Let's smack fatboy.)

My hunch was right. Leo was game for the caper. The plan: At recess, I would approach Yoyi and un-ceremonially throw a punch at him. Leo would stand-by. Simple strategy.

I approached Yoyi. He was sipping from a chocolate milk carton provided for us by the school. Confronting his manatee-like physique with Leo right behind, I released a straight left into his flaccid belly. The chocolate milk he was drinking spilled on my forearm. My fist found no bottom to his paunch. Instead, it sunk up to what felt like my elbow, giving the uneasy sensation I was probing a towering pancreas crowned with a kid's head. My arm was disgorged into the sunlight again. I didn't follow up.

Yoyi just as un-ceremonially delivered a leviathan blow to the side of my head, dropping me to the ground on my back. When I looked behind me for Leo, I saw the back of his wiry frame in full-throttle retreat, clearing the top of a four-foot grassy knoll. I was dizzy and in no hurry to rush the little tank for some more of the same, so I sat up, rubbing my head.

Yoyi bent down, picked up my milk I had dropped on my way down, and shared his observation, "*Tu das como una niña*." He chugged what was left of his milk and walked away, drinking mine.

I stood up but did not pursue it. Generally, you just didn't rush a tank single-handedly. Although, there would be exceptions I would see in my lifetime, like 1968 Czechoslovakia where men attacked the advance of Russian tanks with Molotov cocktails, or Tiananmen Square in China, immortalized by that famous photograph of a lone chinese, arms to his sides, preventing the progress of a Red Army tank convoy. But these heroic deeds had not occurred yet, and even if I had been exposed to them, the throbbing lump where Yoyi's fat fist had collided with my head discouraged any notion of heroic missions, even if he *had* told me, "You hit like a girl."

Back in class, still fuming about my head bump, I sharpened my crayons by rubbing them against a piece of scratch paper. I knew this from before, but it wasted a lot of time. I kept looking at Yoyi with homicidal intent. He just glanced once out of the corner of his eye with gorged-snake satisfaction.

My adrenalin rose, but the teacher was working her way up my row, checking on the students' progress. I was coloring the province called Matanzas in red. Matanzas means *slaughter*. No doubt named after some Native versus European skirmish. I didn't connect the name then, but always found it curious that I had chosen red for its color. Somehow, before the teacher got to me, like in some suspense thriller where the director creates the perfect and unexplainable scenario for the *muhddah*, she upped and left the class. Yes!

There were no second thoughts. If you thought too much about these things, you wouldn't do them. Stepping to Yoyi's desk, I grabbed most of his pencils and threw them on the wooden floor toward the front of the class. Most of the class in the periphery stopped working, looked in the direction of the rattling pencils, then toward us, the source of the chaos. Yoyi did not retaliate as I stood over him with my best lunatic grimace. Instead, he got up, walked to the front of the class, and began picking up his pencils.

When he bent over, a bulbous chunk of flesh spilled over the waist of his pants above the pocket. Acting purely on instinct, I ran to him, leaped, and clamped hard unto this errant chunk with my teeth. Yoyi

11

bellowed and tried to shake me, but I held on like a deranged carnivore. He swung violently left and right, trying to enlist centrifugal force, whipping me like a gator tail. But if anything was coming off, it was a piece of Yoyi, and judging from his wailing, one would think it already had.

"*Niño suéltalo inmediatamente, niño, pero niiiiño…!*"

The teacher dug into my cheeks and teeth using her thumb and middle finger with enough pressure to make me release. I was short of breath, and so was Yoyi. It was over. He was taken to the infirmary for hydrogen peroxide to rinse the bite, which had barely broken the skin. They applied a serving of mercuro-chrome, an antiseptic and coagulant Cubans were very fond of ladling. Naturally, the blood-red antiseptic now made the wound look like the exit hole of an anti-aircraft round. The teacher made me pick up all the pencils and put them on Yoyi's desk.

"*Y ahora como usted es un perrito, póngase en sus cuatro paticas allá atrás.*"

I was sent to the back of the class to stand on my fours "like a doggie" for the duration of the thirty-minute period. After five minutes of this, my kneecaps began to burn. A girl in the last seat of the row closest to me stared randomly, taking a break from coloring her map to study the sociopath. I smiled every time. Yoyi also looked back for any signs of pain, discomfort, or repentance. I smiled again, for different reasons, never once betraying the discomfort in my kneecaps. I was learning early in life, you can't show your ass in this doggie-eat-doggie world.

Between a Tree and a Chain link Fence

"He pissed on the Colonel's ducks," was the orderly's answer to my second-grade teacher when he saw me through the window of the lobby office, standing at attention, with a torn epaulet and a Garand rifle on my other shoulder. Incidentally, the Colonel was the owner of the academy.

"Cadet Yena, *por qué?*"

I was prepared to hold the rifle until the next world if necessary, but I was not going to invite the teacher's ridicule by answering.

"Did a duck eat his tongue?"

When I didn't answer, he laughed, shook his head, and walked away. My eight-year-old shoulder was beginning to burn.

Meanwhile, in the "real" world...

Fidel Castro was still in the mountains, basking in the eulogies of the *New York Times*. Batista, *el dictador del momento*, was feeling the brunt of the opposition, aggravated by a U.S. arms embargo. Uncle Sam was hedging his bets. A civil war was apparently in place, and its bullet-ridden carnage was exposed nearly every dawn. My granddad, a newspaperman, was making enemies on both sides, condemning the gun and bomb-happy tactics of anti-Batista *26 of July* splinter groups and denouncing the brutal measures Batista used to repress any opposition.

Me? I had simply been an eight-year-old boy looking for a place to pee.

During basketball lay-ups in gym class, an eleven-year-old known bully, one guy behind me in line, coughed *un gargajo* onto the back of my T-shirt.

"That's disgusting! *Mojón* (turd) go shower!" he said and laughed with his toadies about the chunk of phlegm he had flung.

I said nothing and did nothing, though it hung on my back, a still warm and dense humiliation. But this guy also towered over me. My turn came. I took my three steps and missed the hoop. The whistle blew. Gym class was over. Bully Boy never got his turn. Maybe it was my payback for that Fat Boy I had once bitten a few years back in kindergarten?

I walked away, taking my time, not looking back at Bully Boy nor the group who had snickered. I regretted not saying anything to him. I thought maybe part of the reason was that summer vacation began this weekend, and our family was going to our beach house in Varadero. I didn't want to be punished for starting something and risk being left behind the first week of vacation—possibly nursing a shiner or a missing tooth.

When I changed back into my uniform in the locker room, I thought about what a bastard this guy was. I felt humiliated, frustrated. If I was honest, I really wasn't thinking about vacation or our beach house when I had remained silent on the basketball court. I had been scared of him, that simple, and it embarrassed me. I looked at the phlegm chunk on my gym T-shirt, which I had placed on the bench on top of my sneakers. What a bastard.

I grabbed it, and as I turned the corner to go wash the hawker off in the sink, there was Bully Boy at the urinal, all by himself with his back to me. I must have been sitting on that bench for a while, stewing and licking my wounds, because there were no other kids around, and he had already changed into his uniform, shirt starched and perfectly tucked in. A fastidious bully.

For an instant, I no longer cared about summer vacation or being beat into an omelet. Fear was not present. It had less to do with courage than the fact the whole universe suddenly had one focal point in that white-tiled windowless cavern. There simply was no room for the slightest deviation of purpose. My intentions fluidly previewed before my eyes like a dream. I followed without reflection. A kid's version of *a good day to die.*

I rolled the T-shirt up in a ball, phlegm-side toward him. Leaping with what seemed like slow weightless grace, I rammed the *gargajo* into the back of his neck with a force I did not intend, making Bully Boy's forehead bounce off the wall, and since he was still holding his wiener in one hand, he slipped and fell. Landing "cat-perfect," considering I was now wearing leather-soled shoes as he was, I turned and bolted toward the exit door.

"*Te mato cabroncito!*"

He hustled behind me somewhere, catching up. Swooping around a locker, just short of spinning out with these useless spit-shined shoes, I stopped dead, grabbed the side of the wooden bench I had just been sitting on, and pushed it behind me with all my life. My sneakers went flying. As he came steaming around the blind bend, I went through the exit door. *Bulls eye!* He must have caught it in the shins because I heard him hit the floor, entangled and moaning.

"*Coño e tu madre!*" (Your mother's twat!) he offered.

I kept running to the end of what was an endless green sports field and hid behind a tree. My breath trembled. I turned, but he was still inside.

I caught my breath, hanging onto the chain link fence behind the tree. Now that I was safe, regret began to gnaw, a disabling and treacherous turncoat. The minute you stopped to think, and always at the eleventh hour, *snap!* You're in its gator jaw. I peeked around the tree, but still no sight of him in the distance.

I'm going to be late for my next class, I thought, *and probably get smacked around after school...I should have just let it go...* No! He was

15

*un abusador…*And besides, I knew deep inside, where it counted, I was glad about it. Proud of it. Yes, proud of it. Second thoughts were always the slurpers of confidence.

My bladder burned. There were some older kids going into the locker room from the courtyard, but no sign of the bully. I would never know his name, but I was sure he wasn't going to forget it. Probably wait for me outside after school.

So what if I'd have to make a run for my car after class? Once inside, our chauffeur, Kiki, wouldn't let that *maricón* touch me. But I didn't like that either. I didn't know what made me feel worse—a beating or the running in front of everybody to have the chauffer defend me. Now I wished I had killed him.

Jesus, I have to pee! I positioned myself between the tree and the fence. As I pissed through the chain link, a group of ducks approached on the other side. Hey, if you got your whole duck world to roam on the other side of the fence but insist on waddling right under where I'm whizzing, then my brother, you're going to get whizzed on. They walked right up, and I peed on their heads. One tried to snap at my pre-pubescent little spout, but I backed off, and it hit its beak on the wire. Then, I forced my bladder harder, extending my magic golden stream, and was able to nail a Muscovy duck on its scrofulous cheeks as it charged from the rear and also banged to a stop at the fence.

"*Chiquillo! Que usted hace?*"

A bald, portly old man, apparently the duck custodian, came out of the back door of the house a few yards from where the ducks were getting hosed. He rushed the fence too. I held my piss and moved around the big tree where he couldn't see me. I just wasn't meant to piss that day. I could hear him lean up against the chain link fence while his ducks quacked and waddled.

"*Desgraciao', pero como tu te atreves?*" (Damn you, how *dare* you?)

I wasn't going to come around so he could identify me, but I was now visible from the locker room exit in the distance, and Bully Boy could spot me. I lay low on the ground.

"Come out from behind the tree, *mariconcito.*"

16

I was getting tired of the name calling and having to hold my piss. So, diplomacy was over. I whispered my answer from the prone position on the other side of the tree.

"Go to hell!"

"*Vete pal Carajo? Ahora tu vas a ver!*" ("Go to hell? You'll see!")

He charged back to the house just in time for me to roll to the other side of the tree and out of view of the bully, who was exiting the locker room, scanning the four winds.

Back in my original position between the chain link fence and tree, I waited, peeked around the tree, and saw him walking toward the classrooms. I had to go to the last class, or they'd call home and report me missing. Nothing to be done. The only strategy, other than bashing Bully Boy in the head with a brick, was to wait until he was back in his class.

In the courtyard, the Cuban flag billowed majestically against a seamless, powdered sky of creamy trade-wind clouds *a la* Winslow Homer. It made me think of big whiskered men riding spirited steeds under just such a sky near the end of the nineteenth century. My bladder stung me again, so I began to pee against the tree, on guard for the old man. Neither he nor the ducks were anywhere around. I worried about him coming back with a stick or something, so I glanced up regularly toward his back door as I peed. "Now you'll see…" usually meant follow-up.

The yellow stream flowed down the mango tree, darkening the bark. I could hear the din of the metal hooks and grommets striking the flagpole in the distance. The clanking metal had rhythm, as if the breeze carried the clanging of the machetes swung by *Mambi* horsemen against Spanish necks and guns long ago, when this big, mowed yard was perhaps a lush killing field where freedom fighters and colonial interests clashed. Their moustaches—I would always remember their magnificent moustaches, if not the circumstances. I peered around to look at the flag.

"*Míralo Ahí!*" (There he is!)

Two ninth-grade orderlies were running mid-field at me, their swords striking the metal rings at their belts.

"*Coño…*"

I tried to climb the tree, but the very first branch was rotten, and I fell on my rear.

One of the orderlies circled my right, blocking my only escape route. Both flanks covered now and a chain link fence at my back. I grabbed a pee-soaked rock at my feet and flung it at the guy who had circled, the heavier and slower one of the two. It bounced off the patent leather brim of his dress cap.

"*Cuidao que tira piedra!*"

Warning his buddy, he took off his hat to shield against further projectiles.

I grabbed one more rock and climbed the fence. The nimbler orderly gripped my left foot. I tried to throw the rock, but as he gripped my fist fast with his other hand, the rock fell. The heavier one came around, and they pulled me down, ripping the button off one of my epaulets. Each grabbed me by one arm. With me giving no fight, we started down the field toward the main building, each at one of my wrists.

The one I threw the rock at addressed me. "*Te gusta tirar piedresitas no?*" (So, you like throwing rocks?)

He delivered *un yiti* (yee-tee), Cuban slang for a short slap to the back of the head.

"*No le des al Mojón!*"

The more muscular orderly told Pudgie not to hit me.

"'*El Mojón,' Por poco me da en la cabeza con una piedra meá!*"

He claimed he was entitled, since I "almost winged" him "in the head with a piss-soaked rock." I said nothing. Twin pairs of black shoes flanked me, spit-shined guard dogs on the lush cut grass. The chrome scabbards rocking inside their belt rings kept a tin-like cadence as they walked.

The trim one questioned me. "Why did you pee on the Colonel's ducks?"

"*Yo no sabía que eran los patos del Coronel!*"

They laughed. Pudge kept imitating the face I had just made, exaggerating my arched eyebrows and repeating my comment as he caught his breath.

"I didn't…know…they were the…Colonel's du-hu-huucks!"

It wasn't *that* funny. And conscience was back, nagging like an asthma attack. *"You can probably forget the beach house this week, y deja que el viejo se entere. Don't worry, Papi probably won't have a place to hit you after the ass-beating Bully Boy is gonna deal you after school."*

As we passed the last classroom and turned the corner toward the main office, the bell announced the end of the school year. Cadets stampeded in the hallways with blissful cheer as fast as schoolie adrenalin could propel them.

"Vacacioooones!"

In contrast, I was firmly attached to my escorts, briefly saddened not to share the collective joy which normally would have been mine too. But some kind of kid intuition granted my second wind.

Most likely, a dusting by my dad was in the cards, to which I wasn't looking forward. In fact, I usually pissed in my pants during a belt whipping. At least I wouldn't have to look for a place to do it. But if Bully Boy got me, I would most likely be traveling the sympathy route with Mami, taken to the beach house anyway, and once there, hopefully get nursed by my cousin Ana, the one with the seashore eyes on whom I now concentrated for strength.

"Así que este es el notorio mea patos!" (So, this is the notorious "duck pisser.")

Inside the office, the Lieutenant sat smug at his desk, sizing me up after addressing the orderlies. I said nothing.

"Y el tira Piedra," ("And the rock shucker") added Pudge, the chunky orderly.

"No me digas?" after the elongated, *"you don't saaay,"* the lieutenant paused, assessing my demeanor.

"Bueno pero, why would you piss on the Colonel's ducks?

I said nothing.

"I am as-king you a qu-e-sti-on, ca-det!" He enunciated every syllable for effect.

I didn't answer, and I wasn't going to answer.

"Okay, if that's the way you want it. *Póngale un rifle en el hombro, que se va a cuadrar ahí hasta que decida contestarm."*

Following the lieutenant's orders, Slim grabbed the rifle, which was bigger than I was, and placed it on my shoulder. I was to stand at attention until I decided to answer him. Pudge had to say something.

."Cadet Yena said he didn't know th-they were the Colonel's duck's, sir."

He giggled.

"Did I ask you?"

"No, sir."

"Very well then. Write yourself five demerits and put it on my desk here. *Ahora*, you're not leaving until four o'clock either…Go outside, find his chauffeur, and tell him to return for Yena at four."

"Yes, sir."

The heavy WWII Garand dug into my tender shoulder, making it throb. Ana's eyes, deep where no one but I could see them, were proud of me. Not to mention that, for the instant that Pudge got his come-uppance, I could have sworn the rifle lightened a couple of pounds. Thirty minutes later, the lieutenant let me rest and wait for my ride, sitting on a wooden bench opposite his desk. Behind him hung a portrait of President Fulgencio Batista, who in the next few months would be unpleasantly surprised and flee the island for his life.

On my end, surprises were also in the works. Surprise number one: when Kiki, our chauffeur, came to get me, the lieutenant had gone to take a call from his wife, leaving word with his secretary that as soon as they came for me, I was free to go.

The whole way to the car, I looked about anxiously, taking no more than two or three steps before looking behind me.

"*Lunín, que te pasa?*"

I told Kiki I'd tell him in the car, to just keep his eyes open for some kid rushing us.

"*Pero si aquí no hay nadie.*"

And he was right. When I looked around, surprise number two: the school *was* deserted! The extra half hour I had done with the rifle had proved redeeming.

I was deserted!

Surprise number three, and best one yet: in the car, I told Kiki what happened. He laughed and said it would remain *"entre nosotros!"*

After Castro's takeover, a classmate from military school told me a great story years later in Miami when I ran into him at his birthday party. In a voice steeped in campfire allure, he recounted the Colonel, who it turned out had been a cruel and corrupt officer in the Batista regime, could not get on one of few planes out. So, he escaped through a trap door leading to a narrow compartment beneath his living room floor.

When the mobs vandalized his home, they inadvertently overturned a massive solid mahogany armoire directly over the trap door, through which the ill-fated Colonel had intended to come out of hiding after the mob departed. Two weeks later, when a group of kids broke into the house, their dog began to sniff and bark at the edge of the armoire. Unable to lift it, they told their parents. The Colonel was found in a puddle of fetid water next to a dripping copper pipe, which he had punctured with a small nail for drinking. The half-dozen rat carcasses he had fed on in the darkness surrounded him.

*Mentally broken—some said by the spirits of the people he had tortured and killed—he was taken away, drooling and mumbling incoherently in a faltering voice, "No me méen los patos! Que no me méen los Patos!" (Don't let them piss on my **ducks!**)*

Mojonus Rex

The acrid smell of the *Partagas* and the violent cough that followed overtook the scent of bait in my hands, momentarily blurring the Cuban seascape raging turquoise and ultramarine blue in the midday light. My cousin's laughter still managed to invade one of my three remaining senses. It was my first cigarette. I was eight.

"Mojonete te vas a morir!"

The cigarette dropped to the sand. After predicting my death by choking, my cousin Pedro kept laughing and wallowing in *his* ability to inhale. He was ten.

I remember thinking, *Where does he get off calling me mojonete?* My father and his father still called him that. He didn't even rate as a *mojón* either. Those were terms of endearment Cubans of every social stratum used on their children. *Mojonete*, a turd-*ette*, was appropriate from in the womb to about twelve years old, though there were exceptions. *Mojón*, just your everyday turd (pronounced Mo-HONG) from about thirteen until your mid-twenties, depending on your maturity and who was calling you that. In Spanish, it had a ring to it.

Pedro was trying to make me feel small because I breezed through things he couldn't do well here by the sea. I had shown him the sergeant majors I caught with a hand line that morning at the dock where my family tied up our eighteen-foot fishing smack, *Mono Chico*, Little Monkey. Sergeant majors were small yellow and black striped fish with tiny mouths, usually never getting much bigger than a wallet. They schooled around the pilings. I tried to show my cousin when to set the hook, but he never caught any. Couldn't get the timing.

Those Cuban cigarettes Pedro had offered were real chest-busters. Lucky Strikes or Camel non-filters were *mojonetes* in comparison. At that time, it didn't matter. I could've inhaled an *unlit* cigarette, and it still would've put me in a world of respiratory upheaval. I was asthmatic and allergic to sundry flora as well. In Havana, I slept with a vaporizer gurgling its mentholated fog from my bedside table all night. On some of my worst days, when I had the wheeze from the crypt, I was taken to the allergist and put on an oxygen respirator for a spell. On other occasions, he would search for allergies, indenting tiny circles on my arm with the twist of a metal tube, then placing tiny droplets of various solutions inside the tiny circles. After about a half hour, he checked for adverse skin reactions. Most of the time, no matter what was administered, the symptoms persisted. Instead of serpents spiraling around a staff, allergists should have a wheezing dog chasing its tail for their caduceus.

The one thing that nearly eliminated my discomfort was summers spent by the trade winds at our beach house in Varadero every year. That year, I rode in my father's new yellow 1959 180 SE Mercedes convertible. I loved the leather smell and the wind rushing against my face. He called the car *El Guevo*—the real word for egg was *huevo* (ooh-EY-voh). My dad had been amused by my mispronunciation when I was younger, and so the name. My dad and I would have been just as happy riding in the back of a rusty pick-up. I was heading to sea.

That was before Castro, before exile from our homeland, before the divorce. All those things were to gradually drive a wedge between my dad and me. He and my grandad wrote incriminating articles in the family newspaper, which often angered many corrupt politicians and their henchmen. President Batista himself would phone my grandmother on occasion with soft-edged ultimatums, soliciting restraint in her husband's often caustic and exposing editorials.

Temporary exile had been a given for any journalists or activists worth their salt in Cuba during most of the Republic's history. Both my granddad and Father had carried firearms to defend the pen. It wasn't as if my dad had been a sedentary upper crust aristocrat in Cuba, and later the life in Miami would serve him unknown turmoil. I imagine losing your country and your way of life as an adult could shake anyone to the roots. But to this day, I still don't know quite how he and I drifted apart. Truth is, the impotence inflicted on many exiles by post-Bay of Pigs U.S. policy could bust just about anyone's nuts. Whatever it was, it was never going be the same. Our closeness would erode within the first decade of *el exilio*.

But in 1959, riding through the mountains on our way to Varadero, my dad composing absurdist rhymes about my mother, himself, and me made me laugh big, as big as the Cuban sky above a speeding convertible.

Tu, seras Príncipe Luna
pero hueles a hocico de oso
mientras que sin duda alguna
Papi es alto, elegante y gracioso

The gates to our beach house had a metal arch that read *Mare Nostrum*. Much later, my mom told me it meant "Our Sea" in Latin and was what the Romans called the Mediterranean at the height of their empire. When my dad and I drove through those gates, my asthma and wheezing lifted from my chest. My soul was in the driver's seat.

My cousin took a deeper drag of his cigarette to stress his supremacy as I regained my breath from the toxic reaction to the nicotine. A few meters away was the sea that would become my *Mare Nostrum* forever. I wiped the spittle off my chin.

"Your cigarette is going out, *Faunillo.*"

Pedro pointed to the sand. *Faunillo* meant "little faun." He was referring to the day before, where some sport was had at my expense. I wasn't going let him know it irked me.

"I'll smoke it later."

"*Pendejo.*"

Normally, being called a pussy would have made me chain smoke his pack and be rushed to the hospital. But days lasted a hell of a lot longer then, so there would be plenty of time to cause a crisis. Besides, I had my own bullets. Pedro was more of a country cousin afraid of the sea—where I thrived like a young dolphin.

"I'll smoke it on the boat. Let's go out."

I pointed to the seven-foot dinghy lying against the sea oats on a tiny sand dune, flanked by an ageless ultramarine horizon. A scene that uninspired postcard photographers and inept painters have gang-banged into the emergency room.

"I want to see if I can find a *picúa.*"

"*No puedo*…We're probably leaving in a little while…and…I don't want my dad looking for me…*que después se encabrona.*"

Pedro's bravado had shrunk like a fish in the sun. His family, in fact, wasn't leaving until much later in the evening. I snuffed the cigarette carefully into the sand, put it in my shirt pocket, and walked to the boat with a sense of control. We pushed the dinghy out into the absurdly transparent water. He said nothing. He knew he didn't have the ante. I removed my shirt, put the oars in the water, and rowed out effortlessly into my element. Pedro diminished in size as more of the shimmering sea came between us. About a quarter mile out, he waved his arm and walked back to the house. *You weren't all that,* Cuz.

I slipped on a mask with twin turquoise snorkels, leaned over the boat, and looked below. The oar made a hollow rumble as it rolled and found its place on the bottom of the boat, then all sounds ceased. A little further out was where my dad had speared a *picua,* barracuda, which had bent the shaft. It now hung in the beach house on the living room wall. A chrome missile, forever brandishing its wicked teeth at the likes of people like my cousin. I wanted to see one in *its* own home.

Turtle grass patches were scattered along the sand bottom fifteen feet down. They might as well have been fifteen leagues, since they were unreachable for a *Moj* (MOWSH). But I still loved it there. There were only a few wrasses and a small porcupine fish around the rocks on this particular patch of grass. A lobster's antennae probed randomly out of one rock near the edge of the patch. The bottom was an expanse of pure white sand where, within an undulating net of sunrays, my dinghy's shadow drifted. An errant cloud with a child's heart.

Suddenly, another shadow advanced quickly over the ridged sand. Startled, I pulled my head out of the water and searched for the other boat. No boat. Slipping my head back in, I saw the leopard ray, brown-black with tiny white polka dots gliding mid-water away from the dinghy. Had it surprised me with my head in the water, Luna the Errant Cloud would have shot its child's heart out his tiny anus. After a few light strokes of its wings, the ray disappeared into the blurred periphery. The tiny polka dots reminded me of the stars.

My mother had a white polka dot on midnight blue two-piece bathing suit, same as the ray's back. Mami was beautiful, armed with a worldly mind, a poet's soul, and a fighter's heart. A triple threat. Upon gazing at my mother, *tout Betes* would sigh: *La Belle...La Belle...*

The *picua* was nowhere to be found, and the sun was beginning to grill my back. It looked like more sand bottom, unless I rowed windward to the reef. The boat had drifted east a ways from the house, and I was starving. Turning the boat toward the house with the starboard oar, I headed back. I loved pulling on the oars. Sometimes, I would row very fast, then peek over at the flattened water flowing under the stern. It smoothed the surface, and you could see the bottom detail without a mask.

I began whistling Elvis's "Hound Dog", but when I tried to keep tempo with my right foot, I lost my rowing rhythm. I had danced solo to it for my mother's friends, one of her whims and part of the price for having *La Belle* for a mother. But another lark, the *faunillo* incident, had caused me some major embarrassment one afternoon at sunset, when she and I and my granddad were supposed to be the only ones around. She requested I pose *nude* for the camera in the manner of a bronze faun she and my dad had purchased in Pompeii. The bronze faun stood *contra posto* in a little pedestal at the center of a shallow backyard fountain, flush with the ground facing the sea. I vacillated, but my granddad, self-professed *cazador de crepusculos,* who had been sitting a ways from us engaged in the sunset, overheard *La Belle's* request. He interrupted the start of his crepuscular pursuit to comment.

"*Vamos faunillo. Diós mio*, this must be the most bashful *faunillo* in all Pompeii!"

Veiled only by the *añejo* light of sunset, striking a near perfect echo of the faun, I had posed: Luna with Sea and Sunset (*Crepusculo*)

"*Faunillo encuero!*"

My cousin Pedro arrived and assassinated me with derision. He had heard the word *faunillo* when my mother was hyping me with the camera and tried to make it stick.

Now, as I neared the shore, his words "Butt-naked *Faunillo!*" began to gnaw. I rowed my dinghy faster in an unconscious attempt to diminish what I thought to be my dishonor through physical exertion. I just wished it had never happened.

My mother had attempted to guard my feelings by telling Pedro, "You're just jealous that I didn't choose you."

A good bullet for her to use, but I couldn't see myself counter-attacking from that angle without sounding rather fruity. I had been on the edge of a, "*Me cago en tu madre,*" those immemorial Cuban fighting words, "I shit on your mother," but his mother was also my aunt and a rare beauty as well. Not to mention the fact that, once after coming out of the sea with my younger cousins, Auntie had demonstrated personal hygiene in the shower by washing our peepees when I was six. An experience which, even at that tender age, had made me quite loopy for her—it also fueled various erotic fantasies through my adolescence which sadly, and to my deep melancholy, never occurred with her present *ever* again.

The fact that Pedro had backed out of the sea adventure in my dinghy had sufficed to demote his rank. So, I felt I had sort of evened the score for the *faunillo* incident. But who the hell liked to tie a game? A draw was just a long rest between rounds. His comments and his cigarettes could go to hell.

In my rowing zeal, I slid over loose chunks of sun-bleached brain coral at the shore, rasping the bottom of the hull before ramming the sand to a dead stop and nearly rolling backward off the seat. I pulled myself up on the gunwale, then stepped out and checked the hull. Minor blemishes. I pushed the boat halfway to the sea oats *by myself* and headed to the house, convinced I was on a roll.

My father was out in the station wagon, getting our cousins who had car trouble. My mother and my aunt, The *Shower Deity*, were playing canasta next door. When I walked in the kitchen, there sat Pedro, eating *tostones* (fried green plantains), which *abuela* had just finished frying.

She offered, "*Niño quieres algo the almorzar?*"

"*No gracias, Abuela*, maybe later?"

"*Bueno, pero no te me antojes después porque yo voy a descansar a la tarde.*"

And I knew better than to bother her during her *siesta*, especially if I had refused food when she had offered. I smelled the sweet lime my cousin squeezed over the fried hog snapper steak—one of the most delicate fish in the Caribbean. I was starving. But *el faunillo* was going to have his day. Abuela placed a big grouper head in a stock pot to boil for a *sopón marinero*, Cuban style bouillabaisse spiced with *bijol*—a kind of yellow orange saffron. *Abuela* Angela was of Afro-Chinese descent, a common mix. Of the hundreds of thousands of indentured Chinese laborers imported into nineteenth-century Cuba, almost none were women, so many of the luckier *Chinitos* burned that fine African diesel.

Abuela had been in the family since my mother was two years old. I was truly surprised when my mother told me she really wasn't my grandmother. To me, she remained my grandma until she died in exile at her home by the Miami River. I took the half-smoked cigarette out of my pocket and held it out for my cousin to see. He nearly choked on a *toston*. He knew, if my parents or his found out, we'd get a thrashing. He kept shaking his head, *No! No! No!* I held it to the blue gas flame under the pot with the grouper head. Abuela chopped onions with her back to me. It was lit now. I brought it to my lips very stylishly and drew smoke without inhaling—as not to lose my pacing with an unplanned coughing fit. I blew it in his direction with my eyes widened, cheeks swollen, and lips flared in the manner of Aeolus, ruler of storm clouds and tempests. *Mojonete* Unbound. Then to his horror, I pulled on Abuela's dress, took a puff, and blew it in her direction.

"*Qué es eso! Dame ese cigarro muchacho!*"

She tried for my cigarette but missed when I weaved to the other side of her. I blew another puff her way and laughed. She tried to lunge, but her age affected her accuracy. I escaped through the kitchen door.

From a safe distance, I paraded back and forth with a cocky gait, puffing to the left and puffing to the right. Even though I could no longer see Pedro through the open door due the brightness of the sun outside, I knew he could see me from the darkness where he sat stupefied. *Abuela* stepped in the doorway.

"*No te pongas atrevido! Bota eso ahora mismo o se lo voy a decir a tu padre. Mira que tu tienes asma, muchacho!*"

I didn't heed her warning about telling my father. Enthralled by my solo performance, I continued my near hypnotic control over my cousin. Oh yes, Mr. Big Shot was paralyzed now. I threw out the butt just before it burned my fingers. When I entered the kitchen, my cousin was no longer there. He hadn't even finished his lunch. I asked *Abuela* for him, and she didn't answer. I attempted a different tack.

"I saw a *raya* and a lobster today *Abuela. Abuela?*"

When she was mad, her silent treatment was seamless. I grabbed the *tostones* from my cousin's plate and left.

I visited the fish freezer in the garage building, which also had servants quarters upstairs. I knelt on an old, padded tube chair, as I had done many times before, opened the overhead lid, and felt the smoky cold air with its slightly muffled fish scent wrap around my face. Bending into the freezer, I rummaged through the frozen fare. In the tepid summer air, their rock-hard eyes got slimy when I rubbed them.

Dozens of yellowtail, with their lateral golden stripes and V-shaped tails, and below them, big-lipped black groupers that could literally inhale prey with their bellows-like gill plates. Light vermilion hog snappers, probably the best eating fish in the Caribbean, whose long snouts were a pattern of thin bright yellow and violet veins. When in danger, they could camouflage to near invisibility behind a sea fan or grass. I loved handling them. Many of these fish had spear holes in or near their heads, a testimony to my dad's marksmanship. The fifteen- and twenty-pound cubera snappers were very difficult for me to lift, but when I managed to push one against the edge of the freezer, careful not to stab myself with its thick, ice-pick sharp dorsal fins, I could watch it dispelling smoke for a long time in an otherworldly swoon.

I had caught some of these yellowtails at night with a Cuban yo-yo—a spool made of wood, which flared at the edges and allowed the hand-line to get payed out like a spinner reel. When the captain found a school, he would drop my hand line down. Wherever the fish would bite, he would tie a knot so I would know how far to drop the line every other time.

It was truly a mythical journey for an eight-year-old, to be out almost all night on this great swelling dark abyss, pulling up fish from its depths. The fish reflecting the light from the boat's kerosene lantern became flashing thick slivers at the end of the line. A couple of people always tried guessing what type of fish it was at this stage.

"*Eso me luce un pargo*...no, no, that's moving like a *rabirubia*."

The captain, Cristobal, a short man with a leathery tan and well-defined musculature didn't have to look. He would feel the line with his callused hands and identify with uncanny accuracy the fish at the end of your line, just by the way it pulled. Once, I caught a *Carajuelo*, or scorpion fish, which made my hook appear as though it was in flames. The captain grabbed my line upon recognizing it and pulled the fish out and away from me. It had poisonous spines. Holding its head tightly with a rag, careful to stroke the dorsal spines against its back, he freed it from the hook and threw it overboard. The bright crimson fish hesitated, then realized it was back in its homeland and disappeared toward the bottom.

"*Eso es rinquincalla!*"

The captain warned me that the *Carajuelo* was "bad news." As a child, he had lost a piece of his heel to a moray eel left unattended on the deck. So, he was always protective.

"*Mojón!* What are you, *turulato* or what!"

My cousin approached and leaned down next to me by the freezer, very worried about my cavalier behavior with the cigarette. He had taken the cigarette pack from behind the freezer by the rusty bolts of the compressor and had gone to hide it immediately somewhere else.

"Don't worry, *no te voy a chivatear!*"

And I would *never* fink on him. But he wasn't totally convinced. In fact, he seemed a little fey and quite apprehensive about the possibility of having to pay the piper for my lunacy. Just then, my father pulled up in the Plymouth wagon with my other cousins. They were making a big hoopla because my uncle had a brand new forty-five—Bill Haley's "Rock Around the Clock." Though it was released in '53, it was new to us kids. He was going to let his daughter, Ana, of the vertiginous turquoise eyes, play it on her portable record player. Ana's 151 proof, child version of pheromone incantation, and a new disc completely crushed the cigarette caper. We followed her up the covered stairs. almost single file, to an open hallway with verandas facing the sea that connected the family rooms.

She attempted to play it, but the little red insert in the forty-five disc was missing, and the spring-loaded one attached to the turntable had broken, so the record spun off center.

"*Ha ver yo lo hago.*"

Pedro, the Cigarette Czar, offered to help. I beat him to it, grabbing the small disc and centering it after a few tries. If anyone was going be a hero to Ana, it was going to be me, *Primo.*

One o'clock, two o'clock, three o'clock rock…We're gonna rock, around, the clock tonight!

The beat ruled, and everybody was jumping to it. My country cousin was attempting a few *rumba* moves, but it just didn't go. I had been watching *American Bandstand* for years, and only the week before, we had seen some news reel showing Bill Haley playing. So, I kind of approximated a few of the moves. Ana was laughing. She was so pretty with her cinnamon skin and big eyes the very color of *Mare Nostrum* just beyond the doorway.

Put your glad rags on and join me Hon'...

I pivoted to the left and threw my head back for a spin just as my father walked through the door with the look of Goya's *Saturn Devouring His Children*. He whisked me out to the hallway. It was twilight outside. The *crepusculo* in the horizon was full-tilt, Judgment Day intense.

"Tu estabas fumando hoy, verdad?"

Was *I* smoking? My heart did triplets. I felt faint. What to do, and with *Ana* there? Not much but live the moment heroically. Hesitantly, I nodded my head yes. My cousins watched from the doorway. Bill Haley was still jamming.

When the clock strikes two three and four
if the band slows down we'll yell for more

"De donde sacaste esos cigarros?"

Pedro cringed at that one. But I wasn't gonna *echarlo pa'lante*. I was no rat. I told my dad, "I found the cigarettes by the freezer." Plenty of people smoked, including the captain and most of my parents' guests, so they could have been anyone's.

"Abuela told you to stop, but you didn't listen. Who do you think you are? *Atrevido!"*

Haley's guitarist laid down the trilling solo *twidiil- twidili-twidili-twidil..."*

As my dad asked me who did I think I was, he grabbed for his belt. My peripheral vision saw my cousins, petrified at this, by now anticipated, *auto da fe*. Next came a warning emphasized by three swift strikes of his belt to my butt.

"Don't let me catch you (hit) smoking (hit) again (hit)! *Me oíste?"*

My cheeks smoldered, pee ran down my legs, and I agreed never to smoke again. Leering for effect, he scanned the audience, transmitting the unspoken message: *Cuidadíto!* Dwelling just a bit longer on my cousin Pedro before leaving.

When I walked back in the room, nobody said a thing. The song was over, and the needle popped rhythmically at the center of the disc with funereal cadence. Out of nervous reflex, I removed the bobbing arm from its unforgiving eddy and placed it at the beginning. My shorts were wet with urine. Pedro saw it but said nothing. In the bathroom, I wiped my legs with toilet paper just as the song began.

One O'clock, two o'clock, three o'clock rock,
five, six, seven, eight o'clock rock...

I felt absolutely deflated. And in front of my boastful little country cousin too. But I knew Pedro wasn't going to say peep because he knew I hadn't given his ass up. And Ana. Oh God! Nothing like pissing on yourself in front of your childhood fancy. I didn't want to leave the bathroom. I hated my dad. How could he do that in front of everybody? I could tell nobody was dancing in the room. Ana asking Pedro if *he* smoked.

"Qué va! Y ademas los cigarros no se los venden a los niños.

No way! Not he. I didn't want to walk out there with my wet shorts. I had to change. I wished I was in my room or outside or being torn to *ropa vieja* by sharks. Anywhere but here. Ana's younger brother claimed he would certainly never smoke. They were all pretty shook up. One thing was for sure—I couldn't hide out in the damn bathroom all day.

Were gonna rock rock rock til broad daylight
Were gonna rock, were gonna rock, aro__und the clock tonight.

I spotted a cap gun on the windowsill I had hid from Ana's little brother the week before. I opened it, revealing nearly a full roll of caps. Damn good for diversionary tactics.

Blam! Blam! Blam!

I came out blasting. The whole crew, including my older cousin, Pedro, flinched, cowered, ducked, or recoiled. Smoke crept out of the barrel. I gave them the Pancho Villa grin. At least nobody was looking at the wet spot on my crotch. I upped the ante. *Blam!* This time, I placed the smoking barrel in my mouth, inhaled, walked over to my cousin, cocked my head back, and exhaled insouciantly in his face. He smiled. Ana worried.

"No! No! *Tío* is going to come back and hit you again!"

Blam! I inhaled, then exhaled into my cupped hands and carried the smoke to Ana with an air of mystery, unlocking my hands slowly with a bit of over-the-top- Abracadabra hype as smoke rose from my palms. I bowed with thespian humility. Pedro applauded, celebrating the *choteo*. Ana's brother joined in, also enjoying the farce. Ana hesitated, then hinted a Giaconda smile. Oh, my fellow cadets! Now Luna was "a storm a flame..." He had "ten hearts...ten arms...too strong to war with mortals!" Little Luna de Bergerac with a Bill Haley soundtrack.

When the chimes ring five, six and seven
We'll be right, in seventh heaven...

I stepped outside into the hallway leading to the stairs, turned, and faced the audience. *Blam!* Inhale. *Blam!* Inhale. *Bam!* Inha-a-a-ale. It was darker now, and the flash from each shot made my eyes glow like the Devil's own hound. A deep maroon dusk hung above the purple-black sea behind me.

Pulling the fulminant deep into my lungs, I expanded my chest, stretched my arms with operatic aplomb, and exhaled a long stream of smoke, at whose tail-end I collapsed on the floor, where I would lay motionless and breathing feebly. The *carajuelo*, that red and mottled scorpion fish the captain had thrown overboard, now expanded its poisoned spines in my lungs. I sucked in as hard I could, but very little air entered. The edges of my vision darkened.

At the end of a floor tile enormity, my three cousins began running toward me. Pedro got there first. I wheezed through my severely inflamed air ducts. Inhaling was like trying to suck a marble through a straw. Ana voiced her distress.

"Lunee, Lunee.....*Se esta ahogando!*"
When it's eight nine ten, eleven two
I'll be going strong and so will you

Pedro ran for my father. His unnaturally hollow footsteps descended the stairs. Ana approached me. "Huuurry—Lunee is turning green!" Her eyes watered. She was scared. Oh God, what I would do for a drop of air. I could feel the contortions on my face. Ana's tears dropped warm on my cheeks, and she wailed. My dad scooped me off the ground and sprinted with me in his arms.

Ana's eyes were precious sentient atolls and I, the wayward spaceman with severed air hose, plummeting toward the end of the universe. The aquamarine sanctuary darkened to the vanishing point…*Ana, I'll never forget you…*

We're gonna rock, we're gonna rock,
Aro___und the clock tonight. Tunto-to TUUUuuuhn!
"No se preocupe Senora ya su hijo esta respirando normal."

I opened my eyes to a soothing heavenly body. I could taste the coppery flavor of oxygen in my space helmet. On the other side of the mask, I was greeted by the voluptuous hills of a mulatto nurse, tethered by a lace brassiere peeking slightly above the first button of her impeccably white cotton uniform. She bent over me with a stethoscope. *O, Yoruban goddess.* Naturally, I was clueless back then, but I still sensed deep to my primal core that my rocket had landed on the right planet. My father sat on a chair at the foot of my bed, relieved. My mother held my hand as I would hold hers one day.

"Concho, que susto nos diste faunillo…pero tu eres idiota? Como se te ocurre chico…?"

Basically, her sweeter and more maternal variation on the American standard, *"Faunillo,* what a scare you gave us. Are you a moron? What were you thinking?"

Seeing that I was out of danger, she felt the slight reprimand was in order. My cousin, Pedro, sat in the corner, attempting to disguise the guilt in his eyes. His cigarette gag had snowballed into an emergency room crisis. Oh, but I harbored no rancorous will. *Al contrario.* For, until our families were forced into exile, I became the unrivaled *Mojonus Rex* of *Mare Nostrum.*

Avenging Angel

"Por qué, Leal, por qué?"

Our third-grade history teacher swung Leal's head back and forth, hanging on to his sizable ears. I felt bad because, even after the teacher had told him to be quiet twice, I had encouraged him to continue telling me about the cosmetic surgery his family planned for his sister. The cadet's name was *Leal de Dios*, Loyal to God. When the teacher let go of his ears, Loyal to God became pale, deadweight, and by all indications, well on his way to meet the Maker to whom his name pledged unfailing devotion. He collapsed. The professor quickly put his forearm on Loyal's lower back to prevent him from hitting the floor. His big ears made bigger by the quarter inch buzz cut, his eyes rolling and the fainting were pushing the envelope of what I could contain from the back of the class. Then, the teacher slapped Leal in an attempt to revive him.

"No sea mariquita Leal!" (Don't be a little fag!)

My guilt notwithstanding, my world exploded in laughter.

Some Cubans had a notion they could shame any man into what they considered correct behavior by alluding to their homosexuality. It was remarkable any man on the island allowed himself to die. *Morirse? Eso es de maricones!*

Loyal came to, and he was sent off, too nervous to cry and too embarrassed to lift his gaze from the wood slats on the floor leading to his desk. In turn, I was summoned.

"And don't you laugh, Cadet Yena!"

The professor twisted my lips, unintentionally snapping off a loose front tooth with his thumb. I felt the sharp edges of the baby tooth on my bottom gum and tasted the blood seeping out of what would become a temporary new hole in my grin. I pulled the tooth out and asked to go to the bathroom. On my way out, I saw the faces of my fellow cadets straining to hold back their laughter.

In the bathroom, I rinsed the bloody taste out of my mouth, then grinned in front of the mirror. I made a tiny bit of my tongue peek through the new gap, making it appear and disappear like some formless pink jack-in-the-box. The tooth was tucked in my pocket to trade with the tooth fairy that night. Back to class, and that was the end of that. I continued the calligraphy exercises, the zigzags and the spring coils on lined paper. But just as unintentionally as my tooth had been snapped, Professor Liptwist would be paid back.

This was Loyola Military Academy, named after soldier/saint Ignatius Loyola. I was attending third grade in a second attempt by my parents to curb my innate tendency to ridicule authority. My grandfather attributed this anomaly to my being possessed by "*un duende Dadaista.*" I now have no doubt the only "Dadaist poltergeist" inhabiting me were his genes.

Leal had been sent there by his father to toughen him up "*a ver si algo de San Ignacio se le pega.*" In all the other schools Leal had attended, kids had ridiculed him with nicknames alluding to the size of his ears. He said some had tugged on them while picking on him.

"And they would tell me, 'Dumbo (DOOM-BO) take us for a ride,' and when I push them away, they hold me *y.* One slaps my ears, '*y los otros,*' They sing, 'Doom-bo! Doom-bo! Doom-bo!' Then, they would run away. I wish they would die."

Hearsay had it that his father had experienced the same difficulty when he went to school. So, that by the time he got to the university, he had reached *ni-una-mas zero* tolerance. In spite of many pleas to refrain from doing so, one fellow student insisted on calling Leal's dad Murci, short for murciélago (bat), referring to his Chiropteran ears.

The last straw occurred at a baseball game, where his dad sat with his girlfriend Concha, Leal's mother-to-be, and the same guy ribbed him as he passed.

"Que pasa, Murci?"

His dad had torn off a loose piece of sun-split board from a bleacher backrest and landed six *tablazos* on Mr. Funny's arms and head, knocking him into unconsciousness before being restrained by his fellow students. The guy was taken to the hospital, where he received multiple stitches on the cheeks and parietal walls. Leal's grandfather had bailed out his son through connections in the Havana police but had to pay sizable reparations to mollify the beaten student's family. The upside—word got out, and his father's tormentors never chided him again. Lest they forgot, they only needed to look at the double black eyes and stitches their schoolmate, Mr. Funny, sported for the next couple of weeks.

But although his father's dominant genes had passed the elephantine lobes to his offspring, apparently they had not advanced his combativeness. Or perhaps it had not manifested yet? A possibility to which his mother, Concha, was not looking forward. Leal told me a family budget had been allotted for both he and his older sister's upcoming cosmetic surgeries in Miami.

"First, *mi hermana* because her *quinceañera* is coming up and then me.

My father said I don't need surgery, that what I need is '*aprender a repartir sopapos,*' but *Mami* says she doesn't want to live another '*episodio de violencia.*'"

Unfortunately, up to now, Leal's tour of military school, meant to "*hacerlo un machito,*" had only succeeded in first providing him with yet one more nickname, *Puertabierta*, associating his ears to the open doors of a car. Second and more recently, getting himself rocked into unconsciousness by his legendary family lobes at the hands of Professor Liptwist for talking to me in class.

Two weeks after the tooth casualty, I sat bored in my usual place in the last desk of the last row by the window. My best class buddy, also bored, sat four rows over in the last desk by the back door. So, we invented a game consisting of throwing invisible pies at each other. The person at the "receiving end" always had to devise a way to avoid being hit by the pie thrower. If successful, the roles where exchanged: the pie-*ee* would become the pie-*er* but only if he avoided the pie *within* the rules.

The first and simplest defense was to move the head out of the way of the incoming pie. Then, it was your turn to throw the pie. Your opponent might catch it with an outward jerk of his arm and exaggerate a slow-motion gesture, leading the pie way back gingerly in his palm, as if whisking an egg out of its trajectory without breaking it. Feathering the clutch, as it were. A favorite of mine was raising a U-shaped tube (an invisible one, naturally) into which, theoretically, the pie would enter and, making a U-turn, return full force to its sender. The rule was, you could only use each defense once per round. Once you ran out of ideas for defenses, you got "pied," lost, and the game would begin again. Every time a fresh defense was executed, we would break into a fit of poorly stifled and debilitating laughter.

After several unheeded warnings from Liptwist, he opted for discipline. He sat us at each side of his desk, facing the class, and dared us to continue giggling.

"A ver si van a seguir con la risita!"

No more than minutes went by before mini-pies were devised. Defenses were adequately miniaturized, and from behind our backs and Liptwist's, the mini-pies were launched with a subtle flick of index and middle finger.

The day before, I had sharpened a pencil capable of rendering the Sistine Chapel ceilings on the head of a pin or, if in a spunkier mood, capable of being stabbed halfway into a reinforced concrete wall. After school, I had stashed it point up in the back pocket of my jeans. While playing in my backyard near some trees, a mockingbird buzzed me, warning I was too close to its nest. Ducking and dodging, I stabbed myself just above the wrist. I squeezed out the broken pencil tip, but to this day, I still have the lead mark under my skin. The next day in class, I rubbed and turned the pencil tip against a piece of paper, restoring it to Florentine dagger status.

It was this very murderous pencil that I now held in my hand, sitting next to Liptwist's desk, facing the class. With my free hand, I flicked a mini-pie at my opponent who, scheming and riotous scoundrel that he was, pushed one nostril in with his forefinger, inhaled my pie, switched fingers, and exhaled the pie out his other nostril at me, full-force. I was felled way before the pie reached me. Constricting my chest and biting my lips only served to amplify the laughter when it burst out as an atonal trumpet *solo*.

Liptwist, fed up with our pie antics, eyes swollen through bi-focals, glared at me with a silent *se acabo la fiesta* decree. Little did he or I imagine just how *over* the party was.

He rose up to educate me. As his arm came down to strike my head, I weaved aside out of instinct. When he lifted his arm, I could see, to my horror, the pencil stuck in his palm. Beyond, rows of cadets, some of them agape, all of them deathly silent, singularly focused on Liptwist's speared hand. He didn't scream or sigh and, strangely enough, didn't retaliate. This four-eyed Polyphemus just pulled out the pencil and walked toward the same men's room where only two weeks before I had walked with my tooth.

It had been truly unintentional, but that was of no consequence to a certain clamshell-eared cadet in the back of the class. Loyal to God beamed at his avenging angel.

Crazy Horse Junior and the Thirty-Year Riddle

My arrow struck him in the center of the forehead. Surprised by the blow, Teo dropped his six-shooters on the ground. All throughout my country, decades of less innocent arrows were coming home to roost.

"*Dios mío ahora sí!*"

I rushed down the small rise in my backyard to where Teo stood bewildered.

"*Me pasó algo?*"

He wanted to know about his forehead. His fingers had already detected blood.

"*Perdona,* I'm sorry, *no se cómo pasó?* I was aiming toward the sky!"

Yes, it had been a bit selfish to worry about my retribution when I had blurted, "Oh my God, *Ahora si!*" After all, *my* arrow had struck *his* head. I had seen even from where I had fired that he wasn't mortally wounded. He would survive. But when you're nine years old and a repeat troublemaker, the first thing that flashes in your mind at the moment of mischief is your father's belt, not the injury you've caused. Yes, it could have been much worse had Teo been struck in the eye, for I had removed the rubber suction cup from the toy arrow. Fortunately, I had not sharpened the wooden point.

I had been in my Indian moccasins and makeshift hand towel loincloth, trying to hunt lizards in the landscaped woodsy plateau behind our house. Though my friend, Teo, always went with the *vaqueros,* I always favored Indians in all the Cowboy and Indian movies, despite Hollywood's attempt since day one to canonize the cowboy. I especially liked Crazy Horse, a Sioux warrior chief my dad had read to me about. I had loved his daring and integrity but dreaded how he had died, betrayed by his own. Cowards who held his arms while a soldier stabbed his side with a bayonet. The keen point frightened me. I knew how painful small stabs could be. Luckily, betrayal was still years away.

Teo had approached me, unruly curls of forest fire hair on his forehead, little wine-red cowboy boots, a short-sleeve western shirt with pearl snaps, sporting twin cap guns in holsters. Spotting him, I had rushed to the edge of the "plateau" overlooking the expansive mowed lawn and stood on a large limestone rock the landscapers had placed on one side of the bank. The rock had been intended as an informal "entrance" on the rise to the small grove. I mustered my best imitation of broken Spanish to assume "Indian" credibility.

"Tu no Pasar por Piedra Grande!"

Teo kept walking. I drew my bowstring back, pointed the arrow skyward in his direction as final warning, and repeated my ultimatum.

"You no pass Big Rock!"

Teo drew his guns and advanced, ignoring my warning. I released the arrow…Eighty feet away, at the end of a long arc, it found the *center* of his forehead. I couldn't repeat that stunt in a hundred tries, even if my dad promised to forego a belt lashing had I accomplished it.

I walked him to the garden hose and rinsed his head while he held his hair back. From many of my own self-inflicted lacerations, I had learned at least one lesson: *Don't let the dirt coagulate in the wound, or it will be hell to pay when Mom has to scrub off the scab.* The water stream made the half-inch pizza-slice flap of skin dance on his heavily freckled forehead. The small triangle of raw flesh was almost an anti-climax compared to the intensity of his blazing mane. He didn't complain.

I told him he should go home and douse it with hydrogen peroxide, which along with the heinous merthiolate, iodine, and the more forgiving mercurochrome were staples of every urban Cuban medicine cabinet in 1960. He told me he forgave me *and* that he would tell his parents he hit his head on a branch. I walked him to the sidewalk, then ran back to the fence at the end of my yard and waved to the paleface just before he entered his front door. He had always been on the outside lane with me all the way, even though we were Indian and Cowboy. A noble Cowboy. But frankly, this last stunt had really scared the *croquetas* out of me.

I entered our house through the den, passing below a much-dreaded ceramic demon face hanging out of reach on a hardwood column across the wet bar—another of my parents' purchases from Pompeii. Out of its deep turquoise complexion, a dark pink pointy tongue sprung from the demon's bearded mouth, mocking guilty souls and naughty children. If its crafty yellow eyes caught your glance for even a fraction of an instant, the jet-black pupils would make you kindling for his bonfire. It spoke.

"*You almost poked his eye out, Luna. Why don't you try it again? Ha, ha, ha…!*"

Looking away, I ran upstairs to my room, although I felt it stalking me until I was well out of view. In my toy closet, I went directly to the back, past the shelves and the box of rubber soldiers and Indians, to a nook where I buried the bow and arrow beneath a baseball glove, a bat ,and a hula hoop, topping it off with an old umbrella. *What* bow and arrow?

I took off my moccasins bearing the bloodstain from the time I had crushed the light bulb against a table to show off for my nanny's daughter. The very one I had shown to my first love, Tere, right after she christened me Luna *(tico)*. So naturally, they had achieved *fetiche*, or icon status. I placed them inside the suitcase on the sofa, which my nanny had packed for a trip the next day to *Mare Nostrum*, our Varadero beach house. I removed my makeshift towel loincloth, buried it deep in the hamper, and slipped into jeans and a T-shirt. *What* Indian?

As I lay in bed, the demon face made stubborn apparitions when I closed my eyes. I felt sleepy. The demon nagged. I shot an arrow and hit the satanic blue-green fiend in the eye. He became serious and appeared emotionally hurt, asking why I had done that to him. He was bleeding profusely out of his eye socket. Suddenly, I felt sorry for him. I couldn't believe I had done it. I looked at the arrow, and this one had a sharp flinthead. I was scared and voiced my acquittal.

"That's not my arrow; mine had a rubber tip!"

"I'm going to have to tell the Indian chief."

"The Chief went out on my dinghy. He won't be back for a while."

Earlier in my dream, I was at our beach house, and Crazy Horse had asked me if he could try my dinghy. Crazy Horse! And he left me his bow and arrow for safekeeping. When I shot the demon, I was convinced they were my arrows. Somehow, I had forgotten. No matter what, now I had done some dirt with the Chief's bow and arrow. I was hoping the demon would die before Crazy Horse came back. But the aquamarine demon walked with the bloody arrow in his hand, almost blending with the turquoise seashore, and sat by the rise in the sea oats next to the imprint my dinghy left in the sand.

"Piojo, me hicistes cojo de un ojo, y ahora no puedo jugar!"

Referring to me as a louse, he said I had made him lame in one eye. It reminded me of my father's absurdist rhymes.

"Y ahora no puedo jugar!"

He claimed that, in this condition, he couldn't play. I knew what game he meant: *Soldiers and Indians*. I looked again, and the demon became my father with half his mouth sewn shut. A breeze had picked up, and a few scraps of newspaper twirled by and into the sea.

"Dad, you can still play. I'll set them up."

He appeared despondent. Luna, the little brave, he have bad trip. In dreams, we mostly accepted every development, no matter how preposterous. We weaved, danced, or flew without asking *why*. Life, no less preposterous, was soon to make many of my fellow Cubans dance, weave, and fly. And when we woke up, *we* would be the answer to our *whys?*

It was late in the afternoon when I woke up in a sweat and with an earnest desire to play with my dad. I grabbed my U.S. soldier and Indian warrior set from my toy closet and took it to my dad's study, or *despacho*. I walked back for the air-powered cork rifles.

I assembled the "stockade," a wood-colored plastic fort made of sharpened log walls that snapped together at the corners.

The last time, I had lost a lot of braves to my Dad's lethal aim because I hadn't had enough cover. So this time, I made ridges and cliffs from encyclopedia tomes surrounding the fort. I built the fort closer to the sofa so I could hide my warriors behind the sofa legs.

There was a knock at the front door downstairs. I ran to the hallway at the top of stairs where you could overlook the living room. I saw my nanny open the door.

"Está la Señora?"

Holy Shit! It. Was. Teo's mother. So. *It*. Was. Over.

The nanny answered, "No," that my mother wasn't home just at the moment.

Teo's mother glanced upstairs. I tried to drop out of sight, bracing my arm against the floor for support, but only succeeded in digging the sharp plastic nose of one of my kneeling Indian bowmen into the palm of my hand. She had caught me, and after pointing me out with a quick movement of her eyes, she moved out of *mojonete* earshot with my nanny. I sat with my back to the wall and pondered the bitter facts.

I couldn't believe it! My *friend* Teo? He said he wouldn't tell. *Que clase de chivatico.* The little rat. *Priquitipao!* (Pree-kee-tee-POW!) Caught with my pants down. Had they beat a confession out of him? I had heard his father discipline him once. Couldn't much blame a little fellow brought within inches of his life or threatened with his worst phobias? Our own minds could be the worst traitor. We all had our weak points. Hell, I knew the belt alone made a fiendish interrogator and then the peeing in your pants; that certainly would finish the job.

But nobody had *seen*. They had *no* proof! He could have stuck to our story. Why did he do it? In my ruminations about Teo's character, I had inadvertently chewed the Indian's rubber head into what looked like a tenderized minute steak. Once again, the way to Indian hell paved by one of their staunchest champions.

The front door closed. I heard the nanny's footsteps. I rushed into my dad's study. Cuban nannies were always good to spice up the stew for the defendant with pre-trial mental anguish. The all-around best, being the universal, "*Deja que llegue tu padre!* Wait until your father gets home! That was diabolical because it was open-ended. Free-range nightmares. Of course, you didn't analyze it back then, and that's precisely why it worked so well on you. Had I known better, I would've grabbed a kitchen fork and charged the nanny *du jour* like some frenzied unicorn. I wouldn't have really stabbed her, but then she wouldn't have known better either.

My nanny never climbed the stairs to deliver the prophecy. Maybe the news of my latest caper, due to its potential for irreparable harm to Teo, like the loss of an eye, was meant to go straight to the highest authority. Who knew?

Back in the study, I decided on a change of strategy. I started to pick up the Indians and the soldiers. Anything with *Indians*, now that Teo had sung like a courting mockingbird, was a red flag. Now, it was back to Operation *What* Indian? My mother walked in the room, looking pretty shook up.

"Luna…"

"Mami, he's a liar! He hit his head on a branch!"

"What are you talking about?"

Oh my God! What a…Why didn't I just grab the bow and arrow, take her outside, and re-enact the crime! She was still shook up.

"Listen, your dad is not coming for dinner. He has some business at the newspaper. Have your dinner and get some rest because tomorrow were leaving early for Miami."

"Miami? I thought we were going to Varadero?"

"No, *mi amor,* we've changed our plans. We'll go after we've come back."

"Okay."

I was relieved. I couldn't have cared if we were going to Madagascar to study native fauna excreta and I had been elected Collector General. My nanny hadn't told. Amazing. I can assure you, I was not going to ask why.

Later, I found out the reason my mother had been shook up. She had been asked by my father to withdraw $200,000.00 that afternoon (1960 dollars) to cover the payroll of my grandfather's newspaper for a year. She could have run into ugly business with Castro's goons. Earlier that day, my father had been granted asylum at the Panamanian Embassy. My granddad was in Spain. My dad had called him a few days earlier and told him not to return to Cuba. There had been a major falling out with the government or Castro—same thing—who began demanding that news be clarified with pro-revolution disclaimers before publishing.

When my dad had asked Grandpa what he wanted to do, Grandpa, the classic romantic, answered, "Let the newspaper go down like Admiral Nelson's ships at Trafalgar, *disparando*, blazing away."

So, my father published articles denouncing the curtailment of freedom of speech, the suspension of elections, the revolution's kangaroo courts, and the ensuing firing squad vendettas. In short, *los muchachos de la Revolución* came to take over the newspaper, and my father and uncles had to rush to the embassy. All this while *I shot an arrow into the air…*

The reason Teo's mother had come over was not about the arrow incident, but to warn my mother that government soldiers had stationed their vehicles across from her house to watch ours.

Of course, I was not aware of all this. I also didn't think anything unusual about going to Miami. Many Cubans shopped there. I had been there in 1956 and '57 when my Mom went shopping.

That night, I ate my dinner with the simple goal of going to sleep without being found out. Tomorrow, off to Miami. By the time I got back, the arrow thing would be old news, if it was anything at all. Maybe Teo hadn't told? Whatever. *Drume Negrito…*

I woke up a bit past midnight, my brown plastic vaporizer still gurgling its medicinal decongestant from my night table. Luckily, this night I could breathe.

"*Deténgase!*"

Shots rang out hollow down the street after a warning to "Freeze!" was apparently not heeded. It was eerie, but I was not really scared. It was out there, and I felt safe in my room. Somnolence coupled with innocence created a near unbreachable sense of sanctuary.

Maybe the *milicianos* (Fidel's men) were capturing the last of the *Batistianos* (Batista's sympathizers) to deal them the quick justice of the firing squad, with the double effect of providing collective vengeance for the faithful and intimidation to the undecided. *Auto da fé.* Tried 'n True.

Milicianos y Batistianos. It was curious that the name of both groups ended in *anos,* which meant anuses in Spanish. Fidel had only been in power a year, but he basked in overwhelming public adoration. There were even Castro dolls. I myself had a red and black 26 of July armband made for me by one of our domestics, which I wore with my olive fatigues—an outfit for which "The Maximum Leader of the Revolution" has displayed an unnatural fondness through the decades. Like the majority of my people, I had been caught in the wave of excitement. Luckily, I was a nine-year-old, so I was spared participation in any type of mob violence or reign-of-terror antics. My alliance *a la Revolución* was limited to sporting olive drabs and the armband, but my heart still belonged to Crazy Horse of the Lakota.

No more shots were heard. I mused on how terrible it must be to die by firing squad. I remembered a black and white picture in a magazine where a man was condemned to death. He had no recourse, cornered like a rat. It scared me. I rolled over and went to sleep, not at ease *at all* with the concept of sin and retribution, crime and punishment. Much later, in Miami, I saw a black and white film where this fat *Batistiano* said to the firing squad, "*Ahí tienen la Revolución muchachos, cuídenla!*" just before he succumbed to the violent quaking which the .30 caliber rounds made when they passed through his body. I'm sure some had been cruel and greedy swine, but still, what a way to get your ticket punched.

"Muchacho!Pero-que-tu-haces-durmiendo-otra-vez?! Espavílate!-que-ya-las-maletas-de-tu-madre-estan-en-el-carro-y-el-avión-se-va-en-una-hora-y-media! Vamos, vamos-desayuna!"

My *manejadora* (nanny) woke me with a machine-gun monologue, instigated no doubt by a large dose of Cuban coffee and the added stress brewing within the imminent exile of the family. Apparently, she had woken me up prior to fixing breakfast, and I had dozed off. She had a breakfast tray for me. I was awakening slowly until an oddity caught my eye. My Indian moccasins, which I had placed in the suitcase yesterday afternoon, were now *next* to the suitcase. I made a beeline to the mocs and placed them back in the suitcase.

"Pero-chiquito-tu-no-me-estas-oyendo? Desayuna-báñate-y vístete!"

After my nanny's Boy-aren't-you-listening-to-me-eat-breakfast-shower-and-dress cannonade, I drank my orange juice out of an anodized magenta aluminum tumbler, which always had several spoonfuls of sugar left on the bottom. I ate some toast and drank my milk, which also had several spoons of sugar at the bottom. Consequently, these drinks got progressively sweeter and grainier as you tilted the tumbler. If I put a quarter of that sugar in milk today, I would break into projectile vomiting. Cubans would put lots of sugar on everything. If you were surrounded by your main product, I guess you ended up using it. Some people lived in yak dung huts.

I took a shower quickly but didn't play with my peepee this morning. Since my discovery of the shower stream climax, I had become quite an aficionado until my early teens. I couldn't drink or smoke, nor did I know about sex at nine, so thank God for shower wiener tickles.

My nanny had left me a red Lacoste shirt and a pair of black slacks over my black loafers. My *first* loafers. I had a bad case of flat feet, so I had to wear lace up shoes with orthopedic inserts for years. Once dressed, I looked at my feet. I loved loafer style shoes back then.

I opened the suitcase for one last check.

No moccasins!

I looked on the couch, under the couch, under the bed. In my toy closet, I lifted the bow and arrow to clear the floor, but I knew they weren't there. I *knew* I put them in the suitcase. I heard somebody in the room. It was the chauffeur, Kiki (Kee-kee), whose wavy, golden-brown, pomaded hair reminded me of the ridges on a Ritz cracker. He grabbed the suitcase. I stood at the door of the closet.

"*Vamos* Hatuey, your mother is already waiting in the car."

Hatuey (AH-TOO-EY) was a famous *cacique*, or Indian chief, burned alive by Spaniards in Cuba centuries ago. As he was about to be torched, Hatuey was approached by a missionary offering salvation in Heaven if he converted.

Hatuey looked at the Spaniards around him and asked, "Are these Christians going to Heaven too?" When the cleric answered, "Yes", Hatuey said, "Then I prefer Hell."

Kiki signaled me, cocking his head that it was time to go.

"I'm looking for my moccasins. They were just in the suitcase."

"Forget the moccasins. You'll get them when you come back. *Y olvida el arco y flecha,* they won't let you in the plane with that bow and arrow."

What was a *bow and arrow* doing anywhere near me?

"*Vamos.*"

I placed the bow and arrow in the back of the closet and left with Kiki.

"*Buenos Dias Mami.*"

I greeted my mother who sat in the back seat. She was distant, distracted. She answered five seconds later and squeezed my hand.

"*Buenos Dias, mi hijito.*"

The next event just about nearly stopped my heart. Teo, the war casualty, was walking up the driveway with a thick pad of gauze secured with adhesive tape to his forehead. He raised his hand in the manner of an *Indian* greeting. The chauffeur stopped the car, and Teo approached the back window.

"*Pero que le habrá pasado al loquito ese?*"

My mother wondered out loud what could have happened to the little loon. Though, the bigger loon was sitting next to her.

My stomach was cramping. I was just about to piss in my pants. I had *almost* made it, *coño*! He stood outside the window. And since I was just short of catatonic, my mother inquired.

"*Que te pasó?*"

Teo, seeing me crippled by fear, said matter-of-factly,

"It's nothing. I got hit by an arrow."

An *a-r-r-o-w*?! Oh no-no-no-no no ! He didn't say that. I thought I was going to throw up all those .45 caliber words he had just grouped in my chest. I looked to the front of the car, and Kiki, the chauffeur, gave me a surprised look. Okay, it's all over. The answer was exotic enough to draw further inquiry from my mother, even though she was visibly stressed with grander preoccupations.

"*Una flecha?*"

"N-no…What am I…I mean…I was *playing* with my bow and arrow and…I…slipped in the grass…I didn't…The sun was in my eyes…This branch…and…"

"Be more careful, Teo, *cuídate chico.*"

"Oh, it's nothing." He shrugged his shoulders then smiled hardly showing his teeth, and moved his eyes to me in camaraderie.

Maybe I deserved the scare for thinking he had ratted me out.

"Well, just be careful. Say goodbye to your mama for me. We have to go. *Adiós.*"

My mother cut him off as politely as possible. We had to leave. At this very moment, there were events which would change our lives and the lives of thousands of Cubans forever. On our end, my dad was heading to Rancho Boyeros Airport under diplomatic immunity, personally escorted by a Panamanian Colonel.

Teo still stood there with a bandaged forehead. He winked his eye though both his eyes closed —broke a smile, and extended his arm for the Indian handshake.

"We'll see each other again someday."

I didn't know what he meant by *someday?* Perhaps he was still channeling our Cowboy and Indian. But what mattered was that he had held the fort. I shook his arm through the car window and smiled. As we left him behind, that turban of gauze and the red boots "dotting" the bottom of his long freckled legs, gave the impression that Teo was slowly morphing into an exclamation point.

At the airport, we got our passports stamped and were escorted to the plane. My dad got there a little after us, and the Colonel escorted him to the plane. One of the Cuban guards addressed my family with an off-color accusation of betrayal as my dad was about to board the plane.

"*Vayanse Traidores!*"

"*Los traidores son ustedes, que han traicionado la verdad, la democracia, y su patria!*"

The Colonel begged my dad to get on the plane as he continued to harangue the regime loudly about their betrayal of the Fatherland. When Dad finally got to our seats, he hugged my mother, then looked where I sat with my cousins across from them. He came and hugged me but quickly gave me the once over with a puzzled serious look.

"*Quien lo vistio de rojo y negro?*"

He asked my mom who had dressed me in the colors of the revolution? She said she didn't know. Probably me.

"*No te preocupes de eso ahora, chico*".

My father was a bit stressed after spending the night at the embassy. Many years later, his question would have some significance.

As we flew over the Florida Straights, an American U2 pilot, thousands of miles away, had just begun a long parachute descent toward Russian soil after his plane was rocketed. As he opened a fake silver dollar concealing a poisoned pin and debated suicide, one of my cousins, Mayito, finished a whole can of Libby's (pronounced LEE-BEES in Cuba) peaches and spent the rest of the flight puking in the bathroom. We landed in the USA in May 1960. We got processed as political refugees, like hundreds of thousands more would in the years to come.

For some people, I would be a Spic here. Some signs would read: "No dogs, Negroes, or Cubans," "Go back to Cuba!" At first, it hurt, but when I got older, I gave it back to the jingoists with a forced Cuban accent.

"Jess, I cang heah to keel all jor leeders ang fock all jor gweemen!"

But I wouldn't have to deal with that presently, and for the most part, I was welcomed. By the time we left U.S. Immigration, it was dark and we were starved. We checked into the Sagamore Hotel on Miami Beach. My father got some sandwiches to go at Wolfie's and brought them to our rooms. My uncles and aunts met at my parents' room and, after a few of our restless antics, sent my cousins and I to eat in one of their rooms. They had just left their homeland forcibly and were understandably frisky, weary, and in need of each other without interruptions from the varied offspring using beds for trampolines and beating each other cross-eyed with pillows.

We never got to the room next door. Instead, we kept going to the elevator, and one of us got the bright idea to go to the roof. Exiting the elevator on the top floor, we took the stairs the rest of the way. The stars were out, and the crescent moon, three hands up from the sea, could still appear to Luna as a tear in Heaven's dark curtain, which if somehow traversed near enough by a spaceship would offer its passengers a glimpse into celestial affairs *del Mas Allá* (the Hereafter.) We ate our sandwiches. My cousin Mayito made his roast beef sandwich talk like a frog. Nobody liked the pickles, so we balled them up in their bags and put that into a larger bag. I looked at the pool, glowing aquamarine in the darkness several stories down. It reminded me of the shore at our beach house.

Oooo-woo-wooo-woo-woo-woo! After making an Indian-style war cry by tapping my lips with my fingers, I flung the bag. After a long, beautiful arc, it landed in the middle of the pool with a splash. Undulating rings radiated slowly, then lapped the side of the pool. Within seconds, out pops a security guard from behind a small rotunda lined by areca palms. He looks up and scans the roof. We crouched down and then shot the eight stories of stairs like rapids. Crazy Horse Jr. rides again! Our leaping steps thundered in the stairwell. Panting, my eldest cousin, Perucho, gave out the strategy by exhaling most of his words.

"When we ge-het…to…our flo-hor, no running! Walk to…the roo-hooms!"

At the exit door to our floor, we all stopped, then walked—some holding back nervous giggles—toward the room where our parents talked. Hungry for air but breathing slowly, we were each given keys to our rooms by our mothers and kissed good night.

"Hasta mañana."

"Hasta mañana, hasta mañana, hasta mañana…"

I lay in bed in the dark, wondering if the security guard would catch us. Just before I fell asleep, I also pondered over the fate of my Indian moccasins with not even a hair-thin clue that this was the first day of decades of exile. That reality surfaces slowly in a nine-year-old boy full of mischief. Damn merciful of the *Grand Frommage*. I was tired.

*　*　*

Several door knocks break my sleep. A man with a flaming head and receding hairline stands outside my door and slaps the side of his forehead, just missing a mosquito. It is eleven thirty at night. I had been watching the evening news. It is thirty years later. I open the door.

"Luna!"

I did not recognize him. But in his eyes, I could tell he knew who I was.

"Soy Teo!"

"Teo…Teo…Teo…" The name didn't gel. "TEO!" I hugged him.

"Coñooooo! I heard the TV, or I wouldn't have knocked at this hour."

As we started a bottle of Havana Club, which amazingly Teo had managed to keep through his latest capers, he told me about how he had been drafted into the Cuban army.

"But I made up my mind not to go to the war in Angola, so one night, I climbed on a mango tree close to the barracks and start screaming, '*Los Marcianos! Aqui vienen los Marcianos No…!*' And I started firing my AK-47 into the sky. *Rat-tat-tat-tat-tat!* I shot every bullet I had at those Martians and kept screaming until they pulled me down from the tree."

I guess he had turned out one wild cowboy after all.

"After that, I was discharged from the army as *un enfermo mental.* But a year later, I joined the Cuban Army Parachutist team, which somehow did not discover my loony discharge records, and I went on to compete internationally."

He now produced a couple of No.2 Montecristo's, and we dipped the cut tips in the rum. Teo, now a crazy-assed *flying* cowboy, continued his tale through the blue smoke as we moved out to the terrace, a three-quarter Moon, Jupiter, and Saturn accompanying us above.

"During a competition in Mexico, I defected and made my way to the U.S. border, *y ahí me escondí* until my sister *arregló* my entry into the U.S. and my papers…"

As result of his fear of retaliation by Castro's *infiltrados,* he lived a very low-key life in Miami "*callaíto*", he said, for years. One day, he decided to look in the phone book, found my address, and decided to drop by when he was in the area.

"*Ante que se me olvide.* I got something special for you." He gave me a very re-cycled and wrinkled paper bag.

"*Mis mocasines!*"

They looked so little, not at all how I remembered them. And in fact, they didn't have beaded uppers at all, and the blood drops must have blended into the darkened brown leather. I beamed at him.

"*Donde Carajo…* How'd you…Where did you find them?"

He told me that one of my nannies had been a staunch sympathizer of Fidel, the one who chose my clothes the day I left—the red Lacoste and the black pants. The colors of the 26 of July flag, the colors of Fidel's revolution, and the same colors that had prompted my father to ask my mother in the plane out of Cuba, "Who dressed him in these colors?" That nanny's son had always wanted a pair of Indian moccasins after he had seen them on me. Seeing that we were leaving the country, she took them out of my bag.

When it dawned on this woman that she wasn't getting our house, the revolution didn't mean the end of privilege, and she wasn't one of the chosen, she began working at Teo's house after his mom died. Her kid came around one day with the moccasins. Teo recognized them and told the kid to give them up. He refused. Teo just grabbed them. The moral upper hand prevailed. He had kept them all this time, and every time he left the country to compete, he always took the mocs with him in case he had a chance to defect.

"Teo, you crazy lovely bastard!"

I hugged him hard. When we stepped back, I barely perceived a whisper of a V-shaped scar in the sea of freckles on his forehead.

"How did you get that on your head, man?"

"Hell, if *you* don't remember. You shho…" He caught himself and smiled. "I hit my head on a branch!"

Some palefaces had the hearts of eagles.

Handjob In The Crib
of Smilodectes

Exile didn't affect you nearly as much as hormones at ten years old. I already knew English, as did most of my cousins, but we had no idea what we had lost or for how long. Miami was just a different place than Cuba to raise hell, grow up, and spring boners left and right…

August 1960 was steaming. When we moved out of the Sagamore Hotel, our original retreat upon arriving in Miami, the family set up shop at Surfside on Eighty-Eighth Street and Garland Avenue. A quiet neighborhood today, nearly comatose then. The families got three houses with adjoining yards. Everyone believed it was a matter of six-months—the U. S. could not possibly allow Communism in its backyard for long—and we'd be back in the homeland, minus *El Barbudo, en un dos por cuatro*. My mother had brought 370,000 Cuban pesos. At an even exchange with the U.S. dollar, it was a small fortune in 1960. A speculator offered her seventy cents on the dollar. She didn't accept. Today, they sit in a closet, a monument to the unpredictable nature of U.S. foreign policy and those who bank on logic.

In Cuba, it was the Year of Agrarian Reform for Fidel. In Miami, the first hatchlings of Cuban exile-CIA liaisons were emerging from their shells and heading toward the poisoned waters of the Bay of Pigs. But the destiny of nations was not on the mind of a pre-pubescent individual entering the Age of the Lunar Crotch Pull.

One afternoon, while my cousins attended summer camp, I decided to climb a banyan tree growing between our house and theirs. I loved to climb the roots that dropped from the branches. They gave that part of the yard an exotic rainforest feel. After climbing as high as the branches would hold me, I found a sturdy fork and set up a crow's-nest. The leaves formed a dense canopy, a secure blind from where you could spy patches of street through small breaks in the leaf cover. Moreover, you could hear most anything approaching within a fifty-yard range or more. I felt at home here.

Years later in an Anthropology course, I found out that homo sapiens were believed to descend from a tree rodent named Smilodectes. In that class, I pictured Smilodectes thriving in a tree very much like this banyan. A fire ant the size of a termite was crawling up the branch toward my crotch. I took a pencil out of my shirt pocket and flicked it off the tree. It plummeted like a skydiver seen from the open hatch of a plane, then scuttled aimlessly among the leaves on the ground. Minutia: mockers of gravity.

This pencil had the eraser bitten off down to the sharp brass band. I scraped the bark, and a sticky white resin oozed down the edge of the branch. I toyed with it, but when it dried on my hand, I couldn't rub it off. Scraping it against a branch only succeeded in soiling the resin with bark dust. I thought of washing it off but decided it could wait. The thought of washing made me think of my nannies in Havana when I was eight.

It began to fuel a boner. Playing Cowboys and Indians in Cuba, I would often hide inside a corridor-like croton hedge. When the game was over and my friends went home, I would sometimes go back and place handpicked bits of earth inside my tiny foreskin and rush to one of the nannies. I would always pop a woody. They would just soap it, rinse it summarily, and be on their way. But for me, somehow I knew I was onto something grand, a lifeforce class motif. Li'l Smilo was hard now. I pulled it out of my shorts to look at it. It throbbed like a second hand on a quartz clock. Touching it a certain way felt better than others. Hit or miss exploration.

The universe converged on my hot little spur. Suddenly, the irregular breathing…then the Big Bang Spasms. It momentarily dazed little Luna the Tree-Dweller.

Whooaa!

It shook my stardust. I had felt this before by letting the shower stream fall on it but had never experienced it spanking-the-monkey style—basic perhaps, but manifestly cosmic. Of course, I did not ejaculate. My DNA was not in solution yet. Shortly after, I tucked Li'l Smilo, who hadn't quite piped down, back in my pants and lay back against a branch in a mild opiate-like stupor. A ray of sun pierced a tiny star in the tree canopy. I made it appear and disappear by opening and closing one eye, pretending the Earth was a cyclop's eye, which he opened very slowly at sunrise and shut very slowly at dusk.

Kaaaaaaaah!

I jerked out of my skin, nearly falling out of the tree. Had not the auxiliary roots from an upper branch been there to grab, I surely would have crash-landed. The crow that had perched briefly above me and screeched its presence shot out of there, wing tips and asshole, snapping a dry twig in its path. We had thoroughly scared the stuffing out of each other.

The low gear winding betrayed the school bus turning the corner on Eighty-Eighth. I couldn't wait to tell my cousins about my discovery, especially my older cousin, Perucho, His Lardness, who was thirteen and thought he knew everything. The month before, he had pilfered a Kotex from his mother and told us that she bled all the time from her *peepee*. That he had seen a bloody one, just like the one he had procured, in his mom's bathroom. We hadn't known whether to believe him or not, but his younger brother, Mayito, the one who had eaten and puked a whole can of peaches on our exodus from Cuba, had snatched the sanitary pad from his hand and had taken off toward the house. Perucho tried to catch him, but His Lardness couldn't overtake him. We had followed Mayito through the front door of their house and into the living room where his parents were entertaining guests, including a former presidential candidate from Cuba. Mayito then produced the crumpled pad and said to his mother crying, "*Perucho dice que te sale sangre por el pipi.*" I guess he thought his mother was going to die because she bled. That night, you could hear His Lardness's lamentations.

"*Ay Papi No perdóname! Nooooo!*"

Instead of the forgiveness implored by Peruchos's "*perdonames*", his dad thrashed him with the belt several more times, mocking Peruchos's plaintive tone.

"*Perdóname? Perdóname? Mojón atrevído!*"

But in spite of the belting he received from his dad and the "*Ay Papi No, perdóname. Noooo!*" we had heard through the windows, said phrase now dreaded by Perucho due to its frequent exploitation (once, even the American kids in the school bus, oblivious to its meaning, chanted it at him), he still received respect for his Kotex contribution to our continuing pre-pubescent sex education. We had not even come close to topping that one. Prompted by that stunt, his parents had sent him and his brother to summer camp to curtail their idle time.

The bus stopped across the street, bursting with that unmistakable kid chatter. My cousins stepped out, the air brakes exhaled, and the bus accelerated. I rushed down, brachiating tree limbs, very much the new and improved Smilodectes. I spotted them crossing the street toward their home.

"Perucho!"

They approached the base of the tree.

"*Mojón pero que tu hacías por allá arriba?*"

That was Perucho, trying very much to sound like Mr. Big Shot, calling me turd and questioning the value of my tree stunts. No problem. I had a story, though suddenly had second thoughts about telling my little cousin, Mayito, especially after his Kotex show and tell.

"Mayito, vete para allá. I want to tell Perucho something."

"No way. I'm staying."

He refused, pretty much as expected. But when we pushed him out of the gate, he began to scream, so we agreed he could stay, provided he kept his mouth shut. I reported about stroking it and what a great feeling it was—this unbelievable tickly feeling.

"Unbeleebol teeckeelee feeleen? *Eso es una paja Mojón!"*

In an unadorned phrase, Perucho said what I had discovered was simply a hand-job. That he had already been doing it for a while. But he cautioned me, as a priest had him, about masturbation making hair grow on your palm. The next line, Perucho delivered in *jerigonza,* a form of pig Latin nannies and parents employed, so that Mayito was not privy to it. When Mayito objected to the new tactic, His Lardness, warping his face to emphasize his claim, pledged aggravated battery. Mayito consented.

In *jerigonza,* you just added a syllable like *ti* or *te* in between every syllable of a word, a cryptic device practical in Spanish because every syllable of a word is pronounced phonetically. Perucho delivered the following:

-ti-**THAT**-ti-**IS**-ti-**WHY**-ti-**I**-ti-**WAIT**-ti-**TILL**-ti-**MY**-ti-**PA**-ti-**RENTS**-ti-**GO**-ti-**OUT**-ti-**AND**-ti-**DO**-ti-**IT**-ti-**WITH**-ti-**ONE**-ti-**OF**-ti-**MY**-ti-**MO**-ti-**THER'S**-ti-**DISH**-ti-**WA**-ti-**SHING**-ti-**GLOVES**.

But he advised rinsing it very well afterwards. I wasn't totally convinced about the hairy palm theory but ti-**PE**-ti-**RU**-ti-**CHO**-ti-**THE**-ti-**RUB**-ti-**BER**-ti-**GLOVE**-ti-**STROKE**-ti-**AR**-ti-**TISTE** had planted the pernicious seed of doubt. That night, though I felt like trying it again, I refrained, keeping my hands above the sheets until I fell asleep.

I dreamt I was in the Banyan tree, lying back, hands behind my head on the same branch I was on earlier that day. Below, my little cousin, Mayito, stood on a bough with a vine in his hand, ready to swing out. He leaped. I felt a tug on the back of my scalp but quickly realized he was not on a vine at all. He was swinging on a ponytail growing from the back of *my* hand! I tried to get up but was fossilized.

I wailed "Let go! Mayito, let go! Your gonna rip my hand!"

My cousin Perucho, now a tubby gargoyle with bird claws for feet, crouched on a branch next to me, cackling hysterically and applauding with oversized rubber gloves.

I awoke, jerking into the sitting position, about three in the morning, spooked. The echo from Perucho's corvine shrieks riddled me with goose bumps. I sat there quietly for a moment. By sleeping on my arm, I had obstructed the circulation to my hand. I massaged my forearm, working my way to the needle and pins on my hand where I discovered, to my horror, that there was something *growing* on it—uncomfortably close to my dad's two-day shadow. I leaped out of bed and turned on the light. Sure as hell, there was something growing on my palm. My heart ran away. But it trailed way behind my rattled psyche. I headed for my parent's room.

Mid-hallway, I turned around and headed back. What was I going to say? "Mom, look, I got hair on my palm!" Death by terminal embarrassment? How had my cousin thought of the rubber glove? Oh, I wish he would've told me earlier?

I'll shave it!

But the kit was in my parent's bathroom. I went out into the hallway again, but the fear of getting caught and having to explain dragged me back. I'll scrape it. I lay down in bed and checked again. Not only was it there, but the fuzzy growth now appeared to have turned browner. The pencil on my night table caught my eye. There always seemed to be a pencil around. I could attempt to guillotine it off carefully with the brass edge. I picked it up, and the brass also had hair! *Ave María!*

But miraculously post- Smilodectian reasoning was in effect:

It. Was. The. Tree. Resin. Cretin-íllo!

The tree resin with the bark. *You did not wash your hands before dinner. You did not wash your hands before going to sleep.* The light at the end of the tunnel led to the bathroom. I scrubbed hard to get it off. It was a stubborn little sap spot.

Back in bed, surrounded by the fragrance of Palmolive soap, I thanked God for not finding hair on my palm. I had survived the first parochial school onslaught on my ti-**GE**-ti-**NI**-ti-**TALS** and emerged confident that Li'l Smilo and God were not enemies.

Al's Matinee Falsies

This boy couldn't stand the pain... This boy... This boy...

I had just danced the freshly released Beatle classic with Mary Thompson, the host of the seventh-grade party. Her unassuming little bumps had rubbed against my chest. My young spur was still pulsing. Being deeply entrenched in parochial school protocol, I knew I was heading to Sin City, with a girl named Mary of all choices. What was next, robbing the poor box?

Mary and her Mom prepared more refreshments in the kitchen, lining up the waxed paper cups of cola, supermarket cake, cheese doodles, and potato chips on the dull formica countertop. After draining a cupful of stale cola, I sat on the sofa's rattan armrest and chewed on the cup's rim, recovering from the narcotic effect of my first slow dance.

"*Quieres ir al cine con Mary mañana?*"

Carlos, who had just come in from the balcony sporting Beelzebub's grin, awaited my answer about the rendezvous. I picked a few waxy flakes from my tongue and put them in the cup.

"How?"

"Ya yo me matié con Ann."

"De verdad?"

I couldn't believe Carlos had already *made out* with Mary's friend Ann. I had yet to kiss *any* girl, ever. He must've done well because he was invited to see *Mary Poppins* the next day with her and Mary. Ann had told him Mary liked me.

"So, Luna, do you want to go or not?"

"Yes, Carolius."

Happy to hear that I would go, primarily so someone would keep Mary occupied, Carlos grabbed two cokes and returned to the balcony, eager to steal a few more kisses from Ann.

Twist and shoooout, C'mon, C'mon, C'mon, baby, now, C'mon, baby...

I was no Chubby Checker, but what was there to it? Besieged by impure thoughts, I continued twisting with Mary. But much to my disappointment, her mother announced the party was over. I had counted on dancing another slow one with her. As I passed Mary, who stood by the door saying her goodbyes to a small group who had left, she took advantage of the momentary lull to ask me if I was going to the movies tomorrow.

"Yes, he *is!*"

Carlos had rushed up from behind me, answered, pinched my butt cheek, and disappeared just as swiftly to escort Ann to her mother's car. Oh yeah, he'd go out there and shamelessly charm the mother too. I felt like slapping him.

Mary and I said our *Adiós.* She glanced back and, assured her Mom was not watching, kissed me briskly on the lips. *On the lips!*

"I'll see you at the movies."

"Okay...," Luna said with an idiotic grin.

My wiener throbbed all the way to the bus stop. I approached my school, Saint Patrick's, a two-story Mediterranean building with Spanish tile and rows of single-hung windows, half a block from 41st Street on Miami Beach. Passing by my first classroom in America, I recalled following our nun to mass the day President Kennedy got shot. A black lady had sobbed at the church steps, maybe not yet secure to worship inside.

From the candy store man to the bus driver, hearts had been broken. Someone had killed their golden boy. It had been a somber day. But in Miami, some Cubans looked forward to another president. This one had betrayed them in the heat of an invasion to liberate their motherland. The children prayed.

But this evening, my mind was in Mary-landia. I fantasized about feeling her breasts but desisted when I realized I had crossed a street and was nearly hit by an *invisible* baked goods truck. Li'l Smilo, the pirate D.J., had been broadcasting sin from his crotch level studios, negligent of the world order.

Mary was not that attractive. Frankly, I had really fancied a Cuban girl named Beatriz. Almond skin, big honey-colored eyes alternately sensuous and angelic—this last combination an ancient and potent aphrodisiac on much wiser men than I. But her family kept her behind five feet of bulletproof prudence. The movies? Alone! *Ni se te ocurra!*

There had also been an Italian girl, Margherite L., who wore glasses— an accessory we stupid assholes shunned away from at that time. She had luscious little plums, maddening lips, and even at that age, a waistline and hips that begged for a pair of firm hands. Many years later, I would remember the dimples she made when I caught her gazing at me. But I had been too busy drooling over the little Cuban idol in the next aisle to notice the shy tenderness offered behind Margherite's near-sighted lenses. The memory of her hazel-gray eyes would provoke a case of gentle melancholia about lost opportunity in the future Luna.

When I got home the night of the party, I began thinking about all these girls with the obligatory hands under the sheets. I created the Bride of Lunanstein. The adolescent Queen of *E Pluribus Uno*. I fused Mary's accessibility and body heat with Beatriz's cherubic face of perdition, *Oui! Oui!* Now, ah, wez feeleeng-uh mai ungry lee-tell ahnds widt Marrgharreet-z tenderg-uh leet-tell mell-ungs. *Oh! Oh! Lord!* All were now part of an ideal and precocious little nymph under the sheets of my adolescent mind. All now willing and delectable donors at the operating bed of Luna The Mad Little Surgeon of Hormone (pronounced with a French *R* and the accent on *mone:* WHORGH-MOAN). The truth was that if any of them would have so much as grazed my *pipi* accidentally, my heart would have blasted through my chest and become another crater on the moon.

The next morning, Sunday, I scrambled powdered eggs and grilled a slice of *carne del refugio*—the pressed canned meat which, in addition to powdered milk and Wisconsin cheddar, the U.S. Dept of Agriculture generously offered at the Cuban Refugee Center known now as the historical Freedom Tower.

After breakfast, it was off to church, where I would survive the Sermon of Father Armstrong dealing with Christ turning the water into wine at the wedding feast. Years later, I heard Lord Buckley's version in his classic riff, *The Naz*. The Beat era wit would've swept this common pulpit cricket off the stand. I would have been a faithful member of Lord B's congregation had he demonstrated a yen for the cloth.

The priest segued from the wine to sharing, unselfishness, *refugees*. How lucky we were, us Cubans in the audience, and how much luckier the Americans. Not because they hadn't lost their country, but because they could offer their country to these Cuban people who had been disenfranchised, some of whom now had prospered and were themselves in the position to assist their less fortunate compatriots. With an aura of pallbearers, two older gents in gray suits began to pass the hat.

"I'm not asking for any miracles. It would be immensely vain of you or I to believe we could match the benevolence of Jesus. But in the capacity allowed everyone, we could aspire, in His Spirit, to ease the load of the less fortunate…"

Men reached for their wallets or fished for bills and change in their pockets. The din of coins and some paper rustling could be heard dropping into the basket working the aisles.

"Whether a donation is small or large is not the point. Only we can judge the fairness of our gift against what God has granted us. And among the many things granted us, the most important—you could say as important as our immortal soul, for without it we shan't be saved—our conscience."

An attractive woman next to me unsnapped her purse and pulled out a *ten dollar bill!* I wondered what noble torrent inspired her generosity. Or in retrospect, perhaps a gnawing *mea culpa.* To me, back then, ten bucks was the down payment on the space program.

"Bequeathed on us the ability to judge right from wrong. So, with your God-given conscience, I ask you to reach in your pockets *and* purses today and share with bliss the fortune God has provided you."

There didn't appear to be much bliss or fortune out here. Dropping the tender became a heart-rending proposition for ye faithful, their faces stern and solemn as if at a funeral mass for the double murder of their parents.

I usually threw in a nickel or a dime. In '64, a dime meant two Milky Ways. So my conscience was at ease with my level of beneficence. However, when the chapeau approached, and I groped in my pockets and realized I had *no money,* the hat man pursed his lips, vexed at the delay caused by my pocket acrobatics. He moved on to the winsome lady who, after smiling sympathetically, dropped the ten-spot. Mistaking the generous young woman for my mom, he changed tack and now smiled at my peccadillo. I was crushed.

How was I supposed to go to the movies with Mary this afternoon?

Unfortunately, I had already spent my allowance on a mail-order plastic submarine advertised on a cereal box. The three-inch sub was powered by an effervescent, like ground Alka-Seltzer, which caused the submarine to surface, release the bubbles, and sound again. Who had conceived this marvel of science? So now, instead of the movies, I could watch this battleship-gray suppository dive to the bottom of my tub while my buddy Carlos made off with the two birds. *No can do.* There had to be a way. And I was not going to ask my parents because they'd probably give it to me but not before subjecting me to a lecture on frugality. And they'd be right. We were going through some hard times. We weren't eating scrambled egg talc and ground cow lip patties for yuks.

After the service, I paused at the end of my pew, yielding the center aisle to an elderly couple. The feeble man barely maintained progress. As he passed, I noticed a dollar bill blooming from a trembling arthritic claw propped against his hip. The old lady led the way. Probably heading to the alms box. Oh! If only he dropped it? My movie *and* my bus fare. Enter my *Guardian Angel.*

"*What was that?*"

"I'm sorry. I just wanted to go…I thought if…I'll give it back next week…It…*I* know, I shouldn't think like that. Fine. I won't even think about it."

After appeasing my *G.A.,* I thought, *You know, it's easy for him to be a goody- two-shoes. He was* already *holy.* My *G.A.* couldn't hear this particular thought. These kinds of thoughts I thought in a special frequency I had devised. By rolling my eyes as far as I could to the back of my head, which made my eardrums flutter, I scrambled the signal, thus my thoughts became immune to angelical analysis.

But Luna had been on the right track. The *G.A.* wasn't facing long time in purgatory or life in Hell. All you had to do was die unbaptized, which could be completely out of your hands, and you could spend an eternity scrutinizing your mired soul in *Limbo.* Oh yeah! It made it a *hell* of a lot easier to preach from a state of grace. The G.A. already had himself a cabin in the luxury liner. The rest of us sea monkeys were just treading ocean in The Storm—the more pompous bragging they heard the Foghorn In The Night.

Not to mention, the *G.A.* had no wiener trying to take over the driver's seat, making it a breeze for his holy-moly ass to pontificate.

The old man reached out to the alms box and tried to push the dollar through the slot. His knotted, balled-up fist twitching at the end of his arm, like an ostrich head on its fractured neck. When he shuffled away, a small corner of the bill stuck out. Visions of infernal damnation battled with a crack at Mary's modest titties. It was Li'l Smilo against centuries of Judeo-Christian retribution.

The last couple of people walked past my pew. I made believe I was tying my shoe to give them time to clear my objective. There were stakes now. The odds were up, so a low echelon demon began to shark around for my young soul.

"Don't think about it. Take it."

"Don't you dare, Luna!"

The G.A. was back in my corner. This kind of crap really made me uneasy, besides throttling up the heart rate. I almost didn't notice a lady dressed in black, kneeling at the side altar with her back to me, praying to Anthony, the Saint of Misplaced Belongings. The *last* thing Luna needed anywhere near him at that moment was an invocation to a retriever of missing things, much less one canonized and known as "Hammer of the Heretics." But Luna was on a mission for Li'l Smilo—an adversary not to be underestimated.

I approached the box, close enough to see the green ink on the bill. I stalked it out of the corner of my eye. One last glance at the lady before going in for the kill, making sure to under-scan, thus conveniently keeping the almost life-sized crucifixion suspended over the Tabernacle at the end of the aisle, out of my line of sight. I reached for the single. Yes! No! Yes! No! Yes! Yesssss!

Out in the sunshine, I rushed toward the bridge three blocks south on Alton Road. My heart was double-timing the rhythms of Babylon. My G.A. must have gotten sucker-punched back there.

Now, on top of the bridge, I was panting, still a bit loopy from the adrenalin. Below me, the mullet schooled lazily in the falling tide of the canal, free of sin. The crumpled bill felt moist in my clenched fist. I had killed game. Bloodied my canines. Now, I could truly feel a kinship to the Banished Tribe of Paradise. My breathing stabilized. From up here, I could see the bell tower above the Monsignor's residence.

"Give it back!"

My G.A. had caught up. I felt a bit nauseous.

"If you give it back now, it's okay."

"Okay. Okay…All right!"

I descended the bridge toward the church. My God, he was right. What was I doing? I had *never* done anything like this!

"Oh yeah?! Well, I'll tell you another thing you'll *not* do, Mr. Holy Pants—go to the movies today. No movie, no Mary."

The fiend wasn't going to allow his new customer to cancel so easily.

"You can always pay it back. You're *borrowing* it!"

I didn't have to think about it long. I did an about-face and was homeward bound again on Alton Road.

I went through the ten blocks to 29th street with a vigorous gait, humming *William Tell's Overture*, flashing back to Lone Ranger episodes I used to see in Havana. It conveniently kept my mind on my walking rhythm. One, two, three, four, five, six, don't step on the cracks. I passed a moribund worm, still gooey, shrouded in a blanket of red ants at the edge of the sod. *Lest we forget the Wages of Sin!* I walked a little faster and gripped the dollar tightly in my fist.

I figured, if someone stopped me, I could quickly ditch it in the bushes. Only one more half-block to go. *Tara-tat tara-tat, Tara-tat tara-tat, Tara-tat tara-tat tarataaaaaata!*

An old Woodie station wagon drove by, burning oil. Its loud muffler drowned my overture momentarily and slowly went around a curve in the distance. A stream of white smoke eerily lingered on the empty road.

"How could you steal money from that sickly old man? From the poor? From the *church*! You think you're going to get away with this, buster!"

Oh God! I felt the G.A. was going to appear out of the exhaust cloud at any moment. I turned around and headed for the church. That was it. I was giving it back, and to hell with this torture.

"No movieeee! No Mareeeey! And what's more—*no titties!*"

The fiend was taking no prisoners. I about-faced and sprinted home, dodging my G.A. momentarily.

This banter had produced an intense impulse to move my bowels. That refugee breakfast couldn't take all that jostling. Once home, I ran to the bathroom. The grand fight between Good and Evil had given me a case of the Hershey Squirts. I examined the crumpled bill while I sat on the bowl but quickly put it away when the eye on the truncated pyramid appeared glaring and accusatory. The Latin quotes around it, *Annuit Coeptis* and *Novus Ordo Seclorum*, didn't help either. It seemed like the more authoritarian an institution, worldly or religious, the more mumbo-jumbo.

It was half past noon. Carlos and the girls would be here anytime to wait for the R bus to Lincoln Road. In my room, I decided I was just "borrowing the money" as the demon said. Naturally, the G.A. had stayed silent to show his disapproval. Not Li'l Smilo. He was tugging on the pro vote lever with tingling delight. As a matter of fact, he *was* the pro vote lever.

I slipped on a pair of navy slacks from *"El Sótano de Richarr,"* or Richard's Bargain Basement. Richard's was a department store downtown that held sales of its irregular or overstocked merchandise in the basement. Many immigrants and people on moderate incomes shopped there. So, I would *never* tell anyone that's where I shopped. But you could get a pair of slacks for five dollars that would normally sell for ten. Occasionally, I would run into a Cuban schoolmate shopping there with his parents. At that point, the party who made the first sighting would usually try to hide behind the nearest clothing rack until the coast was clear. My cover would be blown when my mother would call me by nickname at the cash register. *Luna!* At that point, I wanted to reincarnate as the crotch seam on the pair of madras Bermuda shorts on the last rack.

The garment irregularities would vary. The crotch would be a little tight on some slacks, or the side seams on the jeans drifted toward the front slightly at the ankle—nothing anybody would really notice unless you showed it. It was more of a psychological handicap.

I reached in the drawer for a shirt to go with my navy basement pants. My choice: a golden brown zippered turtle/V-neck combo. It was a little warm for long sleeve velour, but I wanted the look. I spread Vaseline through my hair, parted it on the left, and combed it back. Then, placing my palm in the middle of my head, I slid my hair down to mid-forehead with an "S" motion, giving it that overhanging brim groove. You'd have to get it in one stroke, or you'd have to do it over. I had conceived this 'doo for a Halloween beatnik costume along with painted goatee. Approaching doors with snapping fingers, I'd announce, "Like, trick or treat, cool cat (kitty)." I had gotten attached to the hairstyle, so now I wore it for real. I looked at myself in the mirror. My pants were a tad too short, but my hair relayed Coolsville. My conscience had the occasion to give me the once over in the full-length reflection, but I was ready.

"I'll just save my lunch money for three days and put it back. I just won't eat, okay?"

I reached for the bottle of English Leather on my night table. Next to the cologne, a laminated picture of the Sacred Heart lay flat. Jesus looked at me. Guilt spiked my heart when our eyes met. I averted the warmth of his gaze and slapped on the cologne. Looking again, I fastened on the glowing thorn-ringed heart inside his see-through chest. Glancing again at his face, I sensed compassion. He actually seemed to understand my predicament. A soft celestial voice seemed to say.

"*Go…Go to the movie, Luna. You can pay me back. Just promise you'll never do it again.*"

"Thank you, Jesus. I'll never do it again. *Te lo prometo.*"

I propped up the picture against the cologne bottle, then slipped my black Thom McCann loafers on without socks, confident the Lord was my shepherd. Luna the Happy Lamb did the sign of the cross.

"See!"

I said that out loud for the benefit of the Guardian Angel, who incidentally was not around, or was hell-bent on the silent treatment. Either way was just fine by me. I felt rebuilt and didn't need Weiner-less Wonder and his nagging litanies. Matter of fact, this called for a celebration. Yeah, a little party atmosphere. I put the dollar in my pocket and slapped Manfred Mann's *Doowaddidy* on the record player. Some scholars would argue that this is how empires fall, but Manfred was sayin':

There she was, just a walking down the street singing,
Dowa didi dididum dididooo…

Si Señor! I was cutting some steps now and everything.

Snapping her fingers and a'shuffling her feet…

Imagining Beatriz before me, my partner of choice in these euphoric departures, I jumped up with a half-twist to land, shaking my hips, but it didn't pan out. My new leather soles slipped on the terrazzo floor, ripping my tail seam.

Well, I'm hers, and she's mine, and wedding bells are gonna chime…

I lifted the pullover in front of the mirror and discovered my white briefs rendering a crescent moon out the tear on my pants. Not quite the coat of arms I'd envisioned for my lineage. Thank God, Beatriz hadn't really been there. I dropped my pants, a bit disheartened, hoping this wasn't the G.A.'s idea of harmless tomfoolery. I was not amused.

In my mother's room, I corrected the seam problem from the inside with three small safety pins. It wasn't perfect, but I checked in the mirror, and the pullover covered it. I started the song again to ward off priggish spirits and soon was shaking my hips, lightly enough not to undermine my repair—but quite enough to display heart under adversity.

Doowadiddy diddydum diddydoo....

The front bell rang. I headed for the door, my confidence slightly marred by a jury-rigged posterior.

It was Carlos and the girls. Carlos came through the doorway doing "the swim" and improvising lyrics to *Dowaddidy*, partly in Spanish so the girls wouldn't understand.

"There she was, *te-voy-a-coger las te-ti-cas.* Singin' Doowadiddy diddydum diddydooooo!"

The line about grabbing their titties, he did right in his date's face. Embarrassing. Anne and Mary smiled at his antics. Mary tried to figure out what he said.

"What are *ticas?*"

Carlos the Wayward Minstrel watched me sweat.

"They're a...Well, it's not...*teticas* is a part..."

"What, like ticks!"

"Yeah."

I excused myself and quenched the record player, and off we were to the movies.

On the bus, Mary didn't look as appetizing, which made me less thrilled about dropping the loot on *Mary Poppins,* not to mention risking eternal hellfire. But Carlos, aware of my spreading disenchantment, provided diversion to foster his agenda. He kept caroling *"cogerte las teticas,* ticas, ticaaaas!" periodically and snapping his hands at the air like crab claws to the beat. Li'l Smilo was still on a hard sell campaign. And once we got to the theater and the lights dimmed, he would be in his element.

We walked up to the fifth row, well away from the rest of the theater population, and took our seats. Two minutes after the front credits, when Dick Van Dyke delivered "the Constable is respons*t*able," I knew this petard just wasn't my kind of humor. But I did oblige a giggle or two for Mary, while putting my arm around the back of her seat to test the waters. I spent the next forty minutes—all through Mrs. Banks singing about universal suffrage, the hiring of Mary Poppins as a nanny, and the trip *through* the magic painting into the country side—vacillating on when to put my hand on Mary's shoulder.

A lady needn't feeah, when you are neaaah…

To my right, I saw Carlos out of the corner of my eye, sucking at Anne's face as if attempting to taste the seat stuffing through her.

Feeling I was lagging, I let Mary feel my arm around her shoulder. No resistance. I moved my cheek closer to her. Not a word. I felt her warmth. Li'l Smilo began to register. She leaned her head on my shoulder. I approached her cheek with my lips. She turned and kissed me. I was there an eternity, breathing through my nose. I didn't want to stop. Carlos elbowed my ribs with the silent missive: "shake the lead, *campeón!*" He had another slap coming on the debit sheet. But the movie *was* almost three-quarters over.

We were slouched way down on the seats. I kept kissing her and moved my other hand slyly as possible toward her breast. There was no turning back now from sweet damnation. The rest of the film might as well have been radio, for neither Mary nor I opened our eyes.

I leaned further toward her, grazing the tip of her bra ever so slightly with my palm, almost as if by accident. She didn't say anything. Yes. Catholic girls! My heart drum-rolled.

I had needles and pins on my lips. But I kept steering toward the prize. I squeezed her breast slightly with my fingertips. She kept kissing me. Li'l Smilo was doing figure eights in my shorts.

Supercalafrajalisticexprialadocious!

I gave Mary a harder squeeze on her breast, but something was amiss. To my severe embarrassment, I realized I had been squeezing the padded *armrest* next to her the whole time. She had her eyes closed. Safe. I removed my hand immediately and glanced back as far as I could without removing my lips from Mary, to see if Carlos had seen this potentially never-live-it-down-if-it-got-into-the-wrong-hands *faux pas*. Luckily, from what I could perceive, he was still engaged. Thank God. Now, fully sober, I went after the real thing. The bottom of her bra exuded humid warmth. She had been perspiring. I was getting dizzy.

The End!

When the theater lights came on, Mary sat up quickly and embarrassedly pushed my hand away. Li'l Smilo was still pulsing. I sat back.

Whoaaaaaaa!

I landed on my feet with my butt on fire. Apparently, two of the safety pins had popped during my rub-a-dub-dub and stuck me on one of my cheeky-cheek-cheeks.

Attempting to pull the pants away, I stuck my hand with another popped pin. My young ass had been converted into a porcupine.

Carlos fell to the floor laughing, and his little strumpet joined him with a soprano neighing. He pissed me off. I must have been blood red with embarrassment. Mary laughed at first but, noticing I was rattled, tried to stop the other two.

"Stop laughing. He hurt himself."

I shoved Carlos to the side with a vengeance on my way to the boy's room. Inside one of the toilet booths, I removed my pants and felt my butt where the pin had stuck me. I found a tiny little spot of blood but was no longer bleeding.

While snapping the pins to fasten the seam, I became aware of an awful stench. Turning around, I confronted a heinous pile of stools in the bowl. I relocated two stalls down. What a day. I took Li'l Smilo out to pee and noticed little drops of sticky fluid on my underwear. I touched it and smelled it. I finally had seminal fluid. It tasted salty. When I peed, the stream was gooey at first, and Luna *El Hombre* marveled at it. I finished with the pins and was slipping my pants back on when I felt the presence. The G.A.! So he did have a hand. This whole pin prank was him, after all.

"You're a real fruity punk!"

This time, I didn't care if he heard me. There was a knock at the door. I quickly put Li'l Smilo back in my pants. I didn't want the G.A. catching me like this. He could still scare the piss out of me if he decided to appear. There was no arguing, fruity punk and all. He had the upper hand. I reached for the door confrontationally. But a deeper side invoked, *Please God, don't let him be* really *there!* I held my breath and reached for the bolt.

"Knock, knock!"

I jerked my hand back, recognizing Carlos's voice.

He must have tiptoed to the door and was now expecting the "Who's there?" reply from me. I wasn't in the mood.

"C'mon, Luna. Who's there?"

"Hey, asshole, I don't want to hear it."

I exited the stall. He answered himself.

"Who's there? Al. Al who?"

He almost didn't manage to get it out without laughing.

"Al…Filer!"

I didn't get it. Who the hell was Al Filer? I washed my hands. He kept asking questions and answering for me.

"File this, Carlos."

"Who's Al Filer? Al Filer is *Alfiler!*"

When he said it with the Spanish pronunciation, it was *Alfiler* (pronounced AL-FEE-LAIR) Spanish for pin. Apparently harmless, but Carlos was notorious for giving nicknames that stuck, and that was exactly why I had been wary of being caught with the armrest in my hand.

So, I jumped his precocious little ass and put him in a headlock. It was easy. He was weak from laughing. I slapped his head the couple of times I owed him.

"Al…Filer…," he kept saying. He hadn't noticed I had worked him into the nasty booth.

"*Fo!* Who died in here?"

"You, if you keep it up!"

"I promise, Al. I won't tell anyone about the voodoo doll in your ass?"

He laughed some more. I took advantage and pulled his head within inches of the noxious floating lumps.

"Hey, Luna, come on. I'm gonna puke!" He still couldn't stop laughing.

"Shake on it!"

"Okay, *esta bien*. I'll shake on it!"

On the ride back, Carlos would occasionally break into laughter. The girls would laugh also, although they claimed they were laughing at Carlos. Mary attempted to stop him a few times.

"Don't be a spaz, Carlos."

"I can't help it, Al. Every time I think of how you jumped..."

"He can't help it, Mary. He was born an asshole."

Before I reached my stop, Mary whispered that I was a very good kisser and maybe we could go out again. I told her we would, although we never did.

Except for the few times he called me "Al" back in school, Carlos kept his word. When our friends asked him what Al meant, he said it was between him and me. They tried to pressure him by saying, "What now, *secreticos de maricones*?" But Carlos never broke down on their us-keeping-fag-secrets line of interrogation.

Mary had warned Anne against telling anyone. Apparently, she had some dirt on her. It worked. Bless her homely little heart, for the Al Filer debacle had all the makings of a major image homicide. I thanked Mary. I think she loved me.

The next Sunday, I went to confession. The priest was a Spaniard with abominably stale breath. At that time, I would reveal everything. A few years after that, I stopped going all together, suspecting a number of these confessors were, in reality, vicarious little perverts. When the priest heard about the dollar from the poor box, he made me feel like I had disemboweled Baby Jesus and pissed on His face. I had stolen from The House Of God. These words he had whispered with vigor and drama, reserving a spasmodic exhalation for the word GOD as in:

The house of Go...hod!

The old bastard shook me up pretty bad. What was I thinking? Why had I done that? Oh, a girl. Yes, well, the devil worked through women often. I should beware, for I would encounter this again throughout my life. A good woman could be your best companion, bear your children, offer you solace. But then there were vixens, "who could only seduce and drag you down to perdition, despair and oblivion. Pity wretched Samson." And those were only the worldly consequences!

What did I do in the theater? I told him. Including the armrest scenario, thinking that would mitigate my punishment since I hadn't hit pay dirt. Oh no, because my intention had been sinful.

In any case, the real whopper had been the poor box caper. I was instructed to pray a whole rosary. That's an Apostle's Creed, six Our Fathers, fifty-three Hail Mary's, announce the Five Joyful Mysteries, six Glory Be's, a *Salve*, and a Hail Holy Queen, kneeling on the marble floor in front of the altar. Naturally, the dollar pilfered was to be replaced in the poor box that very week.

"*Ego te absolvo peccatis tuis, In nomini Pater, et Fili, et Spiritu Santi, Amen...*"

So, with the understanding I would undergo the penance prescribed, I, Luna *Penitenti*, was absolved in advance in the name of the Holy Trinity.

Well. After suffering through a rosary on flaming knees, narrowly escaping the nickname "*Alfiler*" (with the obligatory explanation), not eating lunch for three and a half days in order to return the money to the poor box (thank God, Carlos gave me his milk), battling Demons and Angels, developing diarrhea, and being subjected to a minor stigmata on my derriere and hand from a series of popping pins under the likely direction of a rogue Guardian Angel, Al Filer could safely tell you that the piece of arm rest mistaken for Mary's swollen adolescence had turned into Last Stand Hill. But in fact, it had just been a simple case of 20/20 hindsight, for had Al truly paid attention to the title of the movie, *Mary Poppins*, he would have been graphically forewarned from the get-go.

Kiss the Hand
You Cannot Sever

All these cats are always saying "play the song on the chart.
Man, once I learn the tune, I just want to fuck it up.

—Billy Sun Ray, Jazz Pianist. NYC

I had drawn sunglasses on Jesus, attempting to celebrate His Hipness on my terms. Dogma caught up with me in the shape of my eighth-grade nun. When I showed the drawing to my friend Gabriel across the aisle, he tried to alert me with his eyebrows that the nun was behind me. Too late. She swooped down with a liver-spotted hand, the one with the wedding band symbolic of wedlock to the Lord, and crushed the drawing with that vengeful and sanctimonious talon.

"That's blasphemy, young man! We don't mock the Lord in my class. And if you know what's good for your soul, you won't do it at all…What you sow in the Devil's garden will bloom in hell!

Even at that age, I thought her comment a tad melodramatic. My drawing showed Jesus snapping his fingers by the corpse of Lazarus, whom as the story goes, he raised from the dead. The cartoon bubble above Jesus read, "Like, arise, man. Like, arise!" Lazarus, also sporting sunglasses, sandals, and a goatee was in mid-air above his deathbed, effervescing, "What you mean is, jump and swing, big daddy!"

My defense had not gone over well with Sister Tightkeester.

"I was just making him cooler. Doesn't God ever laugh?"

The nun was miffed at my gall to question God and challenge her with the last word, further aggravated by my friends' derision.

"You will all march to the office!"

Taking her literally, I dispatched, "Squad, tensh hut..." My four mates took the cue, standing straight as candles at their desks, awaiting the next command.

"Forward march."

Colonel Luna and his troop stomped the wooden floor to the front of the class, formed a single file, and continued down the hall. My buddy Gabriel trumpeted *March of the Wooden Soldiers* through cupped hands in a jazzy one-two-and-three-four-and-one beat, up to a few meters from the Mother Superior's office. Little did I know at the time, our clever little martial motif was to have prophetic consequences—military school again loomed over the horizon for me. We were made to pick weeds after school until our parents, already notified at work, showed up.

"Luna is a leader. He should be a good leader, not a bad leader like Castro."

Sister T hit my mom with that one-liner at our after-school meeting in the Convent. Oh yeah! If left unchecked, I'd be enforcing agrarian reform projects out on the softball field within the week! She continued about how we stomped military style down the hallway and about Gabriel's trumpeting.

"I think they are a bad influence on each other. They provoke each other's disobedience. So maybe, until they show more *maturity*, it would best serve them to stay apart. Or regrettably, Mrs. Yena, we might be forced to suspend them."

On the word "maturity," Tightkeester provided a condescending side glance, which drove me to the edge of an impulse to shoot her a moon and ask which cheek she'd like to kiss first. *She* could certainly steer you into the Devil's Garden, as she put it.

"I think you are mistaken in a big way!"

"See what I mean, Mrs. Yena."

"She's not mistaken, Luna. It's *her* class, and you are a student there. You don't make the rules. *No te pongas antipático.*"

My mother, to avoid any chance of suspension, showed no tolerance for my questioning the Sister's authority. She made me promise out loud to improve my behavior and forbade me to see Gabriel, indefinitely. I was grounded for the next two weekends and, until summer vacation, no outings on weeknights. As my punishment was dealt, I had a vision—a jalousie window. It blunted my adversarial attitude. So, while outwardly I bowed in the classic gesture of repentance, much to the satisfaction of Tightkeester, inwardly I hatched my deliverance. I did have a *date* this evening.

On the drive home, my mother vented.

"*Yo no puedo seguir así.* I'm going have to do something if you continue behaving like this. Your father is not with us right now, and I'm working very hard to make ends meet. I'm alone."

In fact, she was recently separated, although the official word to me was my father was sick and had to live by himself for a while, doctor's orders. I told her I had not meant any harm with the drawing.

"And the nun crushed it! She didn't have to do that."

"She saw it as *una burla de Dios.* But let's say you didn't mean to scoff God. It was not a drawing class. It was a religion class. *Y explícame* what was the meaning of marching down the hall? *Pero donde tu aprendiste eso?* I don't want you even talking to Gabriel again."

"*No fue* él! I was the one. That Nun *es una mentirosa.*"

"She's not a liar. This is not the first time you're in trouble together. Whoever started it—I don't want you calling him or *juntándote* with him after school. I'm calling his mother. And when we get home, you go to your room and study. Your school is very expensive for me right now *y no me importa sacrificarme*, but you are wasting it. And that's the end of the discussion. *Se acabó!"*

"*Yo od…*"

Recalling my plan, I caught myself just before going off on a litany of the Odious: the nun, religion class, that school, my mom at that moment, etc…I just wanted to get home so I could eat early and say goodnight.

After dinner, I locked the door to my room, waited about an hour, shuffling pages in a few schoolbooks while changing clothes, then turned out the light. Very quietly with the point of a compass, I bent the aluminum tabs which secured the jalousie. I slid three panes away, placed them carefully on my bed, and straddled out the window.

It was winter and already dark when I ran across the Bayshore Golf Course on my way to the beach on 30th and Collins. It smelled like a cool green salad. I was very pleased with my ingenuity. *I'm free, free, freeeeeee!* The air felt cooler when I crossed the mist drifting from the industrial-grade sprinkler streams.

Seven thirty-three floated in the night sky. The big digits, made out of bulbs surrounding the top of a fourteen-story building on Lincoln Road, were visible for miles to the four winds. The temperature read seventy-eight degrees. Its incessant advance had always made me anxious. It seemed like all clocks moved too slow or too fast in relation to my plans.

Rhonda, a Jewess from Rockaway Beach, was to meet me at the Sea Isle Hotel. It was her last night. We had spent last weekend making-out and feely-pooing. I don't know why some people had a notion that Jewish girls made feeble lovers? I would know my share, and most of them went *meshugena* on you. I met her at a teen dance at the Seville Hotel. When the song *Help Me Rhonda* came on, I asked her to dance.

"Rhonda, that's my name."

"My friend's cousin, Ruben La Ronda, died, asphyxiated in the back of a refrigerated truck, when they got captured in the Bay of Pigs."

"I'm sorry, but what's Bay of Pigs?"

"It was the beach where the Cubans were abandoned by—"

Li'l Smilo tugged at me from the Crotch Cabin to change tack, attempt a beach head, and plant a flag of my own.

"Speaking about the beach, have you ever heard of moon tanning?"

"Is that like snipe hunting?"

These girls from N.Y. were nobody's fools.

We laughed and went to the beach anyway. Back then, it was still just kiss and breast feeling, *if* I got lucky, then go home and abuse myself. It went that way until I was seventeen. But believe me, I was ready for more of the same that night.

Almost there, I could see the Seville Hotel with its glowing red clock. I think there were more clocks in Miami Beach than in Switzerland.

As I approached the walking bridge on Indian Creek Canal on 29th Street, I noticed someone at the top. He waved. It was Gabriel! I had forgotten he had planned to come and say his goodbyes to Rhonda's cousin, who'd been martyrizing his little trouser trout. He brandished something in his hand.

I ran to the top of the bridge, glad to see him.

"*Bicho malo,* you escaped!"

He toasted with a swig of Johnny Walker Black snagged from his mother's liquor cabinet and passed me the bottle. A third of the contents were missing, and I could smell it in his slightly slurred speech.

"Iffee die? We die!"

I didn't decipher Gabriel's pledge of chivalric doom to mean literally. That night, he would consume a near mortal ration of the malt, which was younger than him by only two years. But historically, death was, in fact, never too far from heroic deed. I pledged the credo.

"If we die? We die!"

The gulp nearly gagged me. Dying was not going be easy. It burned down my gut—my system's natural defenses, perhaps a bit unmanly now, but in the end not a disadvantage.

We walked around the beach side of the hotel toward the jetty. This was before boardwalks, Sea Bees dredging sand fill, or security gates. Out of range of pool area lights, we sat on the wooden beams connecting the barnacle-studded pilings. I took one more swig, and that was the end for me. I thought that crap tasted awful. Gabriel swigged with a vengeance as he spoke.

"Th'nun called my mommintoo. I'm not ssupposseta sssee-ooo. Your mom called my mom, and they agreed "*sson mala influensjia u no alotro,*" and I'm grounded for a monshh. But I fixshed the penguinssh, you'll ssjee!"

I asked Gabriel what he was talking about, but he would just stare straight ahead, like he was looking at whatever caper he had pulled off earlier, and repeat, "You'll shee tomorrow ha-ha-ha…" But the laugh was wrought in turmoil.

He was getting pummeled on that Johnny Walker. I thought it a good idea to start cruising toward our destination, so we headed for the lobby. Gabriel held on to the bottle, which I thought was an awful idea. When I asked him to give it up, he kept saying, "No, one more…"

Had I known any better, I'd have taken it away from him sooner.

"Just one more…shyou heff 'un too!"

Instead of refusing again, I snatched the bottle from his hand, ran back to the jetty, and buried it before he knew what hit him. Third piling from the shore break. Well out of hi-tide's way. When I came back, he was sitting on the bottom step of the stairs leading to the rear lobby.

"Hahahaha Haaaah! *Mañana* the penguinsh are gonna pissh their habitsh."

"What did you do, man?"

"Can't shsay," is all he kept saying, laughing in a way that was really starting to give me the willies.

He wobbled up the stairs. I thought it convenient to set up shop in an oval salon toward the back of the lobby. Anyone could see from the next town that Gabriel was tenderized. Actually, it was more like pre-chewed. I sat him down in a couch facing a white grand piano. He had gotten unusually quiet.

"I'm gonna go call Rhonda's room. I'll be right back."

Just before I turned the corner, I glanced back. He raised his hand, waving a stately adieu, then just sat there, his hands on his lap, blinking listlessly, uniform with his surroundings. Swell.

This ballroom had been turned into an activities center, mostly for the old Jewish snowbirds. The ballroom had a Busby Berkley groove—oval-molded soffit on the ceilings, crystal chandelier, and a white piano. A groove which naturally came to a screeching halt when the activities director started calling out numbers on Bingo Night or during the "Talent Shows," when some old lady would stand at the mic and do the obligatory "Hello Dolly" over-modulated through a single speaker amp, her dentures tap dancing on her gums. But tonight, thank God, it was deserted, except for an old couple way in the back, playing cards and, hopefully still on the couch, Gabriel the Prince of Autism.

A few minutes after I called her room, the elevator door opened and revealed Rhonda in beach shorts, showing off her tan legs. She wore a sleeveless blouse with tiny blue flowers that matched her eyes.

"Help me Rhonda, help-help me Rhonda…"

I crooned the song, dropping down on one knee. Yeah, I was a bit loopy. She laughed. I went to kiss her on the lips, but in public, she offered me her cheek.

"You've been drinking."

"Just a little, with Gabriel."

Her cousin looked around for Gabriel.

"He is in the oval room."

When we got there, Gabriel had laid his head down on the armrest.

"I guess he's tired…Gabriel! Gabriel!"

I shook him into the upright position. He got up laughing, gave a Nazi salute, and screamed, "Penguinshs achtung!" He sat again, leaned back, laughed, and belched once. Thin vomit poured out his mouth, down his jaw, and streamed unto his baby blue windbreaker. Without saying a word, his head dropped, plopping the bottom of his chin on the soiled nylon. Out cold.

Rhonda turned away.

"Gross!"

Her cousin, the first rat to abandon ship, offered her brilliant conclusion.

"He's drunk! Let's go, Rhonda. We're gonna get in trouble!"

The old couple in the back rose to their feet, visibly agitated by Gabriel's Nazi salute. They ambled toward the front lobby, giving him the once over a couple of times. Gabriel hadn't meant any harm. He had nicknamed our endearing eighth-grade nun, Himmler, after the Nazi head of the Gestapo. But I couldn't get into explaining right now. It might have been futile anyhow. That kind of humor didn't go over too well among the elderly here, and understandably so. Some of them had shown me the numbers tattooed on their wrist in Nazi concentration camps when I had set up their lounges by the pool. It didn't go over too well with the girls either. I refrained from choking him because it wouldn't have done any good at that moment. Not to mention, the up-chuck all over his windbreaker. Let's say he had upped the ante. Any minute, the proper authorities could be heading here from Old Front Lobby Way. Rhonda's cousin had gone back to her room.

"I'm sorry, Rhonda. I told him to…Come on, Gabriel! Come on! Man, get up! Get *up*!"

I tried lifting from behind in an attempt to raise him by the armpits, but I couldn't. I pushed him flat on the couch, rolled him as gently as possible onto the carpet on his back, then dragged him by the legs on the granite floor. Rhonda opened the double doors leading to the terrace pool table room.

"No! I don't wanna die! I don't want to die!"

Once outside the lobby, I stopped.

"Shut up, man. We're gonna get caught."

Gabriel wasn't anywhere near the pedestrian mode. I propped him against the pool table leg, but I knew I couldn't leave him here overnight. Not with any trace of conscience. And I couldn't expect Rhonda to volunteer on this suicide mission for too long.

"What are you going do with him, Luna?"

"I'm thinking."

"You want me to call a cab?"

"A cab, yes, great…! No, wait! I got no money. Hold it, let me see."

Rhonda waited by the double doors. I looked in Gabriel's pockets. No money. I had fifty cents.

"I have a dollar."

Rhonda's offer, though generous, would get us about ten blocks away from here. Perhaps an option not so ridiculous, especially if it was just her and me in the cab. But back to reality—I needed about three dollars and fifty cents more. Staring at Gabriel's vomited and demon-ridden condition did not inspire one to many solutions unrelated to immediate desertion.

I stood up, leaned against the pool table on both arms, and was nearly soothed by the expanse of green felt, momentarily recalling the jaunt across the misty vegetal world of the Bayshore Golf Course. The pool table! *Caballo,* how could you forget? *I knew how to get money out of the pool table.* But I was bound by oath not to reveal our trade. So Rhonda, bless her sweet valiant soul, who still waited loyally by the double doors, had to be dismissed.

"Go ahead. Call the cab. I just remembered I have five bucks at home."

"Where should he come to?"

"To….30th St…to the end…by the beach. There's a back gate to the pool…Thanks."

Thank God, Rhonda was thinking. If it weren't for some of the women in my life, I would've been a more frequent sight a-swirling in the Cosmic Toilet.

As soon as she cleared the doorway, I groped into the potted Areca palm where we kept a hotel dinner knife. I slid the blade in through the gap on the bottom of the locked coin box and pushed the quarters out. It was about four dollars' worth. Gabriel slid off the pool table leg and slammed to the floor.

"No! You son of a bitch! No! No! I don' want to die!"

He nearly stopped my motor. I blitzed eight more quarters out and sunk the knife back into the planter with just enough time to take in a deep breath. The doors opened.

"The cab will be here in fifteen minutes."

She gave me her address on a piece of paper and a dollar. Her blue eyes took the edge out of doom.

"Write me."

"You know I will. But I don't need the dollar anymore. Rhondita, you're the best."

I gave her the dollar back, but before she left, I had her open the door leading to the pool deck. I pulled Gabriel down the stairs gently by his legs. Every time he tried to wail, his head knocked on a step, disconcerting him until we got to the bottom.

"Please don't kill me, pleeeease! I don't want to die!"

He was spooking the shit out of the girl. I rolled him under a sea grape hedge out of sight from hotel rooms. Rhonda and I embraced. But though our kiss was moist and warm, it was jittery on both ends. Somehow, it was already midnight.

"I really have to go. I'm going get in trouble. I hope Gabriel will be All right?"

"He will. I'll write you. Take care. Thanks for your help. Help me Rhonda, help-help me Rhonda!"

She smiled. I was joking, but I hurt a little inside at her departure. I followed her perfect legs climbing the steps. She turned around and blew me a kiss just before becoming a gauzy silhouette through the door curtains. I felt warm. Girls were hard to beat. Luna the Philosopher.

I went out to 30th Street, leaving the gates to the pool deck open so I could keep Gabriel in check. Some car headlights headed my way from Collins. I waved, but it was not the cabbie. Two guys, one brawny and one needlefish-skinny, in bright sports coats drove up in a Lincoln Continental convertible, top down and out-of-town plates. They made me antsy.

"What's wrong, boy?"

"I'm sorry. I thought you were…I called a taxi."

I could feel the purr of the big V-8. The cold air blowing from the air conditioner pushed the smell of their strong cologne. Their faces were sweaty, even though for me, it was cool out.

"You know which way to the Fown'nblew?"

"Make a right up there, and it's about ten blocks."

"Thanks, boy…By the way, you hear the news? They killed a U.N. ambassador tonight, Malcolm X. You know what that means?"

When I said nothing, he offered the answer.

"One less *U*ppity *N*-igger, son. I guess you don't get too many around here."

I didn't understand it, which must have showed, so the driver interceded.

"*U. N.*, U-ppity N-iggers."

They laughed. They seemed a bit sauced.

I didn't like that word. I knew it was a bad word for black people. And *Abuela,* my foster grandma, was black. The one on the passenger seat scratched his thick neck right under his Adam's apple and fired his load.

"We'll give them niggers rights, *and* lefts, and some more rights, heh, heh, heh."

While they laughed I glanced back in the direction of Gabriel, who was still dozing under the sea grapes.

"Are you 'merican?"

"N-no, Cuban."

The driver, the skinny one, called me a name.

"A Spicaninny, Lou."

"And what the hell are you?"

It slipped out. When the skinny driver jerked the door open on his way to me, I wished I hadn't said it. I was stunned but just seconds from sprinting down the beach and out to sea if necessary. I knew they couldn't touch me there.

"I'll fix your mouth, you lil'greaseball."

One of Lou's big hands landed on the driver's shoulder, planting him back in his seat.

"Hold it, Frank. He's got a little *hombre* in him. I like that. And tell you what, somma his people got balls, I know that for a fact. Just don't grow up to be no homo, nigger-lover, or commie bastard like Castro, son, and you'll make a good citizen."

"Let's go get some mossy jaw, chief. Those broads must be at the bar already. I need a drink. I'm hotter than slaked lime!"

Frank gave me a your-life-has-been-pardoned glare, then delivered his farewell.

"You're lucky the Chief likes you, boy."

They drove off. I was real glad and breathed easy again. Those bullies had made me forget about Gabriel, but fro but from the looks of it, he was status quo. Which wasn't necessarily good, just less disagreeable.

I didn't know who Malcolm X was then. Later, I learned he had a lot of poison raging in him too. Understandable, if you factored in clowns like the ones who just left. He had also stood up against bully-ism, even within his own ranks, which in the end cost him his life. I'd heard black people could not overnight on Miami Beach. That included Sammy Davis Jr., who *performed* on the beach—something I found strange because *Abuela* lived with us, and we lived on the beach. I guess no one at law enforcement ever knew. These guys had given me a bad case of the creeps, so when the real cabbie turned the corner, I waited until I could properly identify him. I was nervous about telling the taxi driver about Gabriel, but at the same time, I felt a warning would fare better than Gabriel's shriek surprise.

"My friend is coming too. He's a little drunk, so he might be loud."

"Well, that don't make him the New Messiah, I can tell you that. Where is he?"

I pointed to the side of the pool. When we got to him, Gabriel was still out. We lifted him onto a fiberglass lounge swiftly. He only let out a few yelps when I removed his windbreaker. We carried him to the cab stretcher-style and slid him into the back seat. I placed the vomit glazed jacket on the rubber floor mat.

We got to my house at 12:30 a.m. The front yard was dark. The cabbie grabbed Gabriel and threw him on his shoulder. Not a peep, thank God. I kept looking up to Abuela's window which faced the front yard. My concern was due to her supersonic hearing.

"I don't know what he drank, but tomorrow this boy's gonna feel like a cat run over by a bus. When he comes around, you should give him some water. I'm sure that pukin' dried him up."

I gave the cabbie all the quarters, including a dollar tip, and he left. I knew that the possibility of Gabriel crawling through my window was out of the question. I left him in the front yard, behind the coconut palm where the cabbie had dropped him. The only water he was going to get tonight was if it rained. I was not going to chance another demon-fest. Presently, he lay harmless in his stupor.

As planned, I crawled back in through the window slowly, trying to stifle my breath. I lay in bed and exhaled. *Home.*

Replacement of the jalousies could wait until morning. I didn't want to chance any noise. And anyhow, who knew, there might be an emergency call to the front yard in the middle of the night, and in that case, the escape route was ready. Gabriel's odds were on recidivism.

Tomorrow, I would wake up early and "find" him in the front yard— "My God, what happened to you?"—bring him inside, where he would clean up, have breakfast, then drive him home with my mother or give him bus fare. Hey, whatever happened to him after that was his business. I'd done my share. I didn't leave him in the hotel lobby where he would have been police fodder for sure. He drank the shit. Now he'd have to pay the bartender.

The door to Abuela's room opened. I lay still. She shuffled her slippers toward the living room. I heard the refrigerator door. Relax, little doggie, she went to get a glass of water. There was a knock on a door.

"Lela, Lela!"

Abuela called my mother's nickname. Her door opened. Muffled voices drifted from the living room. My heart began rolling spoon solos inside my rib cage. I shot out of my clothes and threw a sheet over them. I'll deny everything. Gabriel! What are you doing here? That's *all* I'll say. He'll be drunk, talking nonsense.

"No! You son of a bitch. Don't kill meeeee."

Holy shit, he's awake! I bolted up from my bed and started replacing jalousies. There was a knock on my door.

"Luna, *abre la puerta!*"

"Whaaa…? I'm sleeeeping….Huh?"

I offered my best somnolent groans and whines, while I slipped jalousie number two in place. One more to go!

"Open up right now. Gabriel is outside *borracho*. Open the door *inmediatamente!*"

Crash!

To my horror, I dropped the last jalousie on the terrazzo floor, and it splintered eternally. The lights came on like a guilty verdict. *Abuela*, who had opened the lock with a pair of scissors, stood by the door with my mother. They looked toward the window and noticed the missing glass. I stood in front of it, a light-entranced possum in my underwear with the mosquito screen leaning against my leg. My mother moved closer to me and delivered the required question with enviable aplomb.

"What are you doing?"

"I...well....Gabriel, he...I heard a noise by the window, and Gabriel said let me in and..."

"You've been drinking."

"I didn't drink anything...He came. I...He asked me to taste..."

"Don't lie to me."

"I don't want to die, *hijo de puuuutaaa!*"

Gabriel's plea du jour again came home to roost.

"What's the matter with him?"

"I don't know. I was sleeping, then..."

"No seas mentiroso, you're just going aggravate me."

"Mami, no, I heard something...then Gabriel came by the window, and I..."

My mother lifted the bed sheet and revealed my clothes. She grabbed them and extended them toward Luna the Novice Poacher like the freshly flayed hides of some protected game.

"Pero, who do you think you're dealing with? *Yo tengo cara de mente-cata!* "You've both been drinking. *Y ese muchacho* is gonna hurt himself if he keeps *abusando el alcohol de esa forma."*

"I tried to tell him."

"I thought we had reached an understanding this afternoon. Obviously, you chose to be selfish and inconsiderate. But we'll discuss it tomorrow. I have to get up in six hours to be at work. Please put some shoes on and pick up this glass before you cut yourself, and I have to spend what's left of tonight with you in the emergency room. *Que desastre!"*

She walked out. I slipped into shorts and flip-flops and brought back a cardboard shoebox from the garage. As I walked by the living room, I could see Gabriel's legs out in the front yard through the open doorway. He lay quiet now.

Yes, this was a day to put behind you as quickly as possible. Back in my room, I grabbed the largest shard of jalousie too big to fit in the box and leaned it against the wall. The worst part about today was I hadn't paid for it yet. I thought perhaps the nun put a curse on us.

"Luna, come and help *el taxista* lift your friend." There was already dew on the grass. The cabbie grabbed Gabriel's legs, and I was delegated his arms. That puke smell from the windbreaker which I had laid next to him was nauseating. Abuela brought a paper bag for it. She grabbed it gingerly, bagged it and put it in the back seat of the cab.

"*Hijo de puta No No! No me Maten!* I didn't do anything! No. Nooo!"

He was definitely making a hermetic case for severing diplomatic relations *con Mami*.

The cabbie looked perplexed.

"This guy looks too young to be having the DT's."

"What's the DT's?"

"When alcoholics see monsters and animals and boogey men."

He looked up at my mother conspiratorially.

"But Gabriel hasn't drunk but a few times, maybe three."

"That's how you start."

I felt sorry for Gabriel, who now was seeing demons and stuff.

"Take it easy, Gabriel. It's me, Luna."

"You too? No, no! Tell them I don't want to die. Luna, pleeeease, *no! Hijos de puuuuta!*"

Gabriel never once opened his eyes, though unquestionably was seeing some shit. The cabbie crawled in the back seat, pulled Gabriel inside by his legs, and came out the opposite door. I shut the cab door on my side and watched the '65 Chevy Bel-Air taillights disappear around the bend, wishing I were inside, heading to some better place in the future. My mother had gone into the house and was now on the phone with Gabriel's mother. I passed her, stopping behind the hallway wall to eavesdrop.

"No, Luna no sale de aquí en un mes!"

It was a game in the style of conspicuous penitence. I'm sure Gabriel's mother had said he would be grounded for several weeks, so my mother had to throw in a month for me.

"Bueno chica ahí te lo mando. I hope everything is okay. *Te dejo* because I have to wake up early, goodnight. No *claro,* they don't have a clue of what responsibility *is.* I hope they learned something. *Adiós."*

I leaped on my tiptoes and hit my bed quietly. I heard my mother coming toward my room and then change her mind and go back to bed. That was the worst. It left me wondering what was going happen, besides the grounding for a month. We're talking major time: a whole four weekends. *Bueno, mañana* is another day.

Three Miami Beach squad cars were already parked outside the entrance to the school when I arrived and joined the rest of my classmates by the five-foot chain link fence. We congregated there every morning, polarized into girl and boy circles, until the school doors opened. Gabriel's mother's car drove up and let him out. His face looked like road-kill. But I knew his mother wasn't going let him skip school, even if he turned into an Inca mummy before her eyes. He walked up to me in a daze, bewildered at the cop cars as well.

"I wonder what's going on?"

Gabriel shrugged his shoulders at my question. Another kid who wasn't sporting a twenty-megaton hangover was more imaginative.

"I think somebody put a bomb in there."

A patrol-boy who was just coming back from his corner duty betrayed his mollycoddled heart.

"A bomb? Let's move away!"

I imagined one of those old cartoon bombs in which bearded Russian anarchists are always shown pitching. You know, the black bowling ball with the flaming wick. Then suddenly, it dawned on me.

"Gabriel!"

He looked at me, still clueless. I moved closer and whispered out of earshot of the rest.

"What'd you do?"

"Qué?"

"Last night, man! *Qué fué lo que hiciste?* Are you gonna tell me *now?* C'mon! Holy shit, Gabriel."

The little blood he had left in the alcohol pickling his face rushed out. The apocalypse dawned on his pasty, though still inscrutable, face.

"Shit, it must be a good one, Gabriel. Th*ree* cops!"

Suddenly, he held his breath at the sight of something happening behind me. Unlike last night, Gabriel was now seeing these demons with his eyes open. I looked back and saw two officers flanking the black maintenance man who was pointing at him. The two cops nodded and headed toward us.

"Are you Gabriel Benitez?"

He nodded his head with end-of-the-line resignation.

"Son, come with us, please."

They went through the double door entrance closest to our classroom and locked it. Gabriel never looked back. Immediately, some of the other boys came up.

"What did he do?"

"Why is he in trouble?"

I told them I didn't know, and that was the answer they could've expected had I really known. No wonder some people grew up with no etiquette. All of a sudden, I was the spokesman. Even the girls were interested now. No matter how some tried to deny it, the outlaw always held an allure, a fascination. The girls sent one of their emissaries. Actually, she was my pal. Regina was a big girl, an import from California, I think. She was way ahead of us parochial yahoos. If I had known enough back then, she would've made me a fearsome man. The week before, she had transcribed the alleged lyrics of the recent Kingsmen release, *Louie, Louie.* She had even included the word "lay" from the part in the song, "I'll never lay her again." Seeing the word *lay* in a girl's handwriting had given me such a hard-on that I wasn't able make it home. I had gone to Royal Castle, a low budget burger joint and after-school hangout on 41st St., and trounced Li'l Smilo, cross-eyed in the bathroom, surrounded by the smell of fried meat.

When she came up, we moved away from the herd.

"What happened?"

"Between you and me, Regina, I think Gabriel is in the crap house."

"I could have told you *that* genius, but what'd you guys do?"

"I, didn't do anything. All I know is, we snuck out last night and were drinking, and he got messed up and kept saying something about the penguins 'getting theirs,' but he wouldn't tell me any more."

She genuinely felt bad for him.

"I guess we'll soon find out what it was the penguins got! I just hope Gabriel doesn't get in too much trouble—he's a sweet guy."

The senior high entrance door opened, and a nun waved everyone inside. Regina went back to the girls. When they asked her for the goods, she shook her head as if uninformed and gave me a concealed wink.

We were led the long way around the interior courtyard where maintenance men, including the black man who had pointed Gabriel out, were cloaking a large part of the wall with a number of drop cloths. Several nuns milled about, sharing their utter disbelief. The hallway appeared to be a cross between a penguin rookery and an anthropological sight where cave paintings of a controversial nature had been discovered. The whole line of kids slowed down. Our nun, Tightkeester, Gabriel's very own Fraulein Himmler, cracked the whip.

"Keep moving and mind your own business!"

One of the girls in the line in front of us looked back and put her hand up to her mouth, astonished at what she witnessed. Some of the adhesive tape securing the drop cloths had detached. I glanced back, and through the crowd of people, you could make out the spray-paint calligraphy, "FUCK THE NUNS," and Swastikas alluding to the nazi-like tendencies of some of our *monjitas*. The janitor hurried with the stepladder to conceal the coarse bulletin.

"I *said,* keep moving and mind your own business. Unless you'd like some trouble of your own!"

Some in line made hushed comments. I was numb. Wrong or right, my boy had some balls. The *pièce de résistance* came when Rolando, a sheltered kid from the country side who had recently come from

Cuba, asked one of us in a voice a little too loud, "*Que es* Fook de Noons?"

A couple of us almost dropped our guts but recovered just in time. The nun bulldozed through the line and slapped Rolando on the lips.

"Don't you ever repeat that again, *comprende? Muy Malo!*"

As you can imagine, Rolando never lived down "Fook de Noons." That line burned up the odometer. Gabriel was sent home after he 'fessed up to the crime and received a citation. They tried to link me to it, but he told them he had acted alone. His mother's tears and heartfelt pleadings on her knees to the Mother Superior and the Monsignor on behalf of his education and future, and the fact that Gabriel's father, a big air-conditioning contractor, offered to "donate," install, and service a new central air compressor system for the cavernous church *gratis,* kept Gabriel from being expelled that year. But for two hours after school during the week and eight hours a day for the next six weekends, what remained of the school year, he was to do maintenance in addition to painting the wall he vandalized, plus costs incurred. Naturally, if he so much as day-dreamed opposition in class or out, even by mistake, he would be summarily dismissed. And even though from that day on many considered him a bit loony, his ballsy and single-handed act of defiance against parochial school intolerance had already raised him to mythological hero status in the hearts of many others, not to mention my own.

When the nun finally got all of us back in class the day our school discovered the Angry Period of Gabriel *El Muralista*, we were supposed to have read *The Testing of Abraham,* Genesis: 22, about how Abraham was solicited by God to kill his son Isaac. Sister Tightkeester had called on me.

"Why do you think Abraham was ready to kill his son, whom he loved dearly, at God's command?"

"Because Abraham had so much faith in God, Sister, that he thought whatever God asked him to do, no matter how much it hurt, couldn't be wrong because God was all-knowing and all-loving.

"Yes, God is infallible. Very good, Luna. I'm glad to see you finding your way back to the flock."

This time, there would be no drawings. No commentary. Though frankly, in my heart, I had thought it cruel of God to ask Abraham to choose between his son's life and his faith in Him. You had to be a pretty jaded and *Un*-Supreme Being to be going around, trying folk's devotion through filial sacrifice, then seconds before the blade finds its mark, dismissing it with a "Just checking in, Abe. As you were. You loyal patriarch, you!"

Little Luna, not yet aware of the old Chinese proverb, had been its major exponent that morning in religion class. Just as Abraham had been, a millennia and some before. *Kiss the hand you cannot sever.* But Luna, unlike Abraham, could not fly straight for long. At the end of the class, he waited just outside the door of the classroom until all the kids had left. As the nun walked through the doorway, he addressed her.

"Sister."

"Yes, Luna?"

I outstretched my arm, for the first time happy I had read the assignment. Then, waving my open hand over the wooden desks in the classroom, which just minutes ago were filled by the "flock" I was "finding my way back to", and I quoted Isaac.

"Here are the fire and the wood, but where are the sheep for the holocaust, Sister?"

"Young man, Young man…! Don't turn your back on me when I'm speaking to you!"

Boot Camp for the Dancing Dog of Love

The boys weren't helpful when she left. Besides, in the summer of '66, there were just one too many love songs on the chart to be falling in love. Maybe there always had been. Jimmy Ruffin's *What Becomes of the Broken Hearted* alone could exact a torrent of self-pity. Harmless if you had the calloused heart of the older beach-boys who went through "broads" like spoons through Jell-o. But first love at fourteen with a girl that lived 900 miles away did not feel at all like "puppy love," unless they meant the Hell Hound pup.

I was a *pick-up boy*, which didn't translate to adolescent seducer, though the nature of the job facilitated the trade if you were so inclined.

The pick-up boy worked for the beach-boys, usually incorrigible picaroons, tipped by tourists for the provision of mats, towels, and umbrellas at his section of lounges on the pool deck. Every day after school, I made a buck fifty *picking up* beach mats and towels, sweeping cigarette butts, and disposing of sundry trash for the beach-boy. In the summer when the sea was calm and clear, I spear-fished around the wooden jetties for mangrove snapper with a homemade Hawaiian sling using shafts fashioned from the ribs of old beach umbrellas.

If the sea was rough, one of the beach-boys would lend me a surfboard. Anything from six inches on up was considered "surf" in Miami Beach. Sometimes, even the likes of Jack Murph the Surf, not yet notorious for the Star of India heist, would be there with us, riding the swells on rougher days. It was out here in the sea where I met I.V.

She came out to swim in a two-piece bathing suit and had the cutest bubble butt I'd ever seen. As I rode by her on the board, she followed me with disabling "sleepy eyes." Paddling my way back to the break, I passed her and asked *the question* for the first time. That question was worth gold to the beach-boys and would eventually become handy for me too. In fact, some of the guys lucky to just balance themselves on solid ground kept a surfboard around so they could justify "the question" I would presently ask.

"Do you want to learn how to surf?"

Most girls would be interested, but if not, with a little coaxing, they would try it. They'd be lying flat on your board, and you could move them around at your fancy. In what other social milieu, not to mention job, would you have a scantily dressed woman lying prostrate in front of you, sometimes in less than a minute, armed with an excuse to touch her? Perhaps the hotel masseur, but at the time, our hotel masseur was gay, so he didn't count right out the gate.

Although I was not brazen at all, some of these beach-boys were calculating masters of the veiled fondle. But the truth is that whether you were a bragging member of the 4F Club—*Find 'em, Feel 'em, Fuck 'em, and Forget 'em*—like most of these guys or just looking for the true *one*, the surfboard was your ally and broke the ice like a pick.

"I don't know if I could do it?"

"Sure, you can. Come on."

Ivy agreed to the surf lesson in a surprisingly smoky voice for a thirteen-year-old. When she got on the board, the wet fabric stuck to her spherical little butt cheeks. She lay too close to one rail. making the board tilt, so I pushed her thighs over to the middle. They were warm. The small of her back was adorned with the tiniest blond hairs and two dimples. I sent her off on the next wave, lying on her stomach. She held on like a pit bull. Soon, she rode it on her knees, and on her first attempt jumping on her feet, she stood for five seconds on sturdy graceful legs. Hell, the whole ride on waves this size was only ten seconds, so she had ridden for half of it.

"I did it! I did it?"

She wanted to be sure before celebrating.

"You did it."

"I did it! Can I do it again?"

After a few more times, she was doing the whole length of the wave. She was one of those people who had natural coordination. I still had to push her in front of the unbroken swell, then she mostly rode soup, foam of a wave, but she was standing. Her tanned thighs shimmered in the afternoon light. She had the articulated kneecaps of a child, a trait I would still find attractive in adult women for the rest of my life. I watched her ride and was hooked. Not from my wiener end, but from a hollow in my heart. I felt I loved her already. The pool-boy motioned to me from the deck. Paradise deferred.

I told Ivy we could do more next time, that it was time for me to work. She paddled the board to the shore. I swam after her, bird-dogging a hinny of mythological cuteness. From shore, I carried the board toward the deck. I did not want this to end.

"Can I meet you later to play some pool?"

She turned her head, gazing into me with her forlorn amber-greens, and answered in a half-whisper. It spread over my young heart like the shore break smoothing out foot- prints and revealing burrowed life. For an instant, I knew eternity deeper than I would allow anyone ever again to take me with just one simple word. *Yes!*

"What time? We eat at seven."

Moonshine blood rushed through my head. It was hard to come down for logistics.

"Eight o'clock?"

"Okay."

After slipping into a T-shirt and shorts by her lounge, she disappeared into the tunnel leading to the lower lobby.

"Hey, Romeo, when you're through drooling, would you mind starting to pick up?"

The beach-boy I worked for couldn't leave until he helped me stack the mats. I went through the mats in a swoon, piling sometimes seven mats on my shoulder instead of the four I normally brought to the stack.

"We should have that girl around more often. Hell, in a few days, you'll be carrying the whole stack in one load. She really got your little wanger going, huh?"

I didn't want to discuss her with him. I never liked how they talked about girls. One afternoon, I had stepped inside the cabana office when he was just finishing a story about his date the night before.

"I told her, 'Your welcome mat begins between my legs. Now, you either blow or go!' She didn't think I was serious until I pushed her drunk ass out of my cabana and told her, 'For every one of you that don't suck dick, there's four that'll swallow,' and I locked her out."

I couldn't even imagine how to begin to feel like that about a girl. So now, I just grabbed the cover and said nothing. I didn't want her name in his mouth. Standing on a lounge, I helped him heave the cover into the wind. It billowed like a spinnaker sail as we swung it over the mat pile in one stroke. We went after two more stacks.

"Kid, it *ain't* no secret."

"Yeah, I like her."

"I see that. But don't let her know that *too much* though, or she'll have you going through hoops like the Dancing Dog of Love."

"I don't think she's like that."

"Hey, kid, it's war, and they're *all* like that. She is a cute little thing, though, you little pirate."

For these guys, any feelings above your waistline and you were a bozo heading for disaster. We covered the last pile and he left.

I began sweeping under the rows of lounges. What was the point of carrying something like this inside without telling the person you felt it for? I had sensed by the way she looked at me that she probably felt the same. I wanted to feel close to her again, out there in the breaking sea. Her sloping eyelids and her smoky voice became my world. Add to that a smooth responsive musculature that even at thirteen would scramble your signal. Maybe I could visit sometime wherever it was she lived up North? Or ask my mom if she could stay with us?

Come one, come all! To see Luna, The Dancing Dog of Love!

I swept a half-eaten apple from under a lounge chair. The tourist's teeth marks were already browning. I pondered on Adam and Eve's eviction from Paradise. I would've bitten the fruit at Ivy's request in a snap. End of fun and games forever—there had always been a lot of "forever" talk in the Bible. No second chances. No warning ticket. No jury of your peers, if there is ever such a thing. And finally, their offspring *forever* after stained by our disobedience, born in a state of sin. Cosmic hardball. You'd think the Lawd in His all-knowing wisdom and immeasurable love for man, made in His *own* image, would have seen it coming and landscape Eden with something a scooch less pernicious than the Tree of Knowledge. But apparently, the Lawd always seemed to have a penchant for *testing*—a drill I thought should be excluded from a place called Paradise. Adam n' Eve must have been like children! I found it self-indulgent of the Creator. Or just simply damn mean. Paradise with a *trapdoor*. What a notion. *Alaba'o!* That religion class had really pummeled my psyche. But while on the subject of thrashing, some of these tourists could use a little corporeal inducement of their own. The trashcan just a row up, but the tanning dead seemed to find the stroll to ditch the apple a superhuman task. I dumped the satanic fruit and finished sweeping.

The two-mile trek home was spent in a swooning paradise. A pool game...the seashore...perhaps a kiss? I wanted to see her eyes again, sweet lights. *I.V....I.V....I.V.*

Once home, I showered, *did not* jerk-off—rare at that age—crashed and burned through dinner, and was out the door doing barrel turns and loops in the sky.

When walking just seemed too slow, which was most of the journey, I sprinted. Oh, there was no doubt now. I *was* in love. I sprinted at top speed. I wanted to embrace her, marry her, protect her, share every atom of my existence. In reality, I didn't know what the hell I wanted to do, but whatever it was, it was with her. *Us against the damned!* Run I.V., run! The tall Australian pines blurred into the cobalt twilight.

She was not in the pool table room when I arrived at seven fifty-five. A good thing, or I would've been a jabbering cretin when I got there. My heart felt like it was going to jam up. She still had five minutes. I walked around the pool table once, trying to tone down my high. Reason signaled from homeport: Get a hold of yourself, *perrinsillo!*

I sat for a minute. Got up. Where is she? Sat back down for an eon. Walked outside, looked up at the series of black metal dots encrusted in a circle on the wall at the far end of the pool. The mark of the devil. His hands showed five after eight.

I took the knife we kept in the planter and checked the pool table coin box for quarters. Nothing doing. It looked like my friends had been here today, Too many people shown the lick, un-checked sharing coming home to roost. No problem. I had worked today. I had a buck-fifty.

I pushed a quarter into the table, and the balls rumbled out. I racked them, chose the two least warped sticks, chalked one, and banged the cue-ball off the banks a couple of times like I had seen an older guy do once, careful not to upset the rack. The Muzak version of the Beatle's *I Want To Hold Your Hand* played through the hotel's intercom. Less than a year and a half since its release and already a "rock" staple for the Comatose String Quartet.

Where was she? I checked the time. Eight fifteen! Maybe something happened? Her parents didn't let her come down? Then, the horror. Luna the Dancing Endocrinal Bonehead of Love didn't have her room number or last name! I went to the lobby. No I.V.

Inside the dining room, a sea of old timers and a couple of tourist families filled an archipelago of dull mustard tablecloths. No I.V. I hoped she hadn't just said she'd meet me to be nice. Or just not come. Or forget. But how could she forget? No, something must have happened. It could've been easy now if I would've just asked for her room. It could've, would've, should've, typical idiot parlance. It was eight twenty-five.

I returned to the poolroom, on the verge of disillusion really slapping me around.

"I hit this ball and messed them all up?"

There she was! Warm honey on my blueberry heart. The musk ox sitting on my chest upped and went. Irregularly, but I breathed again.

"You did a good job. I thought you weren't coming."

"I'm sorry, but my sister hogged the bathroom, and I wanted to brush my teeth. It was so crowded in the dining room, too, and it took forever to get our food."

"I know I went..."

I caught myself before revealing I had been searching for her inside every nook and cranny. Not that anyone would ever be inside a nook or cranny, unless you were looking for a rodent, an insect, or a small reptile.

"Pardon?"

"I said, I know. I mean, there was a big crowd at the pool today. It looked like they were all eating at the same time.

"You saw them too?"

"No, I mean, but I could see what you mean. They all got to eat sometime."

We got on with the game. I couldn't concentrate. I just wanted her in my arms. I was dizzy from desiring her closeness and inhaling her eyes and lips and skin every time she attempted a shot and looked for my assessment.

She made two shots, but on her third turn, the cue ball came back and sank the eight ball. End of game. After that, we just shot free-for-all, making short work of it.

"Do you want to sit by the beach?"

"Okay."

I drifted toward some lounges on the furthest area of the pool deck. I groped for her hand as we walked, and she grabbed mine. She. *Likes.* Me. My hand had been waiting all its life for this. We sat on the fiberglass lounge, facing the sea. My friends and I had picked this area because the security light was blocked by a sea grape hedge, although it wasn't sanctuary by a long shot.

Once, while the rest of our gang hid behind that hedge, I snaked slowly on the ground between these lounges, up to my buddy Gabriel, who was making out with his date, felt up his ass, and ducked. With unexpected glee, he had escalated the affair by grabbing her titties. She countered by pushing his hands off and cooling him with a very defensive, *"What are you doing, Gabriel?"*

Our buddy Carlos had countered from behind the hedge. "Yes, what *are* you doing Gabriel, you animal!"

I had howled like a wolf from under the lounge, grabbing Gabriel's leg. We had laughed into stomach cramps, never foreseeing that the girl would scare half to death. But when the *canalla,* who was mostly a bunch of good eggs, realized she was on her way for real, we apologized. So now, I scanned the area for my much deserved payback.

"The ocean is so warm and clear here. I'm going to miss this beach. In Rehoboth, the water is gray and cold, even in the summer."

"I love the ocean. I learned how to swim in Cuba when I was four. The water is even clearer there. By the way, you were real good on that board."

"You think so?"

"Yeah, I never saw anybody get up on a board by the third try."

"Now I can brag when I get back home. My sister is already jealous, even though she says she doesn't like surfing."

Her sugar-cured voice and the smell of fresh shampoo in her hair had a heavy pull. I put my arm around her shoulders. We got quiet for a while. I don't know quite how it happened. I turned my head, and our lips touched. Her eyes were closed, and she trembled. We pecked at each other's lips until I couldn't breathe anymore. I didn't even try for her little plums. I was just too high. She embraced me. It was complete. Oh, love! Love was the sweetest fruit. I tried not to think of the apple.

"I really like you, Luna."

"I like you with all my heart."

"I'm going miss you all the way home tomorrow. It's too bad we don't live in the same place. I could really get used to this."

Tomorrow! My world had stopped at *tomorrow,* although I could

have kept nodding my head to her conversation into the next Ice Age.
I struggled to hide the entry wound of "tomorrow"—big-game caliber.
Desperately, I groped for a handle and a breath. The Earth would continue to spin, and tomorrow would be here. Although, I was certain
the sun would never rise the same again. Unbeknownst to me, another
heavenly body was doing spins of sorts. An unmanned spacecraft, *Luna
9*, was making a "soft landing" on the moon. Its pictures would prove
the surface firm enough to land on. But its namesake, thousands of miles
below on a Miami Beach pool deck, could not boast solid ground. In fact,
Luna was now dropping through the trap door of Paradise in a body bag,
searching for words and a soft landing of his own. Ah! The multiform
and erratic gravity of Planet Love.

"You're only gonna stay one d-day?"

"Oh, no, we've been in Florida for a week. We were in Ft. Lauderdale."

I didn't hear a word she said. I didn't want to think. We kissed again.
She closed her eyes, and I could feel her breath, warm on my cheek. For
the first time in my life, I did not feel alone.

"I love you."

"I love you too, Luna..."

I heard a noise in the hedge. I swung around, not in the mood for
games.

"Don't try it unless you want to get smacked!"

A cat came out with a rat in its mouth, jumped up on a wall and
down to the street.

"Ooooo! Is that your pool cat? Who were you talking to?"

"No, I thought...Some of my friends are into pranks, and once
when...Anyway, I'll explain it some other time."

"My God, I didn't know there were rats around here. Can we go back
toward the poolroom? They give me the creeps."

"Sure."

Animal testing would have been a vacation compared to the horrors
I fantasized for that untimely and sporting tomcat.

"Oh, my Go...I got to go, Luna. My dad made me promise I'd be
back by eleven."

Those odious little dots marked 11:40. I wondered if time had existed in Paradise. I was certain the Forbidden Fruit in the story had borne a clock in its core. We rode the elevator to her room. Short ride. Out of fourteen floors, she had to live on the second.

"We're going to the Sea Aquarium in the morning and from there to the airport after we pick up our bags. I can't wait to see the dolphins! If I had to be an animal, that's what I would be. My mother is a Pisces, and so am I. So, maybe in the next life."

"I love them too. My dad and I swam with them out at sea in Cuba."

She was impressed. It was a white lie. Only my dad had swum with them. I felt a little cheesy. We got to her room.

"Good night, Luna. I had a great time. Thanks again for teaching me how to surf."

Goodbye, none-the-less hurtful for being cliché, had Dancing Dog tripping all over his paperweight feet.

"I'll write you if I can have your address. Maybe I'll come up and see you!"

"Of course, you can have my address. I would love you to…"

I wasn't going for Bonehead II. I had found a sweet refuge, and I wanted to make sure I could find my way back to that sanctuary.

She entered her room and came back shortly with her address, kissed me goodnight, and disappeared behind door number 281. Benighted by her farewell kiss, I searched the hallways and hoped for the dreaded minotaur, which I had recently discovered from a story my dad told me. Had he shown his bull-hoofed butt in this carpeted labyrinth, he surely would have died, for tonight, Luna Invictus could not be slain.

I wasn't going to forget the room now, 2-8-1. In fact, years later, on a slow midnight shift as a parking attendant, door 281 appeared in my mind in the wee hours as a free-standing monolith. I discovered that the number of Ivy's room, 2-8-1, in rebus referred to Adam and Eve chewing the apple: *two ate one*. No doubt, the scriptures and an idle mind made a formidable combo. Meanwhile, a future pestilence of TV evangelists incubated. But my walk home on the farewell night had been free of divinations. Instead, I vacillated between fantasies of cuddling up to Ivy's flannel nightshirt in some imaginary bed up north and the more sober task of sampling strategies that would get me to Bethesda, Maryland in the physical plane. Before long, I succeeded in devising a viable trajectory, though not exactly as the crow flies.

I was back in the sea with Ivy before I knew it. The water was warm, the afternoon light sparkling just like the first time. The sun was going down quickly. Our parents motioned for us to please come back to shore, that it wasn't safe to be out there. I gestured with my hand, "It's okay, not to worry," but I didn't have a hand anymore. It was a fin. I looked back at Ivy and saw a dolphin. Somehow, I still recognized her features as being Ivy. We swam out to sea. Now, I was a dolphin too. The water was warm, and it felt great, pushing by my skin when we sprinted. No dads. No moms. No school. No jobs. *No clocks.* We lived in the aquamarine waters of the Caribbean, hunting fish, riding swells, and rubbing up against ourselves forever. Undulating slowly, we circled the blue-green shafts of moonlight deep in the Gulfstream…While curiously faint marching drums drew near.

*   *   *

"Barracks tensch hut!"

The nasty overhead fluorescents came on a few feet from my face where I had been sleeping on the upper bunk. The only moonlight around here had been reflected off Cadet Wilson's pimply butt cheeks, two upper bunks away, flashing as he adjusted the elastic band of his underwear upward from halfway down his ass. We all jumped onto the waxed mirror-like vinyl tile floors and stood at attention in front of our double bunks, forming two perfect files of somnolent ninth graders in their underwear, facing each other. From the end of the barracks, the captain, a senior, made his way toward us, taking slow casual steps in his boxer shorts and rubber flip flops with his hands behind his back. Across from me, I could see first one, then a couple of cadets, trying to contain laughter. They kept pointing with their eyes to Cadet Wilson's crotch, three down to my right, whose bunk springs had been squeaking for a few nights. He was the skinny, somewhat uncoordinated kid with the pimply ass I had seen adjusting his briefs. Turning my head ever so slightly, I spied the boner in his shorts. The captain, up to now overtly unaware, stopped in the middle of the hall, pivoted a military right turn, flip-flopped within a few inches from his face, and dropped the bomb cold.

"Whacking ye olde pud again, eh, Wilson!"

Wilson's face pulsated several shades of red.

"Fifty push-ups! That ought to calm down your hormones, Ace."

While Wilson struggled with the push-ups, resembling a stomped mantis, the captain turned his head and did a mock recognizance.

"Let's see… Anybody else shimmying their shank?"

I was biting my lip.

"Luna, you think it's funny?"

"No, sir!"

"Do thirty push-ups, just in case!"

I did it without a peep. When I finished the push-ups, I got back in my bunk, and the lights went out.

It had been eight months since I.V. left. I was complying with an agreement made with my mother: one year of good behavior at Miami Military Academy, one round-trip ticket to Bethesda to see I.V.

I was doing my absolute best to behave these last two days. *Two* more days, and I'd be out of this kennel and heading to my lady. I didn't talk back or sneak out at night to get pizzas on the Boulevard—well, maybe once—or go AWOL on the weekends when I was grounded with too many demerits. I was attempting the straight and narrow for Ivy, who incidentally had been getting progressively lax in her correspondence.

The month before, when the lure of adventure coupled with the seed of doubt, sailing got stormy for the Dancing Dog, even as he jumped through the fiery hoops for love.

I discovered a small fleet of prams, those boxy little sailboats for beginners, by a small inlet on the bay at the end of the Academy's sports field. In a letter to my friend, Gabriel, I described how we could hi-jack a pram a piece on one of my weekend leaves. We would then commandeer them through a series of canals, for which I had drawn maps, and finally end up in Miami Beach at an empty lot half a block from my mother's house. I mailed the secret mission papers to Gabriel at Ransom, a very exclusive boy's boarding school in Coconut Grove, where he had ended up after his parochial school fandango.

"So, you were planning to steal a sailboat?"

Colonel Grant cold-cocked me with an accusatory query.

"No! What do you mean?"

Against that wet-noodle defense, he produced my letter *with* map.

"I mean this."

The words *how the fuck?* towered inside my skull like the giant stone title letters on the *King of Kings* movie poster.

"This does not become you or your family. I've already contacted your mother and told her not to expect you this weekend or the next. Your friend is also grounded at Ransom. Don't try another stunt like this, buster.

"I, ah…"

"I, ah…Dismissed."

"Yes, sir."

Gabriel had left his blazer hanging on his bunk with my letter inside. Someone found it and gave it to the president of his school, who contacted my Colonel, who in turn summoned me to his office for a coldhearted ambush. From now on, it would be one-man capers.

After sundry promises never to talk to Gabriel again, this time *de verdad*, my mother told me, "*Voy a hacerme la vista gorda*", translating literally to "I'm going make my sight fat," meaning, "I'm going look the other way"—*this* time. But she cautioned that anymore *maldades* and the trip to I.V. was off. So I made a big effort since then to steer for the middle of the channel. For instance, today, a few weeks after Wilson's pud on parade, I woke up an hour early, five a.m., sat in the latrine, and spit shined my shoes for the weekly inspection later that morning. A ridiculous enterprise—but hey, only forty-nine more hours.

When I stepped back into the barracks, everyone was heading out, hauling their mattress on their backs. Gilded by the sunrise, the first cadets out in the sports field appeared to be some kind of man-insect hybrid, suddenly driven out of their nest in their larval state.

The lieutenant, a husky senior, stood in front of the screen door, holding it open with his back. The porch overhang slashed a shadow on half his face but highlighted his sneering upper lip, which he presently began to flap.

"Luna, you're just in time. Grab your mattress and follow the crowd."

"Why?"

"Don't give me any lip, ace. Just grab your mattress…And just for asking, wear those shoes."

Every asshole with a couple of stripes was a tough guy around here. But I bit my tongue and grabbed my mattress. When I caught up with my bunkmate out in the field, he gave me the lowdown in between thick breaths of oozy summer air.

"No one…fessed up…to the beers."

Three cans of Orbit beer, a local brew, had been found in the broom closet that morning, and since no culprits confessed—the obligatory collective punishment. In this case, three laps around the football field, dragging our mattresses on our backs. Even at six a.m., you were drenched after the first lap. I ran carefully to prevent dulling or scuffing my spit shine—the effect anticipated by my ill-intentioned shitbag of a superior officer. It would just be a matter of wiping the dew off. But that didn't change the fact that some of the officers around here deserved repeated side blows with their own sabers.

By the beginning of the third lap, I kept blowing sweat off my eyebrows to keep it from stinging my eyes. To combat the impulse to drop the mattress and cast myself in the bay, I imagined I.V., my Valkyrie, a-waiting at the end of the third lap on her Valhallan steed in the Maryland countryside. But in reality, Ivy seemed to be galloping away. I passed inspection, went to class, then swimming practice in the afternoon, where I spent most of the lap time reminiscing the dolphin dream while I followed the black line on the bottom of the pool.

After practice, I rinsed the pool water off and dressed for mess hall dinner. The menu usually consisted of hamburgers or overcooked spaghetti with greasy meat sauce, canned diced vegetables, like succotash or carrots or peas, and powdered mashed potatoes with powdered gravy mix, all to fit on a molded tray. Rumor had it the food was spiked with saltpeter to keep our sexual urges down. Apparently, it hadn't been too effective on Wilson, or me for that matter. Except I had mastered the art of getting off without making the springs squeak. It was simply a matter of not letting your pussy daze impair your noise registration or breath rate. At that time, I had just turned sixteen, and a girl still hadn't so much as grazed it through my trousers with her fingers. Hadn't seen "live" bare breasts or felt girls' nipples. Pictures of just scantily dressed women would rattle my condiments. And if you were imaginative, then you could really fuel your hand job. Once, a Puerto Rican cadet loaned me a "soft" girlie mag called *Picante* that had black and white photos on newsprint paper of buxom Latin vixens in bras and panties. I took the liberty to shade in with a pencil the dark spots where the nipples and pubic hair would be under the bra and panties. That raised the erotic effect at least by twice as much. I had given him the mag back after weekend leave but forgot to erase the artwork. It became a real crowd pleaser. Luna, Dancing Dog and Stroke Book Artiste.

When the saltpeter rumor first went around, many of us hardly ate. And even though at that age we could have gotten it up attached to a saltpeter I.V. in a coma, we all went to the commissary and substituted our meals with candy bars. One cadet developed a mild case of scurvy, and his parents showed up to the school, demanding an explanation. The powers that be called a powwow, where it was decided the school doctor would make the rounds of the barracks and categorically deny the use of saltpeter. I never needed a doctor's disclaimer. Wilson had been proof positive from the get-go that saltpeter wasn't all that.

After dinner, I checked my mail. For the last nine weeks, I had longed to see my name through the little glass window on my P.O. box, rendered on some pastel envelope by Ivy's feminine hand. *Luna*…a caress, *Luna*…an affirmation, *Luna*…an immaculate conception of sorts, *Luna*, flowing out of her consciousness in a delightful calligraphy. No letter.

Inside the barracks, the cadets shined their brass and spit shined their shoes for the end o' the school year dance that night. The strong chemical smell of Brasso being rubbed on collar insignias and belt buckles was in the air. One cadet, a proud little Sysiphusian, blew on his cap eagle impatiently, turning the Brasso a chalky green gray before its time, then buffing it to reveal the sparkling martial bird. My bunkmate spit shined his shoes in front of our locker, singing The Mindbenders' sappy release, when I approached.

"*We got a groovy kind of love*…Aren't you going to the dance? Aren't you shining your brass?"

"I don't know. I really don't feel like it."

"What are you gonna do, stay here and 'shimmy the shank'?" He was employing our lieutenant's nomenclature to be a wise guy.

"Yeah on your pillow, groovy one."

"You're sick. Luna. Keep your homo wang out of my bunk."

He kept spitting on his shoe. I never completely grasped the physics behind spit shining. I had a peripheral understanding of it, like how the television image works. You spat on your shoe, then applied polish by gyrating a rag on it with the tip of your finger, and it made your shoes glisten like patent leather.

I didn't know what was worse—having to do it, or putting up with the morons that took it all so seriously. Besides, a quarter inch of hair all around my head and a dismal gray uniform didn't make it any easier to approach a girl, even if your shoes were glowing like the Hope Diamond. Dancing in military dress was not in the vicinity of hip at all. Now, if Ivy had been there, then nothing would've mattered because nothing would have existed besides her eyes, her warmth, her voice…

I grabbed Ivy's old letters from my locker, as I had done many times before, first reading her three-week-old letters, then her month-old letters. I would savor the *S.W.A.K.* in big letters in the back of the envelope of the first and second letters.

I sat outside and leaned against the barrack wall. It was near sunset. I re-read her first letter in the golden light. That was my favorite one.

Luna, I've never felt the way you made me feel that night by the beach…I can't believe I truly miss you…I would really love to see you again…Maybe you can go horseback riding with me at my Uncle's…I was so happy to receive

*your letter…My heart pounded when I opened the envelope. I feel so silly
telling you.*

"Hey, Luna did you forget! Luna?"

"What do you want, man!"

"Easy, Grumpy. *Our* pictures. Hey, the only reason *I* give a rat's ass
is my mother bought the book, even though I told her not to."

We were supposed to meet the coach by the pool for the swim team
yearbook pictures. "I" only cared because I could send the yearbook to
Ivy. I put the letters in my back pocket and headed toward the pool with
Jake, who mentioned nothing about the letters. He was a yard eater with
the butterfly stroke, two grades higher than me and had been state champ
in Virginia. Jake also had a lot more experience with girls than I. When
I had told him a few months before that I was planning to visit a girl in
Bethesda, he had offered his parents' house in Fairfax. But he had shown
his doubts about Ivy and me after her last letter, where she had said, "I
don't know if it's a good idea for us to get so serious."

"Sounds like a Dear John letter to me, Luna. You better start looking
for another piece of tail around here, ace."

I had argued that perhaps her parents were trying to influence her,
that she was confused. But he hadn't budged.

"I don't know…When they start getting 'confused,' that's usually a
bad sign."

But on seeing that he had bummed me out on a day before a swim
meet, Jake had tried and succeeded in cheering me with a story about a
girl he went out with who,

"Would jerk you off while she ate a sandwich." He said she loved
"makin' guys sheoot." Although I would've never admitted it, I now con-
fess that I would've been ready to eat pig shit to meet that scamp. But in
truth, back then, I would have been scared shitless. That night, instead of
worrying about Ivy's impending departure, I had dreamt about this girl
eating a peanut butter and grape jelly sandwich while she stroked me on a
haystack behind a barn. The next day, I won the fifty-meter freestyle and
gave Jake a headstart on the medley by tagging him a whole half-body
ahead of our competitors. Jake had true leadership qualities.

When we got to the pool, it was deserted. No photog, no team, no coach. Jake sang one of his favorite lines for these occasions.

"Mama don't peel no shrimp tonight 'cause Sally's comin' home widda crabs."

"You want to check the Phys. Ed. office?"

When we arrived, I entered the open door facing the sports fields. One of the coaches sat reclined, incipient beer belly secured by white Sansbelt shorts and egret legs resting on a desktop. Upon noticing me, he shot up and in two violent shoves had me outside the door.

"You knock on the door and ask permission before entering here, Cadet!"

He returned to his desk, sat with his back to me, and resumed his conversation with the other two coaches, who were now repressing grins and sneers.

I knocked this time, going through his dumb-assed charade. He said nothing to my question. But one of the other coaches said the swimming coach had gone home sick, and the photo shoot was postponed for early tomorrow before we went home for the summer. I stepped outside and walked back toward the barracks with Jake.

"What do those assholes think? It's Holy Tabernacle in there?"

Wap! "That's right."

I felt the sting of a sucker slap starting to buzz on my left cheek.

Colonel Grant, who had been heading our way, overheard my comment when Jake and I turned the corner and felt it his duty to discipline me as he passed. I had to stand at attention and *fucking* salute him.

"For *you,* it is. Is that clear?"

"Yes, sir"

"As you were."

When we got a little distance, I vented.

"I'd love to punch that son of a bitch fuckin' bastard."

"Easy, Luna. He's an asshole. Hey, this is your last night."

"I hate this shithole academy. I'd really love to kick the shit out of that bastard."

"Hey, Luna, he's just taking shit out on you. Don't let him piss on your parade. If you ever run into him on the outside, then whip his ass into a cheese soufflé. All you wanna do now is get the hell out."

"Yeah, well, I'd really like to tear this shithole academy to the ground, starting with the Colonel."

Jake got closer to me and lowered his voice.

"Check this bulletin, ace. Last year, he caught his wife blowing a cadet. Yeah! An *un-der-age* cadet, in the back of that used Coup de Ville he gave her for their fifteenth wedding anniversary."

Jake's gossip stunned the anger out of me. It took some sting out of the slap. My anger was displaced by erotic fantasy. I still remembered his "sandwich girl" in sharp focus. The boy had a million of them.

"So, the kid told his mom. The Colonel's wages are still garnished every week, I heard, to pay them off so they wouldn't go to the authorities."

My image of the Colonel, begging for his life through a bloody lip while I poured gasoline on him, dissolved into a picture of a Caddy's backdoor opening and revealing his wife's horrified big blues eyes, the cadets gizmo still in her mouth. I wondered how that would feel, a woman's mouth on your wiener…For an instant, I intensely wished *I* would've been the underage cadet.

"Hey, Luna, that dance starts at eight…You're going, right?"

"I don't know…I might just hit the sack, man."

"Hey, up! Off your knees, fellow no alibis. Hup, two, three, four. If I don't see you, I'll come drag your ass over there, you hear? Huh! I feeeel good, ta-ra-ra-ra-ra-ra-raaah, like I knew that I would, ta-ra-ra-ra-ra-ra-raaah!"

Jake left, alternating from a mock march to James Brown footwork. How did he find out about the Colonel's wife? Had he made it up? It really didn't matter either way because it had its effect, humiliating the Colonel and taking my mind off the slap and into fantasyland. With that kind of talent, I was certain Jake would some day lobby for a big corporation or weasel some plum job in the government, getting dirt on foreign dignitaries while showing them a "good time." I always wondered what the hell he could ever have on me, though.

I really still wanted to bust that Colonel's face. Cocksucker! Though, literally speaking, it was his wife who would fit that handle. Who the fuck did he think he was to be slapping people like that! The slap began to eat at me. *Asshole-bastard-motherfucker!* Yeah, but I had Ivy, not him. He wasn't capable of *ever* having an Ivy. God, I wanted to see her more than anything in this world right *now*. She could take the pain and humiliation, which was a broken pick in my chest, and dissolve it with just a glance. I felt like trashing the barracks, then going and smashing his face into the corner of his desk. Easy. Just one more day, doggie. You can't let the Colonel, or any other asshole, blow a whole year of putting up with assholes? One more day, you bastards. Just one. More. Day!

The barracks were empty. I took soap, shampoo, and a towel out of my locker and went in the showers. I was alone. All the cadets were already at the dance. The water ran warm down my chest and my thighs.

Impure thoughts snaked their way to center ring to duke it out with frustration.

The screen door to the barracks had a rusty spring, so it would report any intruder long before they entered the latrine. A rare stroking op. She licked her ruby lips in anticipation and looked me in the eye, telegraphing a meet-your-maker blowjob from the driver's side of the Caddy. I produced a ceramic-tile-piercing boner. Slowly, she grabbed my shoulder, bent over me, and the back of her beehive hairdo eclipsed my crotch. Just before touching myself with the tips of my puckered fingers to simulate her lips, Ivy was approaching outside the caddy door! She would not appreciate Luna jerking off to that inbred bitch, or anyone else for that matter. I had a momentary loss of focus. But Li'l Smilo would not drop the itinerary. He was in control of the bobbing wrist. The beehive came back and pounced on me, consummating my double-edged fantasy—getting off while chastising the Colonel. Ivy would never know, and unfortunately, neither would the Colonel. My breath was agitated as I watched my issue slip down the drain. Sorry Ivy. Thank you, Ma'am. Fuck you, Colonel!

"Glooooria, G.L.O.R.I.A. Gloooria..."

The band had stoked the cadets into an egg headed frenzy at the gym, extending the last chorus by twelve bars for audience participation. There weren't that many girls to go around. And frankly, I didn't find any I liked. What girl in her right mind, except for some of the cadets' local or flown-in girlfriends, would come to an end of the year dance at Miami Military Academy to be bum rushed by a pack of sex-starved cheesedicks?

I spotted Jake in the distance, hyping something, making gestures with his hands to illustrate something big. He was talking to an over-dressed and overweight Cuban girl. He walked through the sea of beat-nodding cue ball heads toward the entrance doors of the gym where I stood. He spotted me. The band started on the Troggs' *Wild Thing*. Jake was a carpetbagger with a prospect.

"Hey, ole dude, *que hay!* Luna, this is Miriam. She's Cuban, just like you."

"*Hola.*"

"Hi."

"We're gonna go see if that ole manatee-o is still feeding out by the inlet."

He said this in earnest, like we had both seen this manatee attraction pretty much on a nightly basis. He nor I, nor anyone else for that matter, had ever seen or mentioned the presence of anything in that inlet except schools of mullet, needle fish, or the occasional blue crab. He headed out with his chunky Cuban in a satin dress who was at least twice his girth. Jake was an active member of the no-pussy-is-bad-pussy cult. Short and sweet had its merits. I, in turn, craved for redemption—a pretty tall order. Love always required performances without nets from its dancing dogs. And you never knew which payday its check would bounce. It was eleven thirty and half an hour before tomorrow. I went back to the barracks. But I couldn't sleep right away. I took out Ivy's last letter and jumped on the top bunk, facing the foot end where the security light outside my window made a bright, though slightly keystoned, square on my tight-as-a-sausage blanket. I read only the top part of Ivy's last letter. In the gym, the band played its last song, the Moody Blues' *Go Now*. Its piano *decrescendo* ramrodded my soul.

We've already said…Tuntun tuntutuntun…goodbyeee, ah ah ay. Tuntun *tuntutuntun, If you got to go, dahling, you better go now.*

"Thank you for the varsity letter. I put it on my white V-neck cable sweater…"

I skipped over the "you shouldn't have sent it." That part always made me feel queasy.

I want you to tell me what you intend to do now

Cause, darling, let me tell you, I'm still in love,

still in love with you now, Wowowowo-o-o-o….

The song wasn't helping. My eyes moistened, but the next line held it in.

"You quick little dolphin. I wish I could have seen you swim…"

I stopped reading there. The rest started with, "Maybe it's better if we don't get too serious…" It reminded me of the day she left and what the beach-boy had said. Ivy and I had kissed goodbye in the lobby. When her cab left, she turned between her mom and dad and waved through the back window. There I stood, a thousand pianos hanging from my heart. Outside on the deck, the sun had been still baking at four o'clock and the tourists still greedy for a tan. I sat on a lounge toward the end of the pool deck where I had kissed her the night before. I began to write her a letter on Sea Isle Hotel stationery, which had the logo of an island around which I drew two jumping dolphins named Luna and Ivy. Mine was doing a flip by the stars.

"Hey kid, that ain't no good. She'll probably be back with her boy-friend this very evening."

I flipped the letter and blushed slightly at having been caught in my loopy reverie by the beach-boy and my immediate boss. But after the initial embarrassment, I was angry and felt he had trespassed my intimacy.

"That's not true. She doesn't have a boyfriend. I'm gonna visit her next summer. You don't know everything, okay, and I really don't want to talk about it. Just mind your business."

"Hey, it's okay kid. It's just puppy love. We all go through it. Wait until the next little honey comes out here, maybe a little older, and if you're lucky, maybe she'll give up a little poon tang. Sh-Yeah, you'll be writing, writing this one off."

He pointed to the letter.

I slipped the letter in the envelope and into my shorts' pocket. I didn't want his predatory finger anywhere near her.

"Forget it."

"Hell, boy, I'm telling you, either you or her will meet somebody else before next summer gets here, bank on it. I'm trying to save you the heartache."

"I don't want to meet anybody else."

"Oh, you got it bad. Well, I'll tell you what. No matter what happens, C.Y.A., kid, and if it don't go right, you got an ace in the *hole*. If you get my meaning, ace…Let's start picking up some of the mats. See if these buzzards get the message that it's quitting time. If the moon tanned them, we'd never go home."

We lined up in front of the pool in our tank suits—tallest in the back, shortest in the front. It was seven a.m. It felt a little chilly in the morning breeze. I was still drowsy since I had slept through breakfast.

Jake, standing directly behind me, waved his fingertips up to my nose. They exuded a musky smell.

"That senorita had one wet snapper. I might be visiting here very soon, Amigo."

The yearbook photog, a cadet with half-inch-thick lenses, took the picture, capturing Jake's impish grin and his hand just off my nose…and it made it to the yearbook like that. Jake the Show and Tell Debaucher. Good conversation piece perhaps, but not the thing I had wanted to send Ivy. Back in the barracks, we all exchanged addresses, though we never wrote. I had not made any real friends here, just established alliances. Jake would never come back to Miami to claim his snapper dinner. We all waited, sweating a bit in our parade dress, with our duffle bags jam-packed in front of the main office for our parents to pick us up. My mother, still a sultry beauty, came in her new '65 Mustang—a very cool car, even though it was only a six-banger. As we drove away, the old Colonel and the younger coaches looked at her wistfully, trying to catch her eye as she passed. I felt vindicated somehow. Eat your hearts out, jack-offs, and go back to your white trash wives forever.

Passing the Colonel who had slapped me, I waved goodbye and smiled, crossing my eyes when he looked, and flipping him a stealthy bird with middle finger on my nose bridge. He did not know quite what to make of it. He pretended not to see it. On the way home, I asked my mom if we could go get the ticket.

"What ticket?"

"The ticket to Bethesda, to see Ivy."

"There's plenty of time. I have to get back to Burdines's. They're having a sale, so I have to work the floor tonight. By the way, here's a letter for you. I think it's from her."

She handed me the pink envelope. I turned it around. It was *S.W.A.K.E.D.*! I looked at my name. I didn't want to open it just yet. Yes! To puppy love—if that is what they called it.

We climbed the first bridge of the Julia Tuttle Expressway heading toward Miami Beach, the panoramic view of the bay on either side. A V-shaped flock of pelicans just cleared the the top of the lamp posts above us. The sky was cloudless. *Yes, life!* An Olympic smile spread over my face. I held the envelope like a map to an enchanted island.

"Well, are you going to open it?"

"Yes. Can you drop me off at the beach? I want to open it by the sea."

"*Muy romantico,* my son! But how are you going get home?"

"I'll walk. Just take my duffle bag."

She dropped me off at Thirtieth Street.

"*Con este calor* in that uniform, you're gonna sweat to death!"

"I'll be okay."

She quoted from Virgil's *Aenid* with mock thespian oratory.

"O wicked love, to what do you not impel the human heart!"

She winked. I smiled, a bit self-conscious. My mother did not belong selling department store couture. And were it not for a despot in our country intolerant of dissenting views, she would've not been.

I didn't walk more than ten feet from her car when the June heat descended on me like a biblical plague. A trash bin dispelled the sweet and disagreeable stench of rotten fruits and cigarettes. I took my tropical wool military dress coat and flung it into the container. The polished brass ornaments clanged on the metal walls. *Kiss my ass, y'all! Hup, two, three, four.*

Once on the beach, I kicked sand on top of the spit shine and ground it in with each shoe sole into a matte finish. *Shine this!* I walked to the shore break, and I felt the seawater seep in my shoes. Yes! I held to the letter like an amulet. It was five-thirty in the afternoon, and the pool deck was almost deserted. No one walked the beach. I screamed.

"*Que se cuadre tu madre!*"

After mentioning their collective mamas, I threw my dress cap like a discus. The brass eagle above the patent leather brim strobed a few times, switching the sun as it spun, before splashing in the sea almost at the end of the jetty. I then sat on the piling, my scuffed black oxfords in the water, and opened the letter.

Dear Luna,
I have sealed this letter with a kiss
for you being you. The reason I haven't written in
so long is because I was afraid to tell you I've
gone back to my boyfriend.

I looked up for a moment and noticed, through misty eyes, my water-logged cap near the end of the jetty, slightly bobbing in place as if marking the spot where the drowning man had last been seen.

I didn't want to hurt your feelings.
I hope you forgive me. But if you
hate me, I understand. Please don't write me
anymore. You would only hurt yourself (I'm sure
there's some cute girl drooling over you as we speak).
I hope there is lots of surf and life is good to you.
You'll always be special in my heart, Luv, Ivey

Why belabor the effects of this unadorned sayonara, which not only exploded in heaving lamentations, then, but way in the back of Dancing Dog's psyche for a spell. And though his heart at times still leaked like poorly mended porcelain, the singed pooch still danced, like it was his first dance, like it was his last dance, through each and every fiery hoop. But word has it he got better at choosing his songs and sniffing out the trapdoors.

Last Bus to Delinquencia

I hated the taste of liquor. At sixteen, you just drank to prove you could. If eating dog shit would have put you over the hump with your peers and the girls, give us three scoops. So naturally, we had a couple of drinks.

When the Chattahoochee River rock struck, some people hit the floor in frenzied surprise. No, Chattahoochee River was not a new rock-a-billy tune freshly spun by a D.J. to a packed dance hall. There was, however, a rush of teenagers who thoughtlessly boarded the damaged bus. *My* Venus flytrap.

It was a weeknight. The party shut down at eleven, and a group of us headed to the bus stop. In 1967, Miami Beach's public transit system was in the Stone Age. When the last L bus on 17th Street finally turned the corner heading east at eleven-thirty, we flagged it down.

The driver didn't stop. He passed by, looking at us like we were organ grinder apes for his amusement. The light turned red at the corner about half a block down, so he had to stop. Most of us were bummed.

"I can't believe that bastard."

"What an asshole."

"Is that the last bus?"

As friends and acquaintances cackled, I *picks* up a lemon-sized rock from a landscaped garden near the bus bench. A smooth, oblong, solid, Chattahoochee River rock. I *pitches* it high into the night, trying to land it on the bus roof—for that mallet and kettle drum intro—foreshadowing a demand for satisfaction. Hey, we might be apes, but *tool-wielding* apes, James. When the rock concludes its arc, the tinted back window of the bus explodes in place. *Holy Shit.* Within the bluish glow, people scramble to the floor, trying to escape injury at the arrival of the second missile which never came. The traffic light turns green, but the bus doesn't move. My mates, in what can only be described as a reversal of the schooling instinct, all dart *toward* the predator, which still lies in wait by the curb at the end of the block. The side jaws open, and one by one, the schoolies enter its maw. The last I saw, they were taking their seats on the other side of the shattered tinted window. I stood, incredulous, until their world diminished to a thumbnail-size fish tank, and the bus turned the corner. Bunch, Of Dumb, Fucks. I walked home.

"Luna Yena, please come to the office."

After the loudspeaker attached above the blackboard of my general math class delivered the announcement, a few people in the class looked at me, wondering what the story was. I had no idea. Just seconds before, I'd been in fraction division hell—how one number on the top is divided by the diagonally opposed number on the bottom of the other fraction, and in between that, daydreaming about spear fishing and unattainable girls.

Once in the office, I was escorted by one of the main desk elves to a counselor's cubicle.

"I'm Lieutenant Ratter with Miami Beach Police. You were at a party last night?"

"Yes."

"Do you know anything about the broken bus window?"

"No."

"Well, last night after the party, one of you threw a rock at a bus and busted the back window. Do you know who?"

"No."

"Where were you?"

"I said goodnight, and I walked home."

"How come you were the only one in my list, except for the girl that gave the party, that wasn't on this bus?"

"Because that bus doesn't go in the direction of my house."

"Where's your house?"

"Twenty-ninth Street and North Bay Road.

"Do you know who might have thrown it?"

"No."

"If you know anything, you better tell us now, or if you're his friend, tell him it's to his advantage to step up. Because we're gonna find out, and we're gonna get him. The only difference is, the less cooperation we get now, the more we're gonna bust his ass later."

"I don't know."

"Go back to class for now."

The Lieutenant turned to his go-for.

"Get Shelly Reinberg in here."

My first thought as I walked down the hall was identical to my last thought the night before concerning my little group. *What a bunch of dumb fucks!*

I went back to my general math class, which now felt more like the Catacombs than it had felt before. The teacher didn't help. He was one dry, boring old man who paid more attention to the violation of dress code, like not wearing socks, than making the class interesting and fertile. At this point, though, it would have taken a *Playboy* centerfold doing squat thrusts on the teacher's desk to dislodge my focus from what had occurred and its likely finale.

After the bus had turned the corner on Washington Ave. that night, the driver had stopped at Lincoln Road, locked the bus, and called the cops. The B.O.D.F.'s on the bus claimed they were at a girl's party but knew nothing about the rock throwing. The cops questioned the party's host, and she gave them all the names of who attended. She didn't have to give them *my* name. I wasn't even *in* the bus. But hey, they can't prove a damn thing unless somebody blabs. Still, I had the uneasy feeling that possibly my ass was up for grabs. The bell rang. It was lunchtime.

I walked across Dade Boulevard to a 20th Street sundry shop where I would usually eat a candy bar for lunch. The rich kids would go to Ollie's for his spicy burgers and fries. Ollie was in his mid-forties, and his small grill made its lion's share at lunchtime. He ended up selling the recipe of his *8 Secret Ingredients Hamburger* to the Lum's franchise chain and became famous. I would see his face on their menu for the first time years later, coming down from mushrooms at the Lum's across from Peacock Park in the Grove. Drenched in cultural ignorance, when approached by the Pakistani waiter, I would assume the lotus position on the red Naugahyde booth bench and, awash in reminiscence, sing his name like mantra. "Olllieeeeeeeeeeeeeeeeeee."

But now, I bit into my Milky Way, somewhat curbing the lust created by the scent of Ollie's grill. Shelly Reinberg approached me, a bit rattled from his interrogation.

"Listen, man, they called me in there twice already. They think I did it. I'm seventeen. They can put me in jail. You're just sixteen. They can maybe write you a citation, and I mean, *you* did it, Luna. It wouldn't be cool if I had to take the heat because…"

Heat was what I was feeling in every one of my tortured hormones. Anne Fine walked by, and I slowly sipped the full lips of that dark-haired Jewish girl, whom I most likely would never get close enough to even smell because I didn't have the wallet, the standing in her clique, or the nerve to get rejected. My whole world existed to devour her every move, her every gesture, monitor her every changing cell. My breath was timed to each bend of her adolescent knees, which ruled just above her tall palomino-colored suede boots. Had she approached, ripped my soul out, and right there in the middle of the street, lifted her skirt up and pissed on it, I would have found it clever, endearing, and poetic, and precisely for that reason, I would never have her.

She entered Ollie's with the rich little Punk du Jour, *absolutely* unaware of my existence. Shelley broke my reverie.

"Hey, Luna."

"Yeah."

"You like that broad!"

She ain't a 'broad', Shelley, I thought. But why bother to school him? Like she was *nothing* to him, like he could just snap his chubby little fingers and she'd come and beg to eat his dingle berries, right?

"Listen, man, so what's gonna happen? 'Cause I shouldn't have to go to jail…After all, I didn't do it."

"Okay, God damn it! I'll go tell 'em who did it. I'll tell them it was me, even if it was you morons that got caught."

I had said that, never taking my eyes off of Anne Fine, who had dipped an Ollie fry in ketchup—a capital sin in front of Ollie—placed it in her mouth, and licked the spices off her fingers. Her presence had inspired the heroic journey, the quixotic charge. Just then, between bites of her seasoned burger, Anne looked my way and smiled. Could she have heard me and recognized one who would not easily recoil from the dragon? Had I said it that loud? Her booth was on the other side of a plate glass window? Whatever, schmuck, don't question this sliver of luck. She knows you *exist* for whatever reason. I smiled back, accepting my good fortune. As I bathed in the light of her recognition, David Goldstein walked past me, and her gaze followed *him* through the door. He lived in the Sunset Islands, an upper crust landfill on Biscayne Bay with bridge access and guardhouse checkpoints. Last week, I had seen Anne getting into his brand new metallic blue Le Mans convertible. He kissed her cheek very close to her mouth and sat beside her. Sir Luna, Grand Asshole and Fugitive Vandal? Slim chance. I looked to my left, but Shelly had gone. Let's face the music.

The cops hadn't returned from lunch, so I was asked to wait in the counselor's office, temporarily the bona fide interrogation center. The worst part about this whole thing was my mother finding out. Facing yet another authority figure and explaining, promising never to do it again, perhaps enduring some type of lecture about the company I kept and how it would affect my future. But it would not stop there. She would then phone my father, who since the divorce naturally kept a separate residence. Then, he would also feel it his duty to make a presence and an inquiry. He was really not around much, except when I did something wrong. He had grander things on his horizon. He would be the first to offer proof of human rights violations to the United Nations—that Cuba's political prisoners were undergoing torture. He was a well-known journalist seeking the liberation of Cuba. I was not looking forward to weighing down his agenda with my two-bit act of vandalism. Soil his name…you know, the whole-fucking-nine-yards. I was the wayward offspring of a failed marriage. He was a public figure. On a more sanguine level, exiles expected his voice on the radio once a week, denouncing the atrocities of Castro's regime while they drank their *cafecitos* and licked each other's wounds about the Bay of Pigs betrayal, or delivering the same question year in and year out from decade to decade, *Cuando usted cree que se caiga El Caballo?* When do you think the horse (Castro) will fall?

And my mother truly had her hands full, although I didn't see it then, what with being a single parent, struggling with me. An astute, intellectual, and romantic beauty who came from a politically elite newspaper family in Havana, now exiled here in 1967 Miami, where a lot of the local crackers considered Cubans a type of "mango-munching nigger." She worked a part time for $50.00 dollars a week under a philistine Cuban banker, who, envious of her integrity and family name, made advances but lacking the class, the upbringing, or the noble heart to attract her, compensated her rejections by frequent criticisms and digs in public about her secretarial performance. And now enter the vandal. You can see how I would've rather saved everybody the aggravation?

"I know who did it."

I didn't even give them a chance to fully step through the door.

"So, who did it?"

Officer Ratter didn't want to waste too much more of his time on this punk shit.

"Hold it. I talked to him, but he wants to make sure you don't tell his mother."

"Okay, that's no problem. It will be strictly confidential between he and us."

I extended my hand, and he shook it, sealing the deal with no hesitation.

"I did it. And I'll pay for it."

Triumphant in truth, standing straight and tall, I looked at him right in the eye. He addressed his rookie.

"What did I tell you, Jim? It was the little mango muncher all along."

He scanned the list on the clipboard with his index finger, found what he was looking for, and dialed the phone...

"Are you Luna's mother?"

Son of Chaos

*The only difference between a madman
and me is that I am not mad.*

–Salvador Dali

Within ten seconds of releasing the tourniquet, the hotels barricading the eastern dusk to my right lost their armature. Miami Beach was a snoozer in the spring of '68. I had gotten off in the back seat of a Corvair convertible, traveling with the top down on Collins Avenue without the fear of tourist rubber-neckers or the Pigs. The LSD I had main-lined bum-rushed my control room and spun the dials. The sea side city undulated.

At the top of Haulover Cut Bridge, which passed over the Atlantic Ocean access at the end of Bal Harbor, I tossed the "works" forty or fifty feet down into the out-rushing sea. I pictured it carried across the Atlantic—which in reality would never happen due to the northbound, five-knot Gulfstream current—by wind, storm, and current to West Africa, where the acid-tainted syringe, riding a final wave, would impale

135

itself in the back of an unsuspecting fisherman netting his catch near the shore. Suffering hallucinatory revelations, he'd be hailed the new prophet and finally made king of his tribe.

"You through with the spike?"

Chris, the driver, wanted his needle back.

"Yeah, I dumped it over the bridge."

"What are you talking about?"

"It's going to West Africa."

"Did you really, Luna!"

My friend Luis, sitting next to me, searched my pockets.

"I don't think he has it."

"Jesus! Those are hard to come by. Handle your drugs, man!"

We were heading to Thee Image, up at 183rd and Collins, a con-verted bowling alley re-designed with meditation room and "black" lights. Surprisingly, they booked some of the top bands of the sixties, like Grateful Dead, Led Zeppelin, Frank Zappa and the Mothers…Tonight: Cream, with Ginger Baker, the meth monster, on drums. Unbeknownst to us then, Thee Image was one of only *two* psychedelic music venues in all of the south in 1968, the other being Vulcan Gas Company in Austin. And though admission was under five bucks sometimes, we didn't have the full fare. On those occasions, we'd hustle the line outside and usually came up with the ante.

We passed all the neon signs and exotic statuary on the drive-way-to-driveway motel row north of 163rd on Collins. I stood up in the back seat to better address the tourists.

"Yes, I am Luna, Son of Chaos! I, who cast the spike into the sea! I, maker of Prophet Kings in West Africaaaaa…! Repent, you work-a-day zombies of Neo-Babylon!"

My other buddy Tommy, who had swallowed his, was just getting off and was beginning to work his cheeks with laughter. All of us had had a big pasta dinner at Chris's. They had swallowed *their* tabs, and because of the food, it would be a while before they peaked.

A hippy couple on the sidewalk gave us a peace sign to confirm their solidarity.

"Hey, keep cool, Luna. I'm still holding weed. These Sunny Isles Pigs will have a fucking field day."

That was Chris again, the organized one. He owned the car, had an apartment and a full-time job. His roommate, Bob, spoke from where he rode shotgun.

"Luna, Chris doesn't want to bum your trip. Just cool out a little till we get inside."

"Okay, man," I capitulated.

At the next red light, a couple of tourists ogled at the car full of long hairs. I crossed my eyes and sprung halfway out of the car, a la jack-in-the-box, about a foot away from a couple crossing the street, in a mock attempt to grab their pizza, arms flailing in a wacky freestyle.

"Son of Chaos returns!"

Silly was simple and satisfying. Shocking the *petit bourgeois* was mandatory Dada antics in those days. And it didn't take much to rattle cages. The tourists spooked, first into immobility, then into flight and away from the drug-crazed hippy hostiles. The man had dropped the boxed pizza at the curb, but the woman, a corpulent dominatrix, made him return to fetch it. He did, at first hesitantly as a grackle approaches a bowl of dry dog food, but when the light turned green, he ran, scooped it up, and almost hitting the deck in the act, bolted back toward his tenacious and pie-aroused partner.

Both Gabriel and Tommy wailed in the back seat, still giddy from a murderous bud of Colombian Black they had toked in Chris's corn cob pipe. I fell back in the back seat and joined them in my acid-propelled laughing fit. We were attracting attention but couldn't stop. Chris, not amused, made a left turn into the parking lot and, happy to have arrived, let us out to go park the car. He and Bob had tickets. We had always suspected Chris and Bob, who were a little older than us, of being queer, although they came across as spiritual abstainers of sex. Once, when I was hanging at his apartment, Chris got into a long diatribe about how sex was just mutual masturbation—each person just trying to get off on each other, which to him implied a debasing activity. I, a virgin still, had no aspirations to annul Li'l Smilo in the bud, trucking down *La Via Dolorosa* to become the first Cuban celibate master. Instead, Li'l Smilo and I wished every day for a lady so we could debase ourselves irretrievably.

"Son of Chaos!"

Impersonating a wigged soothsayer, arms flailing overhead, I rolled my eyes spastically and addressed the incoming carloads of concertgoers. Noticing a group sharing a giant bag of chips, I shook my head from side to side to the syllables delivered in a one-cylinder-marine-diesel cadence:

"Po-po-po-po-po-po-potato chips! Po-po-po-po…"

Overtaken by weakness, I eased into a sitting position on the pavement in lieu of crash landing on it from a laughing seizure. To be able to laugh at two silly words over and over to the exclusion of the universe was truly a state of grace, or a grand predicament. The smart thing to do was to get out of public space and the likely predations of law enforcement. Luckily for now, the Fates seemed to be humored by the acid-headed waggery. Chris and Bob weren't counting on the Fates, so they ditched us like egret droppings.

As people drove in, we provided the entertainment for them, and they for us. One guy stuck his head out the window of a rusted pickup.

"You dudes are on some good drugs, huh?"

We nodded our heads, laughing in agreement, and he gave us the peace sign. Each passing car was a world. Another passing motorist inhaled on a joint, held his breath, and smiled. A cough attack changed the channel on his face.

We laughed at his face until our stomachs twisted into knots. Tommy wanted to start working the line. By this time, I couldn't care less if I ever saw Cream. I could have just stayed here, laughing at cars forever.

But Tommy talked us into at least trying to get into the concert. Besides, the entertainment value subsided when the cars stopped driving by. Luis tried the first people who looked like they had something to donate.

"Can you spare some change, brother man? We're trying to get in."

"You're not gonna get in tonight. It's sold out."

The guy making the announcement was a well-heeled longhair. He must have owned a head shop, dealt grass, or been a rock impresario.

He sported a billowy deep purple silk shirt tucked inside black velvet bellbottoms, which broke the crease impeccably over a pair of new black lizard ropers to match the straight brown hair flowing with sheen from his black leather hat. Hippy with bank account. His patchouli-scented girlfriend was delicate in a suede petticoat top, revealing silken skin and a hint of peach-sized breasts through the leather laces. Her loose cotton skirt, which ended just below the knees, was simple, though masterfully tailored to cling and release in all the right places. In other words, understated though still nut-buzzing couture.

"I like your Indian moccasins," I offered in a trance.

"Thank you. They're Navajo."

She smiled like a fairytale and melted me into a mutual acid swoon. *Wow!* I think we must have gotten the acid from the same place. Yeah, but she was staying with Long Green, so keep it your jeans, Flowerino. She gave me a peace sign as she walked inside. I gazed and smiled like a lobotomy victim, just short of drooling. The fiery tips of her roan-colored mane grazed slightly just above her oscillating rump as she disappeared into the crowd.

Don't you love her as she's walking out the door...

I hated to panhandle. Never had the face for it. And frankly, on acid, I had no clue what kind of face I did have, if I had one at all. On top of that, I was not in a concert head. We went to the front of the line, where Tommy talked to the ticket taker.

"How about a couple of tickets for three stoned hippies."

"Bro, I'm jammed packed. Look behind you. I don't think it's gonna happen.

"Tommy, let's go."

I didn't feel like staying around. Gabriel kept panhandling, just in case. Money always came in handy, and we had a crowd. The line didn't move much, and we got bored waiting. Tommy remembered that the last time we were here, we had stashed a pipe across Collins in an Australian pine hedge next to a motel. We foraged, and Gabriel spotted the clay pipe. It still had Colombian buds in it. We smoked at the beach, where I felt some connections to shaman rituals. Native American themes always emanated from my drug-induced nature jaunts. Orion rose from the eastern horizon. I imagined the Tequesta smoking some ceremonial pipe by the same sea and constellations and timelessness, or just having a damn good uncivilized time before European *Finishing* School. I got up and walked with my bare feet to the shore break. I let out the quintessential Indian war cry I remembered from the Indian and Cowboy movies of my childhood.

"Woowoowoowoowoowoo!"

"Hey, Crazy Horse, let's go to my house, and we'll drop another tab."

Tommy, Captain Beyond, was calling from where he sat with Gabriel, who, taking one last drag of the pipe, burned the contents to a feeble orange ember before it went out. In a few weeks, Tommy would be in a bind for the rest of his life. But at this point, even Luna, Son of Chaos, maker of prophet kings, couldn't foresee that. And hey, another free tab sounded like a great idea at the time.

We caught a bus to Tommy's house, or more precisely, Tommy's mother's house. She was gone to the Keys for the weekend.

"This guy read Walden Pond!"

"No, Walter Pound. The name is Walter Pound. See? Pound!"

Bam!

The wino slammed the stainless steel tubing on the backrest of the seat in front of him while he held on with the other hand. The bus was empty except for the nurse sitting on the side bench behind the driver way up front. She had picked up the quarter I had dropped on the way in and handed it to me. Tommy and Gabriel had paid and gone to the back of the bus, where Tommy had misunderstood our pickled fellow traveler, who wore a medium-sized supermarket bag for a Chef hat. Gabriel worried about the man's hand.

"You're gonna break your hand, man."

"Nah, it don't hurt. See?"

Bam!

He struck the pipe again and showed us his white-knuckled fist. As we approached a streetlamp, Tommy interrupted.

"Duck! Here comes a meteorite. Wooooosh! Hah-ha-ha!"

"What the hell is he *on*? What on earth are you on, buddy?"

I was looking at the enlarged pores on the winos nose which, reinforced by its vermilion tone, resembled a strawberry with nostrils.

"Here comes another one. Woooooooooo!"

"Holy fuck, Tommy. That really looked like it was coming at us!"

Gabriel had joined Tommy at dodging meteors. They were getting loud because the grass had boosted them into their by-now-full acid peak. I looked toward the front, and I could see the bus driver looking at us in the visor mirror. He addressed us.

"All right, let's watch the profanity back there!"

The nurse was looking straight ahead. Tommy and Gabriel missed it altogether; they just ducked at the next street lamp and laughed. I started to straighten out, remembering my last bus fiasco, whose busted back window I was still paying off at a dollar a week with thirty-five weeks to go.

"Hey, cool it. Stop cursing."

With glazed eyes and stale breath, the wino went on a roll.

"Profanity, pfff...Life is one big profanity, but nobody says nuthin'... And this ain't no spaceship. It's a big turd, and the light at the end is the open asshole of lechislachors and the hemorrlhoid shtinkin' pigs that harass substratum. But nobody says nuthin'. Nobody gives a shit on a rolling donut about substratum..."

I closed my eyes, and the wino's imagery combined with the acid had sent me on a scatological kaleidoscope. Donuts spun like wheels out the ripped-open backsides of big empty gray suits, while cops, the spokes on those wheels, reached up to handcuff us as we drifted weightless through the donut hole and ducked out of the way, like Gabriel and Tommy had dodged the "meteors." Oh yeah, it was all getting very sci-fi. I looked outside, saw our stop coming, and pulled the cord. Our eject button.

"This is it! Tommy, Gabriel, come on!"

Bam!

"See? It don't hurt. You just gotta stay numb. Substratum gotta stay numb."

141

We exited, and as the bus drove away, Walter Pound rested his head against the window glass, bending the near-perfect vertical creases of his paper bag hat.

In Tommy's bathroom, fascinated by the thin yellow stream pouring out of my pee hole, I squeezed and released "Smilo," attempting to spurt S.O.S. in Morse Code with the flow—*dot-dot-dot dash dash dash dot-dot-dot*—and watching the wave rings on the surface of the water lap against the edge of the bowl. I pondered the phenomenon of the urethra. I, Luna Yena, had burst out of one just like it as "primeval ooze." I was the sperm cell that made it. I was a *winner*!

After pissing, I washed my hands. One hand washes the other. It *really* did. I started to laugh. I caressed one and then the other. But there was an argument about which was "the one" and which "the other."

I was ambidextrous, not taken to mean I could do the same thing with either hand. Throwing a football or a baseball or batting, I was lefty. But I played tennis righty. I also wrote and painted with my right hand, but shot a gun with my left. I had cut the tendons on my right index finger when I was five years old, so my trigger finger was no good. The last phalange did not bend on its own. So, the left hand told the right that *it* was "the one" on account that the right hand was the gimpus. It slapped the gimpus, and the gimpus slapped it back. I laughed. It was *all* about hands. Hands that applaud, hands that insult, hands that caress, hands that injure, hands that bring the newborn into the world, and hands that execute those same newborns for a myriad reasons…

Hands…hands…hands…hand-to-hand, handout, handy, out of hand, hand-me-down, hands-on, handjob, handover, hand-to-mouth, bird-in-hand, hands down, give a hand, hands above the sheets, wash your hands, hand over fist, hand in the cookie jar, winning hand, backhand, like the palm of my hand, handheld, ranch hand, handmade, don't bite the hand, handle it, hand it over. Let's join hands…Hands had built everything in this world and could destroy it all. These things with ten fingers on them carried out the wishes of our brain. I looked at myself in the mirror. My face was "breathing." (t had "patterns" on it. The face of my brain!

Wow, man! We were essentially brains...! With bodies growing below it to get "the brain" from point A to point B. It even "grew" a face so it could make it easier to communicate with other brains! So, we were really, at the core, just a bunch of brains being carried about in a hard bone case, like a crane operator in a cockpit, with legs and arms and dicks and pussies, raising cane all over the planet and making more brains. *Holy shit!*

The sound of the faucet stream in the sink, which had been nonexistent all this time—however long that had been—" came back" with a tone resembling the hiss on a blank audio tape. I cupped my hands and splashed water on my face. One, two, three million times. Yes! *Water!* The life-giving fluid. I wet my lips. I drank some. It was cool. Water gave you life. Oh yes, I liked water. Ahh! Down my face. Down my chest. More! I breathed in, and some of the water went down the wrong pipe. *Cough, cough, cough!* Multi-colored cluster bombs shattered into an asphyxiating vacuum, then I inhaled fire gas. *Cough, cough.* I inhaled again with a violent wheeze. *Oh, I'm gonna die!* I thought. *Oh shit!* I inhaled slowly and tremulous. My ears buzzed in a high pitch. My chest burned. My heart ram-rodded my chest. I bent over, holding onto the sink, and dropped on my ass, gasping. Oh...Oh...Oh...My God. Oh...Oh! This life-giving water could kill you! Every damn thing was a double- edged sword...

My ass cheeks felt a spreading coolness. I was sitting in wet shag carpeting. My splashing had gotten out of hand. The water was still running—the "hiss" inside my head tapes. I stood up and looked at myself in the mirror. My pupils were wide open. On closer inspection, I found it dilating and contracting in short spasms. It reminded me of Tommy's cockatoo when it got excited. My cloth headband was twisted and halfway up my forehead. I removed it, pulled my shoulder-length hair back, and re-fastened the headband. *Man, you're really vain*, I thought. *Everybody else is in the room, tripping out, grooving, and you're here, worrying about your hair.* Fucking plastic asshole!

I left the bathroom, thinking a little less of myself. That ol' ego loss black magic.

In the room, Gabriel was laid out in a bed, staring at the ceiling, who knew in what planet. From his bed on the other side of the small room, Tommy saw me walk in and held up another acid tab.

"Here's your other booster, spaceman."

"Oh, no, man. I'm really fucked up. Let's just do it tomorrow at the love-in."

"No, man. If you want it for free, you got to do it now."

"We don't really need it. Hey, Gabriel?"

Gabriel didn't respond.

"Hey, *I* dropped another one. That doesn't mean you have to gun your cosmic chopper."

"All right, give it to me!"

I knew I didn't need it after my hands-and-brain-and-water trip in the bathroom. I was plenty fucking "boosted." I sat next to Gabriel, who was still immobile on his back and hardly blinking. The ceiling seemed to be staring back. I looked at the tiny purple mind bomb which ticked on the palm of my hand.

"What do you think, Gabriel? Should I drop it?"

"I'm tripping out..." was all he managed to offer after my many attempts to engage him, and he only had the one tab.

What the hell. I dropped it. Tommy smiled from across the room. His mouth became a big orange clown grin, the pointy corners of his mouth turning into tiny day-glow telegraphic dots outward into space. I lay down next to Gabriel, who was still speechless. I stared at the ceiling. Within minutes, an undulating series of colored veils kept turning upon itself in one small spot.

"Hey, do you see the colors too? Gabriel, Gabriel!"

"What?"

"Do you see the colors moving? It's intense, like a movie projector."

"Yeah."

"Are you fucked up or what?"

"Yeah."

That's the last I got out of him, in monotone.

"Check the sound here, Luna. It's a trip."

I went and lay next to Tommy, who faced two big speakers, one on each side of our heads, and blasted Blue Cheers's version of the "Summertime Blues." It was twenty- megaton electric guitars.

The ceiling pulsed and spread rotating carpets of saturated hues. Imploding filigrees of paisley-like silks…Now translucent. Now opaque. I was hitting overload, so I closed my eyes. Not the recommended anti-dote. The music set the speed limit, and I slid forward through spinning mandalas, warping and stretching as I penetrated them at dizzying speeds, Wow! There was no conscious thought. Just hold on to your surfboard M' Gremlin.

There ain't no cure for the summertime blues!

Then, the guitar break.

"Whooooooooooooooah!"

Universes collided, or maybe it was just a monumental rush. Spaced out, spread out, stalled out. I plummeted and blacked out. Time and space *and* continuum not accounted for…Zip!

When I came to—which wasn't really "I" since I didn't know *what* I was, much less *who* I was—I did not recognize my surroundings. I didn't know I was in a bed, in a room. There were no names for anything. No words, just a sentient dawning. I didn't know if I was a woman or a man. I eventually recognized a man next to me but not that it was Tommy. *I am a newborn child*. With my eyes, I follow a translucent figure walking across the room with a hammer. He approached an anvil, and when he struck it, the figure disappeared. The clanging sound immediately delivered my identity. That translucent figure is *me* and me is *Luna*. I looked next to me, and my shoulders were touching the man's shoulder beside me, who I now recognized as Tommy. What made me come and lay here? Why was I lying next to Tommy? Was I…queer? It was the only place to lie down, asshole! It was this, the floor, or Gabriel's cot across the way there, where he was still doing his best impression of the Mummy at Rest.

But where the fuck did that come from: *Am I queer?* Oh my God, *was* I queer, and now through a double dose of lysergic, I had received the psychedelic boot out of the closet? I got up and sat by the foot of the bed, concerned. Well, one thing was for sure, I wasn't battling any urges to rip Tommy's pants off and savor his gizmo. I looked down at the top of my feet, stained with brownish rivulets. The soles where almost black from everything that had stuck to them since earlier in the night, from Thee Image's parking lot to here. My bellbottom jeans, besides having the ass soaked from my H2-O shenanigans in the bathroom, had a frayed tear. The white T-shirt had a brown stain from foraging into the pine hedge where Tommy had stashed the pipe, and I was lying here, *being* the waste my parents had told me I was becoming. A druggie that'll never amount to anything…*Soy un mierda*. A common turd. No good for anybody…I'll never find a woman…Who the fuck's gonna want this broken compass with a dick? What am I gonna do? What the fuck am I gonna do? Bad fucking medicine.

All night long, I put myself through the Stations of the Cross, which wasn't really the Stations of the Cross because I hadn't lived enough to truly crucify myself. I would master that art later. But nonetheless, I thought I was crucified. And believed it. *Substratum*, whatever that meant. I felt deeply near its vicinity…My stomach was in knots. Gabriel and Tommy were passed out. No inward scrutiny there. Lucky bastards. I had nearly drowned in the self-generated shit monsoon of my own worthlessness. For all our bravado, we were all such fragile monkeys at some point. Yuan Wu's "Do not establish any views or keep to any mental states, move with the mighty flow, so that when the wind moves, the grasses bend down," was no doubt a worthy gun with which to carve the clean-up set, but Luna the Hodad had just wiped out, bared soul on *diente de perro*.

I went to the bathroom and pissed. No revelations this time. Washed my face and rather greasy forehead, and pulled my hair back. I powered up the small lamp on the table in the breakfast nook. The warm light made the kitchen cozy. On the wall across it hung an impressionistic painting of a sailfish, leaping out of the sea in the foreground, and a female angler, sitting in a classic Fifties sports fishing yacht with outriggers, rolling in the swell a short distance away. Beyond the horizon was the tip of the Eiffel tower. A Tommy's Mom original. Her ex-husband, before she met Tommy's Dad, was French.

I made a golden find in the refrigerator—a bowl of *kimbombo* soup I had seen Tommy's mulatto Cuban maid cooking two days before. I was in a food trance now, no ruminations. The "brain" wanted to eat and was not fucking with uncertainties. I put some in a pot to heat on the stove. A muted blue dawn illuminated the floor to ceiling breakfast nook window. I took an ice cold Schlitz from the refrigerator, a beer brand I had always assigned to the trailer-park crowd. It was delicious.

The soup was like a gumbo, cooked with tiny shrimp and okra and mashed balls of potato and plantain, but the cook had also used tiny bits of conch. I could smell it heating up. The gas stove made short work of it, while I sipped the beer and engaged on the blue flame flaring outward from the bottom of the pan, mimicking the pre-dawn light. I poured a steaming big bowlful, then scooped a helping of homemade cornmeal on it from the refrigerator to cool the soup a bit and snagged another beer. His mom kept a collection of sauces, both store-bought and homemade. I picked a homemade labeled *Habanero and Tamarind*. Ah, Fruits of the Earth and Sea! My tongue relished all the blends and, occasionally, an ice-cold swig of beer for relief. I was conducting a Symphony of Flavors, lost in the world of taste, texture, and succulence. I finished the last spoonful and sat there, still stimulated from the drug but without the edge. Sometimes, it was just a matter of eating! I still felt gamy, sticky. The "cat" clock up on the wall with a pendulum tail said 6:15 a.m. I stepped outside and rubbed my feet on the dew all the way to the dock, a cool salad for my feet. The food felt warm inside. The bay was glassy and reflected the pilings supporting the dock. A mockingbird sang from the very heart of song itself.

I took my clothes off and looked at the reflection of myself, lit now by the first orange rays of the sun. Luna, Son of Chaos, didn't seem so damnable at all. I dove into my own image, feeling the seawater define my borders. I was no longer on trial. I surfaced and backstroked, pushing a stream of water between my front teeth. My whole body smiled. The mockingbird sang. Armature had its place.

Split Your Cheeks

I outlined the white in her eyes with the hot wax seeping from the tjant-ing needle. I had found sanctuary, a place where discord had a chance, where sometimes it was even rewarded, not punished just for its own sake. The next day, I would dye the burlap again. Abruptly, a nasal feminine voice requested my presence at the office through the speaker above the classroom door. Beyond the horizon, the shit monsoon was a-brewing.

"Luna, *what* now?

"I don't know."

My friend, David, working on his batik, gave me an okay-whatever-you-say look, not quite sure I was giving him the whole enchilada.

"Hey, I really don't know. I've been going to all my classes. I'll tell you when *I* find out."

The clock above the blackboard showed 2:55 p.m. Last class of the day. School let out at 3:00 p.m. I started cleaning up my stuff. Mr. Minacci, my eleventh-grade art teacher, had been observing.

"Luna, I'll watch that for you. I'll be here until around three thirty. If you're not back by then, I'll put it away."

That was nice of him. Throughout my life, many gays had allied to my contrary nature, willing to lend a hand. I don't know if they did it in the hopes of nuzzling up to my wiener, or because they also had to suffer for being different and going against the grain. And truly. I didn't think about it. I wasn't in the position to curtail my alliances according to anyone's sexual preference. My friendships had never been determined by it. I'm sure he had observed that this Luna spun giddily around the mound of Venus, not planet Penis.

Some of my street friends would have given him a cold shoulder. Back then, you didn't associate with "queers," lest you'd be taken for one or risk being deeply chided. I considered him hip in his own way, meaning he was over thirty, and we accepted each other. I found out later he had a loose hand for students' good work—many a blue-ribbon winner got lost en route from the exhibition back to the school. One of my own blue ribbon winning temperas on paper had been found "missing." That was the highest compliment Minacci could pay you. His predilection for young rebels would bring him post-mortem local news celebrity for a day.

Decades later, he was stabbed to death in his apartment at the hands of an adolescent hitchhiker. Some of the "lurid" details included the discovery of dead birds in his freezer. The report tried to make him into more than just your everyday fudge packer. Oh yeah, he was some kind of necro-ornitho-sodomizing pederast. Truth of the matter being, if you want to draw or do anatomical studies, the best way to keep dead birds is in the freezer. Michelangelo used to sneak into the morgue at night to dissect cadavers in order to fully absorb anatomical mechanics. The main reason Mikee didn't keep the cadavers around, besides the stench, was fear of violent rebuke, if not execution, from the Renaissance Church. For Mr. Minnacci, tabloid television news would perform the auto da fé.

Walking the hallway to the office, a corridor well-traveled, I wondered:

What the hell now? Maybe I didn't *do* anything wrong. Hey, maybe they're calling me for something else. Might be a message from home? Why so negative?

The sucker punch is one of those things, along with getting "juiced" at a fuse box or catching your wiener tip in a zipper, that no matter how many times it happens, it always feels like the first time. But truth was, I *had* been doing pretty well scholastically—somewhere around a B+ average? Had some A's too, like art class and phys ed. Finally, I had discovered that if you were a disciplinary problem, and on top of that an F student, you were cannon fodder. But if you had close to an A average, then "but he's smart, the boy," a renegade worth turning over.

At the main office, the chunky-but-tight secretary in her twenties gave me a conspiratorial wink, followed by an inquiring grimace.

I answered just palms up, that I didn't know. Just a few weeks ago, she had witnessed, with slightly disguised relish, when my buddies and I had been wrangled back to school in our surfing baggies by the police. The truant officer followed shortly after, drenched and squeaking in his soda-soaked oxfords, declaring, "I don't need this. I really don't need this…" When we had pegged him, spying on us from his car at the beach, we left one guy surfing as a decoy and the remaining three of us went around the block and bought family-sized Ritz Cola bottles. We shook them as we approached from behind and ambushed him, holding the bottles like Tommy guns and spraying him down where he sat behind the wheel. We all received citations. My second. Three, and you went to juvenile hall.

"I'll tell Mr. Mamon you're here."

I felt like a fish mid-way through the dry season in one of those African ponds where the water level is quickly evaporating, waiting uneasily for the stork beak, the eagle talon, or a crocodile's jaw.

"Hi, Luna, how are you!"

Mr. Mamon, the vice-principal, gave me a slightly constipated and hyper-solicitous smile.

"Fine. What's up, Mr. Mamon?"

I was curt. There is no love lost between a stranded fish and a crocodile.

"Dr. Lechman wants to see you…"

Lechman was the principal, and who looked like an effete version of Trotsky without the goatee, for whom Mr. Mamon faithfully bulldogged.

"How are you doing in TV History?"

How am I doing in TV History?! Oh no, I thought, some real shit was coming down. I played along, trying to read between the lines.

"I got a B plus."

There was a lull while Mamon jittered mentally with whatever he knew and I didn't.

"How's your English and Math?"

"I've been doing fine."

"Good, good!"

I couldn't believe I was AN-SE-RING him! Mamon continued with the squirrelly small talk in a ridiculous attempt to camouflage the obvious: buying time.

"What *is* the problem?"

"Go wait in your counselor's office. We'll be in there in a minute."

I smelled cul de sac, checkmate, *emboscada*, three hundred and sixty degrees. Just last week, I had an encounter with Mamon. Between classes, some of us met in the Boy's Room to smoke a cigarette in under thirty seconds. You'd piss and pass it around—more a ritual rule breaking than pleasure. Easy to be friends then. By the third set of lips, the cigarette was a glowing vampire fingernail with a filter. On my way out the door, I had exhaled the last drag inadvertently into Mr. Mamon's face, who at that instant happened to be approaching the bathroom door from my blind side into the hallway. Instant Karma, cause and effect—three days of detention. But this time, no matter how I shuffled it, I could not make the connection. All made the more disturbing by Mamon's Mr. Friendly shtick.

My counselor, Mrs. Fischback, had not been too judgmental in the past. On the contrary, she was the one who had helped me dig about "good grades" as defensive weaponry. I knocked on her door.

"Hey Luna, what can I do for you?"

"I don't know. Mr. Mamon asked me to wait here?"

"Have you been doing okay?"

"As far as I know? I have been coming to school every day. My grades have gone up two letters in most of my classes…"

"You haven't been writing any more letters for your mother, right?"

Mrs. Fisher said this with a good-natured smirk. I shook my head.

She was referring to a deficiency notice I had received in world history. Mr. Mamon had been involved in this one too. Instead of taking the note home as expected, I wrote under parents' comments, "Mr. Smathers, I recommend that you engage yourself in a highly spiced meal of freshly laid bird droppings", and then forged my mother's signature. I had shown it to my friend over some laughs and ditched the crumpled note out on Par 3, the small golf course adjacent to my school. Well, wouldn't you know…Some dickhead picks it up and returns it to the office. That had been another chapter for the Sucker Punch series. I had waited here in her office for Mamon, just like right now, and I had answered exactly the same to her inquiry about what I'd done.

"I don't know. Do *you* have any idea?"

Deja vu of an unsettling order. I glanced at a copy of "Desiderata," framed and hanging on the wall above her desk as she spoke.

Go placidly among the noise and haste…
Exercise caution in your business affairs
the world is full of trickery…
You are a child of the universe, no less than
the trees and the stars, you have a right to be here…

"No, I haven't had any reports on you since the last time we talked. Don't take it personal, Luna, but with you, no news is good news."

Knock, knock.

Who's there? Federal Bureau of Narcotics Agents.

Who?

"We're arresting you for the illegal sale of LSD, and anything that you say will be held against you."

This announcement came from the scrawniest, homeliest, and worst dressed of the three tear-drop-Ray-Ban-wearing crackers blocking the door. If you looked up "Holy Shit!" in the slang dictionary, you would have seen Mrs. Fisher's face, and just a few pages after, under *J*, you would've found mine under "Jesus F. Christ!" They were about to handcuff me, when Mr. Mamon stepped inside.

"Don't handcuff him. I wouldn't want his friends to see him handcuffed."

He then put his arm through mine, and drawing me close in sham paternal intimacy, Mamon dispatched the following *guapería* with a stale corn beef scent.

"He won't run from me. But if you run boy, I'll hurt you."

I said nothing. I just stood there, arm in arm with this portly sack of smegma.

The beanpole cracker, with the ready-for-the-flood pants, who had read me the Miranda Rights, also had to have his posturing.

He grabbed me by the belt loop directly above the crack of my ass and shoved me ahead. I began to walk. After no more than eight steps, he tugged hard. giving me a "wedgy."

"Not so fast, boy. If you try to make a getaway, we'll shoot you."

I slowed my pace. *What getaway?* I thought, you shit-filled corn dog. We walked outside. It was about a quarter to four. In the parking lot, a crisp afternoon sun highlighted the royal palms. When the breeze waved the fronds, for an absurd and slightly melancholic instant, I missed the seashore. Most of the cars had left, augmenting the feeling that the game was over. I looked around, hoping to recognize one of my friends among the stragglers. I *wanted* someone to know I was in trouble.

"Come on, walk. We ain't got all day!"

Beanpole slammed his body into mine, still trying to prove something. I just reacted and moved a little faster. My head was into thinking when and who I would call. I wasn't going give him the reason to play at what *he* thought was a man with two armed guys as back-up. *Oh celestial joy!* But to smack him around with the fat end of a cue stick!

A vaguely familiar voice came from the back seat of an unmarked Dodge Polara.

"That was great acid, Luna."

His goatee made me twitch. I flashed on a weathered Karman Ghia. A cold, greasy feeling permeated my chest. Some bastard sold me out! No, man, it can't be Tommy, man. Wally, what a screaming fucking creep! When had I sold him anything? It wasn't enough to arrest you. These motherfuckers liked to demoralize you, try shake your foundation.

They handcuffed me and put me in the back seat of a squad car and drove off. Mamon, visible through the rear window, nodded solemnly at whatever he was being told, then shook hands obsequiously with the Federal Crackerie. I was headed for Dade County Jail. But first, I would be held and questioned at a Miami Beach holding cell.

"I didn't sell anything, and I didn't get *anything* from anybody."

I repeated the same hermetic phrase over and over. After three to four hours, I was driven across Biscayne Bay, handcuffed to a wino in the back seat of another squad car.

"There goes your life, junior. I bet you're sorry you were selling LSD now."

"I didn't sell anything, but what's the point of telling you?"

"Okay."

He drove for a while, glancing back at us periodically in the rearview mirror, then spat his poison again.

"You're Cuban, aren't you?"

"Yeah."

"Well, let me tell you, you'll be lucky if they don't deport you back to Castro. Is this the way you folks thank America?"

The cuff ring, not locked in place, dug into my wrist when I leaned back on the seat.

"Sir, is there any way you can loosen these cuffs? They really bit down when I leaned back."

"Sorry, pal. If I stop for you, then I have to stop for pops also, and with all due respect, I'd like to drop you boys off and go home to my old lady."

Pops, cuffed to me, had years of cheap liquor creasing his face. He came out of his watery-eyed trance and slurred his mind.

"Y'un hafta whirr bout me, copper. Hancuffsss dumbar me none. You can't doo shiddamee. Cops ain shit, kid. When they by theysels I—"

Slam!

I flew into the grill partition face-first but was able to spring a forearm block. Pops wasn't so lucky. His nose was bleeding, and his left cheek looked like a nine of diamonds from the grill pattern.

"Sorry, fellows, I almost hit that dog."

The cop was lying. There was no dog.

"You shonnafa bisch. You busted my nouusssh."

"Settle down, pops. I said I was sorry. And here I thought you were a tough guy."

"That wasn't cool, man".

"Tell your 'cool' hippy friend here, or Yippy, or whatever the hell he is, if he don't like handcuffs, he should'na been selling LSD."

I didn't respond. The rest of the ride, Pops kept wiping his nose and saying, "You shonnaba bish, you busshted my noushe. Why'dja bussht my noushe, you coward shonnababish…"

It was 1968. Just about all over the world, Peking, Mexico City, Paris, Chicago, it was *them* and us. "Down with the establishment!" "Fuck the Pigs!" "Power to the people!" the whole nine—which I never completely bought. But what this cop did was bullshit. It would've been bullshit in 68 B.C., and it would be bullshit in 6068 A.D. For some reason, law enforcement seemed to attract all the trash that, without the badge, would be powerless trash. Unfortunately, there was lots of trash on *our* side also. I felt abandoned and disenchanted—ever vigilant against manipulation by either side. In the name of *the movement*, fools gave acid to women to get in their shorts. Racist motherfuckers grew their hair. Self-styled messiahs of all breeds, including Castro, "This is the year of the heroic guerilla!", vied for your soul while they stole everything but the grease off your grill. Oh yeah, the Dream and the Summer of Love would die a bloody fucking death. A toast to the ones who died in combat. You didn't miss a damn thing, man. You took it with you. Sergeant Pepper was going to get buggered with his own heart. And the Majarishi put the sand in the Vaseline. But hey, enough talk about buggering and Vaseline. I was just about to enter the gates of Dade County Jail. I'll break the suspense right now, chillun'. I never had my oil checked. But I did get severely raped by a brutal and stubborn stool at home after a clip of ten crapless days in my cell.

We drove through a chain link gate and headed toward a guardhouse where a correctional officer, framed by a bulletproof window, glowed in the cold fluorescent light. Once there, the cop opened the back door of the squad car and walked us up to the guard holding the clipboard.

"Yena and O'Malley."

He looked for our names, marked something, then focused on the blood caked on Pop's upper lip and chin stubble.

"Joe, don't tell me you ran into that dog again."

"Yessir, that dog must be part proctologist."

"Why is that?"

"Because he only comes out for assholes."

"Ha ha ha ha."

Pops, still too drunk to give a shit, trimmed the forced laughter.

"Yarw the pig. There was no dog. *N'you* bushted my noush, you shonofabitch, cow'rd."

"Hey, watch your mouth, Pops. There's still plenty of crooked walkway between here and inside. You might trip and tug on Tiny Tim's tender wrist there, and I might just let him slap you around with his free hand."

"Leave him alone, man."

"If I were you, I'd mind my own business, Tiny."

Officer Joe said those words in a soft tone but with inordinate contempt. He walked us through the door. We stood in an open area where processing was in effect—fingerprinting, mug shots, phone calls. Once released from our cuffs, Pops and I parted ways toward different holding cells. I was hoping I wouldn't get an acid flashback like I had three months ago, when my dad and a cop had whisked me from the airport, nipping my plan to run away to New York to visit my dream girl, Didi B., who had lit up my life after just one heavy pettin' night on the enchanted sands of 30th Street beach. At the Miami Beach station, where my dad had taken me for a lecture, the wall directly behind the detective's desk began "breathing" paisley patterns. Not what you would call a visual aid toward getting a grip. But at this time, the errant chemistry seemed to be well anchored, wherever.

In the holding cell, on a narrow wooden bench across from mine, a shirtless black man held a piece of yellowed gauze against his paunch, which protruded from an unbuttoned short sleeve shirt. When he peeked at the wound, he lifted the gauze cautiously as if preventing air from escaping a tire, lest his life might seep out. Even from across the cell, you could see the white fatty tissue lining the entrance wound. There was no blood.

"What happened to you, man?"

"Got shot."

That's all he answered and dozed off. He came to a few minutes before they took him upstairs, checked his wound for the last time, and cursed as he stood up. "Muhfuckin' ho."

Shortly after, holding my breath at the far end of the cell, I pissed in the jammed stainless steel toilet, which dripped with large curd vomit along with something resembling weak coffee with crushed nuts. I hoped to forego an encore by the wretched expeller of these ingredients.

The four hours in Miami Beach and three here waiting for fingerprints and cell relocation had worn me down. But as the adrenalin subsided, clarity ascended. And now, the goateed creep in the back of the unmarked car, "That was great acid you sold me, Luna," and the weathered Karman Ghia started to make sense.

One night in front of his parent's house, my friend Tommy introduced me to Wally, a "hip" older guy. Not finding a place to split an LSD tab Tommy had given me, I asked Wally if I could use the fender of his Karmann Ghia. I split it with a house key and licked the residue off the faded fender, to everyone's amusement.

That month the GOP convention was scheduled for Miami Beach, and the Yippies, grandstanding radicals of street theater and tormentors of the political status-quo, had threatened to disrupt the pep rally, perhaps by even spiking the Miami Beach water supply with LSD—a threat never executed at the Democratic convention in Chicago. Needless to say, law-enforcement was frisky. Any longhair was suspect.

The town of Ojus was named from an Indian word meaning "plenty," and sure as shit, plenty went down. It was toward the north end of Miami and west of U.S. 1. There, in a converted clapboard house surrounded by vacant lots, sat Miami's first "headshop." The back room wall was papered with black light posters: Day-glow Hendrix, Peter Max's *Sergeant Peppers*, MC Escher's *Metamorphoses,* beads, peace signs, ankh jewelry, and sundry tribal curio which I really couldn't afford then and wouldn't buy now.

A genuine flower girl entered while I waited for Tommy to score. Angelic, with a flower drawn on her porcelain smooth cheek, she took a mock toke from a four hose brass water pipe display that sat on the glass counter like a totem. With a voice from the back of her throat, as if she did"t want any of the make-believe smoke to escape, she quipped,

"This…is…very…aromatic…hemp."

Wit, my favorite aphrodisiac. A charming Nordic Wood Nymph. Before I galloped into an unbridled 60's fantasy, she disappeared through the beaded doorway. While the bead strands where still swaying, Tommy came through with a smile, patting his shirt pocket. He reached in and gave me twelve tabs wrapped in tin foil. We had scored for all our buddies back at the beach.

"There's a friend of mine here. You remember Wally? He wants six tabs. You want to sell it to him?"

We had bought four extra for us. He pleaded.

"Fine, sell him three, if you want.

Tommy didn't have a car, and I didn't want to do the exchange at the headshop. Frankly, I didn't want to do it at all. I just wanted to leave.

"Tell him I'll meet him at the Little General Store."

I stepped outside, not really feeling good about the whole deal. The land surrounding the headshop was mostly empty lots and weeds. The nearest house was two blocks away.

The flower girl passed me as I kick-started my bike the second time. Her boyfriend was at the wheel of a VW camper. She offered a peace sign and a smile. The plates were from California. I knew she wasn't local. Goodbye loveliness. The brake lights glowed once at the crossroads, then the noisy four-banger wound through the gears, and the camper faded into the starry night. Things seemed benevolent again.

The battery in my 160cc Honda had been skittish for a couple of days. It didn't want to kick-start. I tried push-starting it. As the clutch engaged, the headlight revealed a pothole just ahead on the deserted road, then dimmed again when the pistons didn't fire. I tried five more times. No luck.

Frustrated, I gave the tabs to Tommy, who got into Wally's old Karman Ghia and went to the convenience store. I was glad because I was no dealer and it had been his idea. Too much paranoia.

After three more runs back and forth in front of the head shop, my bike finally fired, and I met Tommy at the Li'l Generals' parking lot.

As Tommy straddled the bike seat behind me, Wally said, "You guys better clear out. There's a lot of heat around here."

Every time I thought about that snake, I felt he deserved to have the back of his skull probed slowly with an ice pick by a psychopathic hitman.

Shortly after the Li'l General Store deal, Tommy was busted driving his car smacked out. They had found a load of stuff: an assortment of barbiturates, paraphernalia (needles, etc.). The narcs who searched his room found three pounds of weed in the closet and three spoons of heroin. On the way out, the rookie carrying the shit got too close to Schmeckle, Tommy's neurotic cockatoo, who wore a metal collar against self-defoliation. Schmeckle clamped on to the rookie's forearm. A spine-chilling yelp caused the cops up in front to draw their weapons in alarm.

They tried to take the bird to animal services, but Tommy's mom, who was well-heeled and had connections in city government, prevented it. They did take Tommy, all smacked out with a shit-eating grin, saying, "Schmeckle don't like the lit-tle piggies."

Three weeks later, Wally would be in the back seat of an unmarked car in my school's parking lot, twisting the dagger with, "That was great acid, Luna!"

It was 2:45 in the morning. I was alone in the holding cell. Someone lighting a cigarette in the cell next door reminded me of incense. Naturally, it smelled nothing like incense. Perhaps my head and spirit, weary from mulling over who, what, and why for the last twelve hours, was seeking inspiration. I summoned a Valkerie. Maybe I would run into her in the park some Sunday. I had never tripped with a woman. Ah, the flower girl from Ojus, off to some Enchanted Forest. I chase her through the ferns and dry leaves in the cool air of fall. Her sweet laughter cauterizes my betrayals. She leans back on the trunk of a great tree and pants from the chase. Drifting in her gentle azure eyes, I press against her. The firm pubis within her skirt is hot against my thigh, her breath erratic in my ear. My fingers travel the rough contour of the tree bark toward her hips. The opulent, soft plum lips eternal as they graze mine. Her tongue is warm, profane, delicious…

"Mr. Yena? Come with me."

An officer built like Baby Huey, the cartoon character, opened the door to the holding cell with clanging keys. He escorted me toward the search room, where I would have to undress. I still had a hard-on from my flower girl fantasy, a condition I had to rectify before dropping my shorts. As I walked down the corridor, I imagined Mr. Mamon, our vice-principal, sitting on a stool in the search room and demanding fellatio, his pants down and gathered at his scuffed wingtips, his wart-riddled salami nestled in a gray fright wig… *What hard-on?*

I undressed in the overhead fluorescent light, and the guard looked under my armpits.

"Now, split your cheeks."

The thought of having to bend over and reveal my anus at this guy's command was extremely unnerving. Opting for levity, I pulled the corners of my mouth up with my index fingers, raising my cheeks in a Cheshire grin.

"I don't have time for your antics, Mr. Yena. If you like, we can provide *assistance.*"

"That's quite all right. I prefer self-service on this one, chief."

I bent over and spread my butt cheeks. I recalled uncoordinated endomorphs like him, usually former patrol boys in junior high, would never take showers with the rest of us after gym. They'd get dressed, sweaty and stinky, and high-tail it out of the locker room. Occasionally, someone would bank a basketball off their forehead on the way out.

"Take your belt off and empty your pockets in this bag."

I threw in some change, a pen, and a wallet with my restricted license.

Baby Huey handed me over to another guard, Mr. Perez, a stocky Cuban in his late thirties with overgrown eyebrows and the voice of a gravel dump truck. In the elevator, he read to himself from an arrest sheet. Out on the fourth floor, he unlocked a barred door. Once through it, he slammed it shut, making a finite cavernous sound for effect, no doubt. And it was. After the second door was slammed and locked behind you, the unequivocal feeling was "you was stayin' a spell." What if there was *a fire* in this place? It would probably not be a pretty sight, *jailbird*.

"*Vendiendo eL eS Dee, no?*"

Mr. Perez interrupted my thoughts of conflagration to let me know that *he* knew why I was in here. And his tone expressed a righteous disgust. Never mind that he looked like a debaucher of stray pets.

"I didn't *sell* any LSD. Why don't you just take me where I'm supposed to go."

It was five-thirty in the morning by this time, and I was tired of having to schmooze with every one of these Barneys.

He looked at my shoulder-length hair contemptuously.

"*Si? Esta bien*".

We continued down the corridor. He whipped out his billy club abruptly, attempting to intimidate me. Instead of striking me, he jabbed open what resembled a mail chute on the wall. This he accentuated with his pelvis, a thrust alluding no doubt to anal penetration. Grabbing me by the back of the hair and pulling me down so I could see and be seen through the open slot, he growled at a group of black men playing cards around a table.

"I gah sung gwhy poossy heah fo' ju."

He yanked out his billy club, as if from a vanquished posterior, and the chute door swung shut. He urged me with the club to keep walking. He had no intention to stick me in that particular cell. It had all been a ruse for his amusement while he showed me who *gwas dee* boss. I said nothing. I was handcuffed. Though even if I wasn't, there was nowhere to go. But there was always the comfort of your thoughts. *Oh, Mr. Perez! The gods should've pissed in your crib as you slept, drowning your greasy post-fetus ass before you were sprung on this planet.*

Where did the county find these gargoyles?

Finally, we arrived at my accommodations. Perez opened an off-white steel safe door with a shatterproof glass porthole. He removed my handcuffs. I fought off an impulse to pivot and tag him with a left hook. That would've been suicidal. I entered the barred holding pen within the cell. It was dark by comparison to the fluorescent corridors. Perez closed and locked the safe security door, then operated the sliding barred gate by turning what looked like a large sailboat steering wheel, peering through the porthole as I was released into the general population of my new residence. The next time I'd see this creep would be three years later at Jackson, the county hospital's emergency entrance, wheeling in an injured prisoner. Had my friend not been there to grab and caution me on the consequences, I might still be in jail today. I stepped into the main cell. Perez worked the wheel until the barred door slid shut again. It was a long way back to the sidewalk, citizens.

I was too tired to think. Sometimes a blessing. It was 5:45 a.m. People were sleeping. I found an empty cot by the wall, but it had no mat, only the bare spring grid. A guy with two mats under him slept right across from it. But I wasn't about to wake up anyone at this hour. I sat on the floor with my back to the wall and dozed off in the ashen glow of dawn.

Shit! A searing pain jolted me awake. I opened my eyes to hovering ribbons of fire. I slapped at the flames engulfing my feet. Beyond them, huddled in the corner of the still dimly lit cell, eight or ten guys laughed. I ran and doused my feet in the sink above the toilet bowl, then rinsed the ash-fringed serpentines of tissue, which the pranksters had weaved between my toes. I really wasn't burned. What was I supposed to do? Bum rush the whole lot of them?

The cot with two mattresses was empty now. Saying nothing, I walked over, grabbed a mat, dropped it on the empty cot, and fell asleep. What a world…

Roll call came three hours later at 9:00 a.m. I awoke, still groggy, offered a perfunctory, "Here," and hit the sack again. I had by-passed my breakfast—flaccid toast and eggs, navigating in half a cup of syrupy sweet coffee spilled by the rough handling of the molded tray cart from the kitchen to the cell slot.

It was difficult to encourage a bowel movement, sitting on one of the two toilets in the middle of the cell while twenty-nine people gadded about. I'd crap when I got home.

Across the cell from me, a black man sat at an aluminum picnic table, rolling a cigarette from a pack of Bugler. He skimmed every bit of tobacco spill off the table edge back into the bag like it was Acapulco gold. Across from him, another prisoner, playing checkers with wads of newspaper for chips, watched as he smoked. Near the end of the cigarette, the inevitable question, "Can I have the short?" The smoker gave the checker player the resin-stained cigarette butt, which he inhaled with delight and did a triple ninety degree move, eating three of his opponents "checkers" and landing safely on the corner. He exhaled and, with a throaty voice, announced the events with panache.

"Three mo' caaasualtees, brothuuuhhhnn, yyeeah!"

A few cots down from me bunked a stocky, middle-aged Italian with a massive member, which he lathered profusely when he showered. A few of the guys sat around his cot now, bullshitting about his escapades.

"Hey Bandini, whatchu gonna do when you get out?"

"Rob another bank."

Laughter from the audience.

"It's the only ting I know hadda do!"

More laughter from the audience. A cozy community.

It was nine p.m. on the second day. I was not bailed out and now was sorry I had given up my dinner. Luckily, I had kept a piece of white bread, which I now quickly devoured and dozed off.

Woke up at 5:45 a.m. When the hell were my parents going to bail me out? Or at least contact me? This was not Calcutta!

No word from the outside, man. That gets eerie. It was getting old, and it would get ancient. I spent *six* more days doing this boring routine, where you run out of thoughts to think except, *Get me the fuck outta here!* By this time, I would play games at roll call. The guard would call a prisoner's name three times. According to jail protocol, if there was no answer on the third call, he would have to put out an all-points bulletin. So, I would let him call me three times and then emerge from the toilet partition like a jack-in-the-box, bobbing my head.

"I'm still here, man. I'm still here."

But soon, the energy would dissipate. Then, I was again just another asshole sitting on a bunk, waiting to get out.

"Fuck you, man! Give me that back."

"I ain't givin' you shhhit. You owe me one."

The white guy went to grab his candy bar back and received a smack on the lip from the black man holding it. They wrestled to the floor; the black man was in a headlock, getting punched. When they rolled, he knocked his head against my bunk leg. I sat up.

"Okay. That's enough. That's enough."

Bandini was attempting a truce.

They rolled over a couple more times. The black man broke loose, still holding the candy bar. The white man went over to the sink and washed out his bloody lip. The black man checked his cheek and head for blood. There was none. He ate the Heath bar.

My theory: if you took thirty of the most upstanding successful members of our community and made them live under these conditions, they'd be ripping their throats out within a week. So, what was to be expected from *the dregs*? But my theory, though minimizing prejudice, did not advance bail. I had to concoct a theory to get my ass out of this zoo, and at this point, I was barren and taking a beating from self-pity.

"Mr. Yena, you have a visitor." An announcement from the cell P.A.

Some of my cellmates looked at me, a little desirous. Anybody that got out of this shithole, even momentarily, elicited mild envy from most of us. *All right! I'm outa here.* Yes, yes, yes! Adios, motherfuckers!

As I entered the visiting booth, I saw my mother and stepfather, approaching with the how-could-you-have-done-this-to-us look. We communicated through the bullet- proof glass using an intercom which processed my mother's voice into early-Japanese-transistor-radio fidelity.

"How are you?"

"Fine. What's going on? When am I getting out?"

"Soon. We got you a lawyer. Your bail is set at five thousand, and we don't have the money. The lawyer said you'll have a hearing to lower your bond soon. Do you need anything?"

"I could probably use a few dollars to get cigarettes, candy, tooth-paste, and stuff."

"*Bueno te dejamos quince pesos,* see you when you get out. Please be careful. *Chico tu te metes en cada cosa?* I just don't know sometimes...I love you."

"*Gracias*, Mami. Bye."

My mother and stepfather left. The guard motioned me to vacate the booth. I was escorted back to the cell. *Five thousand* for bail. Jesus Christ! And in 1968 dollars.

I couldn't really believe that they didn't have five hundred to pay a bail bondsman. Maybe the lawyer had assured them that I'd be all right, that I'd be out in a few days, not to spend the money. No sense in throwing away good money that could go in his pocket for my defense, right? Or maybe my mother wanted to teach me a lesson, see if I might fly right after this. Frankly, I didn't know who to trust now. I was very frisky.

I had gone to jail once before, but only for three days, for what the cops had labeled "Grand Auto Theft"—preposterous-sounding felony for what had really occurred. This little rich punk from our high school shows up to our turf, Thirtieth Street Beach, with a 650 Triumph. Needless to say, it made my bike, a 65cc Yamaha, look like a rectal polyp. He said it belonged to his cousin.

The tags were expired by two years, "because my cousin is away at college, but if I pay for the tags, my cousin said I could use it." Punkette continued, "Right now, I don't have the money, and I'm paranoid to ride with expired plates."

I never did buy his story. In all honesty, he hadn't said it with con-viction. I don't think he expected me to believe it so much as he wasn't going to rat on himself, but the last offer overrode any suspicion or self-preservation instinct.

"Do you want to trade for a few days?"

What do you think?

I drove the Triumph the next day to my high school, and the students cleared the entrance to the parking lot to allow me right of way at the very spot where usually I would have to sit on my 65cc Yamaha and wait for the self-absorbed and bovine caravan to pass. When I revved the 650, the numb nuts scattered and enviously eyed *the wild one*. I even caught a couple of mini-skirted tenth-grade vixens turning their heads. Yes, power!

The possibility that I was riding a stolen bike and its consequences began to gnaw at me beyond the novelty and power procured, so I decided to ditch it and get mine back. I took it for one last drive, fully opened at 110mph, across Julia Tuttle. Biscayne Bay to either side of me blurred from the wind tears streaming out the corners of my eyes and onto the hot road. Finally, I left it with the keys in the ignition at the parking lot of my old parochial school, St Patrick's in Miami Beach, just below the bell tower, from where the large *Christus Rex* staring west out of its niche could witness the Triumph's destiny beneath its keystone eyes. I met Punkette at 30th Street beach, got my Yamaha back, and gave him a ride home.

That evening, I had gone fishing at Haulover Cut, next to the very "ritzy," racist, and anal Bal Harbour. I was on the north jetty, cutting bait on a rock, when a light beam flashed off my filet knife.

"Put that knife down and come up here!"

Above me, the state trooper, hat silhouetting against the purple sky, pursued my eyes with the pesky beam.

"What's the problem?"

Come up here turned out to be handcuffs, getting in the back of the car, and being charged with grand auto theft. Apparently, the punk—as I had imagined—had stolen the Triumph, which they traced by the '66 tag hanging on the back of *my* Yamaha when I gave the cop my registration. We had forgotten to exchange tags.

But here was the double whammy: the engine numbers didn't match the title of my original bike either. So *my* bike, the one my dad had bought from a "friend" of mine, had *also* been stolen by the guy who sold it to us. I spent three days in jail that time. My dad told the judge he had bought the bike and had a check to prove it. They let me out under his custody. In the end, the case was thrown out of court. But this time, it was going on seven days. When the big metal door closes behind you, I don't care if you're there for only ten minutes, you're their gerbil.

Though now, back at my bunk with a fifteen dollar largesse in my account, thanks to my mama, I was a mildly substantial gerbil. One tube of Colgate, one toothbrush…after six days my teeth were furry. I was marking items on the commissary sheet with improved cheer and an overall salutary effect. I had bank now. Let's see…Milky Ways, yes, six. Hershey's almond bars, four. Heath Bars, three. Reese's Peanut Butter Cups, six. And one pack of Top roll-your-own tobacco.

The next day, my supplies were delivered in a plain brown bag. I sat on my bunk and ate two Milky Ways in two bites each. Next, two peanut butter cups. This blessed little decadence was truly an obscene show of privilege, especially within view of less fortunate jailbirds. I stopped myself there, took out my toothpaste, loaded the toothbrush, rolled the bag, and stashed it under the pillow.

I could've kept going, but I heard chocolate was a constipating agent, and it was day seven, and I still hadn't crapped. The last two times I had tried, I made more faces than a complete collection of Chinese opera masks. Oh no, purging this freight was not to be a public spectacle, even at the risk of surgery.

I straddled the toilet to brush my teeth over the sink. I felt my incisors with my tongue, and the fur had been sheared. Ah! The minor pleasures of basic hygiene.

Most of the inmates were sitting at the picnic tables, watching *The Untouchables* in black and white, with Richard Arness as Elliot Ness. Not the program of their choice. More like the guards trying to jab home: Crime doesn't pay.

Whenever the criminal got caught, there was booing and protests. I rolled cigarettes out of my new pack of tobacco and gave away rather long "shorts."

"Fuck that pig. He'd a been smoked ham in da hood."

The TV sat about seven feet up on a shelf out in the corridor, right at the dividing wall between our cell and the one next door, so the cell population on each side would crowd the dividing wall to watch. The TV guide was abridged from the Sunday paper to avoid arguments over programming.

"Man, that fool shootin' that roscoe like some faggot. That gansta ain't shit."

"Dat mu'fucka leaving his prints all over de place. Dat some bogus shit."

Near the end of the show, one of the agents approached a captured gangster, who stood against the wall, hands up, legs spread, then whispered in his ear, "This is the end of the road."

"Buuuullshit! If that Fed got that close to me, I'd grab that piece and pistol-whip his wise ass into the next fucking world."

Suddenly, the silhouette of what looked like a slipshod jousting lance tipped by a twelve-ounce boxing glove approached the channel knob of the TV set from the other side of the wall. One of our guys had already gone and come back with our sawed-off broom. Holding it by the bristles, he began a fencing match for control of the TV knob with cheers from both sides, until our guy knocked their broom to the corridor floor. One of them reached out and retrieved it.

Then, a voice announced, "Hey, man, Miss America is on Channel 4."

"I'm down. Let's dig some tang."

Sounds of approval from our side. This time, the original broom samurai stretched, reached, and turned the knob with absolute immunity. On closer inspection, what had looked like a twelve-ounce glove was a piece of pillow foam wrapped tightly in the shape of a fist at the end of the broom stub.

"Our next contestant is from Alabama…"

"*Coñooo! Esa guajira tiene diez libra e bollo.*"

"I love to bend her over and long dick that bitch."

"I'm more of a gourmet, boys. My first course would be sniffing her farts through silk panties."

"You a sick muthafucka, Bandini!"

Another Black didn't agree.

"Whatchu mean, playaah? I'd go through a yard of her shit just to lick dat belly button…from the insid., I ain't afraid a-eatin' no pussy, now, nigga. I'd leave that trim looking like a mango seed."

Yes, there were some entertaining moments. You have to figure, these guys weren't in there for following the program. The festive mood made me want another candy bar. I went to my bunk.

No candy.

Just my toothbrush and my toothpaste were in the bag. That really pissed me off. They could've fucking asked. Then I thought, *really?* Earth to space cadet? I had given them, whoever "they" were, no reason to respect the hippy. Respect around here was gained through reputation, and reputation came with violence.

"Hey, can I have some candy, man?" One of the black inmates was fucking with me now.

"There ain't no fucking candy, man. I know a bunch of you took it, so I hope it gives you the shits."

He left smirking. I'm glad he left it at that. I didn't need the scuffle, and if he got stupid, it would've come to that. Right now, I just wanted out of this hellhole. I had set myself up for it, though. I should've known better. I should have bought just enough to eat that day or share the shit. You know, the political gesture. Though they had no right to take my shit, hoarding always begat larceny. According to Chatwin's, *The Songlines*, Aborigines of Australia "believed that all 'goods' were potentially malign and would work against their possessors unless they were forever in motion."

So metaphysically, I had one less worry. But in my heart, I lusted for a double-gripped backhand on this clown's face with the bristle end of the channel changer broom. Trouble was, you couldn't just get into a scuffle here, then go home. This *was* home, and you had to sleep *sometime*. There were thirty people in here, and that made for thirty potential problems. So, you save the scuffle for something more serious. That didn't mean that it didn't smolder in my chest. The anger nearly choked me.

It made me tired. I lay down and thought of the beach, the sun, the surf. It would be winter soon, and I'd be out of this shit hole. We'd be going up the coast to Sebastian Inlet or Fort Pierce and freeze our ass off at sunrise in the gray-brown water. My reverie took me to one trip in particular we had taken a few months ago. After a few tokes of Panamanian Red on the road, I had commented to Tommy that the word "fort" in Fort Pierce was there because this had been a fort. Fierce battles probably had transpired between whites and Indians in the very place where we now slid on the shoulders of waves on resin-coated foam lozenges.

"Luna, where is the rest of that acid?"

I had assured Tommy I hadn't dropped any, just free verse. With mock reverence and ceremony, he christened me Luna the Surfing Sage. After the rest of the joint, we stopped at one of the myriad mom and pop grills on US 1, just south of Sebastian. Tommy poured a hill of sugar on a bowl of oatmeal. While he scooped spoonfuls of the over-sweetened pap into his face, he parlayed the following to the elderly owners:

"It's a little known fact, but Luna"—Tommy pointed at me—"the Surfing Sage from Havana, is attempting to draw national attention to this little known fact. The evening of a ferocious attack by the Seminoles on Fort Pierce, many troops were beset by gastric problems. Mr. Pierce himself suffered a great assault of flatulence that blew a hole in his britches. And that is why "the Sage," here, is leading a petition drive to rename the city just north of you Fart Pierced. Are you in?"

I had spat out my blueberry muffin on the counter, further aggravating the owner, who was not amused. For starters, his great aunt had actually been family—Pierce's step-sister.

Glaring at me, he had threatened. "If you don't pay up right quick and get your foul-mouthed friend out of here, I'll have the missus call the *po*lice."

I had left the place, eyes watering, abdominals straining, and gasping for air. More a case of serious stoned giggles than clever humor, though his cadence was seamless. But who cared? God, we laughed a lot more then. We were forced to stop the car several times on the turnpike *en route* to Fort Pierce due to debilitating laugh attacks. During one of our stops for gas, laughs, and cokes, we had met the babes, tourists from Montreal. Norine and her sister Emelie. They had seen our surfboards and asked where they could rent some. We were still laughing when we met them. We told them we were going up the 'Pike and that they could use ours if they liked.

Now, I dreamt we were in Miami Beach, with the girls trying to decide where to hang—their room with the air conditioner or Tommy's place with the stereo. In the dream, the girls, sunburned to the color of radishes, were for the air-conditioner. Tommy wanted to listen to his Hendrix and get some more weed. I, on the other hand, was the only one who woke up. I wasn't at their hotel room or at Tommy's. When I looked beyond the foot of the bed and saw the bars silhouetted against blue dawn in the windows—*You ain't going nowhere, m'nigga*—my eyes misted, then I lost it, crying quietly, trying to swallow and control the spasms. Impotence riddled me. This was the *ninth* day and no damn word.

I can hear the ex-cons, the hard timers, laughing at me now. "Nine whole days. Aw, poor little spic faggot!" And they had a point. Not to mention the plight suffered by many of my Cuban countrymen—political prisoners, especially *plantados*, who refusing to wear the uniform of a common criminal had to go the distance, twenty or thirty years in underwear or rags, rotting in some dungeon. Oh no, compared to them or Mandela or the gangster testosterone of the maximum security boys, I was light years away. I was a product of hallucinogens and a pacifist peerage until further notice. But like everyone, I would pay for the consequences that destiny saw fit to invoice. Plenty o' crosses to go around, little doggies.

The doors opened, and in stepped a new customer whose demeanor severed my bout of self-pity. Black tank top, tank briefs, and sandals. A black Hercules with some teeth missing and stringy goatee that hung off his chin like Spanish moss. He sported long, thin, fresh crimson cuts on his powerful arms, back, and legs. He was quiet and composed. One of the black guys asked him what happened.

"Twelve guys jumped me with razor blades."

The Apostles' revenge?

Shortly after the Black Titan of Gillette showed up on that ninth day, I was called before the judge, my bail was lowered to one thousand dollars, and I was out. I was definitely ready to leave. My mother picked me up. I stepped *outside*.

"I hope that you have learned something from this. I tell you things, and they go in one ear and out."

The whole ride back home, I was mesmerized by motion. The trees on the boulevard sped by. I stuck my arm-wing out the window and sliced the air at thirty-five miles an hour. I almost got dizzy with the motion. *Liberty.*

"I've had trouble sleeping at night, knowing you were in there. That something could have happened to you, *chico tu te buscas cada problema.*"

"I was okay."

"*Tu amigo David ha estado llamando* to ask what happened, but I thought it wasn't anyone's business, *asi que no le he dicho nada.*"

"Thanks, *Mami.*"

God bless her. Whatever the reason I wasn't bailed faster, the fact was, I *was* bailed out.

"If I was you, I wouldn't tell too many people."

"Did he say he'd be home?"

"He didn't say, but again, if I was you, *estuviera derechito como una vela,* it's not over yet."

"I'm not doing anything."

"*Dime con quién andas y te dire quién eres.* You didn't end up like this from doing nothing. *Si tu te acercas donde estan salpicando caca, vas a oler a caca.*"

I smiled at my mother's second guilty-by-affiliation proverb, the one with the "caca" imagery. But I assured her I'd be cool. No doubt, she was right. I was nowhere close to home free, even if I wasn't guilty. And I was not a citizen yet, just a refugee, so, they could deport my greaseball butt pronto if they so wished, just like Officer Joe had said. So C.Y.A. had to be the order of the day.

When I got home, I called Tommy. There was no answer. I wondered if he had made bail. I called David, who said he'd be on his way with a couple of the boys. I called Tommy again. No answer.

At eight, the car pulled up. David greeted me first. I hadn't seen him since art class at 2:55 p.m. nine days before.

"Hey, jailbird!"

I stepped in the car, and we drove off.

"I hope you weren't one of the ones who went in a tight end and came out a wide receiver!"

That was Luis, with the Cuban's fondness for dick and ass metaphors. He lit up a joint.

"Wouldn't you like to *know!* You're just jealous *you* weren't surrounded by a daisy chain of hungry convicts in the shower."

"Here, bro."

Luis passed me the joint.

I was euphoric but extremely paranoid. I still couldn't believe I was out. I scrutinized every car at every intersection and alley. A spooked cur, to be sure.

Looking out the back window and seeing it was clear, I brought my head down to the joint. Colombian Black, the shit that had made me hear hammers and anvils the first time I smoked it.

"Hey, man, it's cool."

"Yeah, but it ain't cool in *there*, man. Not cool at all. I just don't need to make a round trip tonight. I think I'd blaze away. Luna's Last Stand." I passed the joint and stuck my arm out the window again. Cheap thrills, man. "Damn, it feels good to feel the air. To breathe the air boys!"

I took a big breath of the air coming in the open window in an attempt to inhale this wonderful exterior world.

"Don't worry, airman. We got you covered. Where do you want to go, bro?"

'To the Grove, *Mariguaneros!*"

Coconut Grove was a village by the bay. A few small businesses, including a leather shop, head shop, health food store, some silversmiths and a nautical shop. The spiritual and cultural center of the grove was

Peacock Park. Right across the street was a Lum's restaurant. That's where I went first. The maw preceded the spirit in some of us low-level re-incarnations. Especially the ones who have been eating Dade County Correctional grub for the last nine days.

I ordered a Sloppy Joe, fries, and a Coke. *Fuc-king fries!* The Sloppy Joe was tangy, on an un-toasted generic burger bun. A communion wafer would be tangy after jail food. Black pepper, Tabasco, and ketchup for the fries: a picnic for a stoned soul.

"Hey, where the hell is Tommy?"

The table got quiet. The mirth was buried for an instant. Gabriel spoke first, answering my question.

"*Esta jodio* in a bad way, bro. He'll never walk again. He's at Mount Sinai."

"Jesus, what happened?"

"Car accident. Him and a couple of guys were fucked up on smack and hit a tree. He broke his neck in two places. He's a quadriplegic now."

"My God poor Tommy, man. I don't know what to say. I'll go see him tomorrow. Major fucking bummer."

The word "bummer" seemed out of place. I felt stupid after I had said it. Yeah, I'd say it was a fucking *bummer,* to be paralyzed from your neck down for the rest of your life.

"But hey, he's still Tommy, bird-doggin' the nurses and cracking jokes. They love him. His mind and spirit are intact." Gabriel's attempt at the silver lining.

"And according to him," David added, "his dick is intact also."

A few days later, I would see Tommy at the hospital. If his spirit was damaged, he didn't let on. But the motor control of his arms and hands was shot. No more walking, no more surfing, no more fishing, no more Kama Sutra, no more pretty much jack shit. No matter how you stacked it, not a pleasant sweep. The Wally snafu: Wally had been up for doing big time Upstate but had *rolled-over.* As long as he kept setting people up and busting them, he could remain on the outside. Supposedly, Wally set Tommy up, and since I was with Tommy, even though I had sold him nothing, I went down for the count too. The worst thing of all was that from that day on, and for a long time after, doubt would creep over Tommy's loyalty. But because of his physical state, I would never confront him with it.

After we ate, we crossed the street to the park. David lit another joint as we walked through the oaks toward the swings at the far end. My paranoia was easing. The three beers had helped. I felt good inside. I took one large toke, held it, and passed the joint. We hopped on the swings.

I swung hard, reaching a good height in line with my friends on each side of me. The stars were visible through the live oaks surrounding us. New moon. I started on the first Beatle tune with an exaggerated Cuban accent.

"*Gwat gwoo ju do if I sahng ahooro toon.*"

My friends responded in over-the-top effeminate Cuban.

"*Gwood ju essstandup and gwak out on meeee…*"

Tommy went to court in his brand new wheelchair. The judge, in a surge of compassion, just gave him probation.

"I hope you have learned the lesson life has taught you, Thomas. For you have paid far more dearly than any punishment I could now administer."

A few months up the road, my case was thrown out of court by a different judge: lack of evidence. Luna, using up a vast reserve of luck, had survived yet another Harlequinade.

La Venus De Wally's

"You know, if you're about seventeen years old and about
this tall, right? And you ain't figured it out yet...,

What you need! (Cymbal Crash!) What you want! (Crash !)
Anything. I can do anything. I can do...
I'll be your mama, baby. Yeah your mama, babe.
Whoa your mama, babe...

Tell Mama, JanisJoplin

She wasn't beautiful—treacherous adjective—but your first one doesn't have to be. In fact, in some places, the guys' "first" wasn't even from the human species. So, I was ahead of the game. Besides, La Venus had a special feature.

It was still 1968, a year so dense it felt like ten. Martin Luther King and Bobby Kennedy were assassinated, the Vietnam War raged on, Jimi Hendrix was blowing "heads" away with otherworldly licks, and I had been expelled from high school for allegedly dealing LSD. The case was

177

pending. Material wealth was passé, but it would come back with a vengeance in the Eighties. My worldly possessions: one pair of bell- bottom jeans and one T-shirt. No shoes. Barefoot was hip. I made four dollars for two hours work, picking up mats in the afternoon, and slept rent-free in a cabana where they stored mats at another hotel, or on a pile of mats outside under a canvas awning at one end of the pool deck. But I *was* squeaky clean. Most of my day was spent in the sea, surfing, swimming, or diving. Every couple of days, I would go to the Beach Maisonettes, a Mediterranean-style apartment complex half a block away on Indian Creek and 30th Street, and wash and dry my clothes for sixty cents in their coin washer/dryer. For ninety-nine cents, I could eat the early bird dinner special: soup, main course, two vegetables, dessert, and coffee or soda. I was seventeen. What else did I need?

Pussy

That's right. But *La Venus de Wally's* was going take care of that. Sally worked at Wally's, a small coffee shop in the lower lobby of the Sea Isle Hotel where I made a living by the aforementioned unskilled labor. She flirted with me on and off on the mornings I went there for breakfast after some psychedelic all-nighters. I don't know exactly how it happened, but we decided to get together one night.

A half-moon directly above bathed the expanse of some two hundred white fiberglass lounges, arranged in perfect rows of twenty, in a cold sepulchral light-- like so many marble slabs in a morgue. Perhaps at another time, alone and wounded, an ideal breeding ground for Poe-*esque* or Baudelarian melancholy. But tonight, under the trance of Sally's bewitching pheromones, other *duendes* would just have to take a number or leave.

Clouds scudded under the stars, and we could smell the sea in the east wind that oxidized the metal frames of the awning at the far end of the pool deck. My home. There we went, weaving through the rows of lounges, not far from where I had kissed Ivy, my first love, three years before. An eternity.

I sparked up, took a deep pull, and passed it to her. She inhaled, revealing the moist interior of her lush lower lip. She seemed to be clutching a thought momentarily, then she smiled and exhaled. I smelled the hemp as she addressed me.

"I've been struggling all week about what I'm gonna do with my life. I thought to myself, 'Sally, you're twenty-one. What are you going to do?' and I just figured it out. You know what I really want to do for the rest of my life? Not *worry* about what I'm going to do for the rest of my life."

We, the worriless of the world, laughed and finished the joint. Sally's shoulders shook when she laughed. It was contagious.

Twenty-one, a voluptuous "older" woman to the seventeen-year-old Luna. She sported an "unfashionable" pair of pearl baby blue prescription cat glasses on a very plain round face. I was not looking at her face. Already buzzed from the Colombian leaf, I peered at her full honeydew breasts. Moving closer to her, I felt the moist heat rising from the abundant curves bound tightly in her pink waitress dress. We said nothing. I kissed her. She slipped her tongue in my mouth like a snake dance. I groped for her nipples, burrowing my fingers between cheap bra and ripe breasts. She leaned back on the pile of mats. I grazed the inside of her thigh, advancing my other hand. A short ways up her dress, I found what can only be described as a sweet fat pussy, already yielding its honey. Pulling her panties aside, I slid my fingers and palm along her wet trench. She gasped, spreading her legs wider. Sally reached down and touched my pulsing wiener, which tried to rip out of my one and only pair of jeans.

"You're wet, too, Luna."

I owned no underwear. A few beads of semen seeped through the worn denim. She pressed her index on the wet spot and rubbed me in small circles. *Holy Moly!* I felt faint and would've passed out if at that very moment a roach the size of a small dog had not galloped across my foot. I kicked high, and it bounced off the awning, smacked heartily unto a fiberglass lounge, and scuttled to the floor, fleeing into the darkness, completely oblivious of its impertinence. Sally, entranced by her Venusian heat, failed to notice the acrobat roach. In a bedroom voice, she checkmated the virgin.

"Let's go to my place. I live across the street."

This was *it,* man. The Big Bang! To tell the truth, I was nervous and self-conscious, crossing Collins Avenue with a railroad spike shimmying in my pants.

We bumped and grinded in the ancient elevator that, with the din of a medieval drawbridge, took forever to get to the second floor. She fumbled with her keys while I stood there, skirting an out of body experience. Then, with a quick turn of her wrist, she unlocked the louvered door to her studio apartment—two steps and we were in bed. She removed her dress, revealing large roseate nipples through the bra's lace.

Li'l Smilo tingled. I sat on the side of the bed facing the other way, quite shy at the prospect of her seeing my hard-on. She slipped out of her panties, and I rolled beside her. We kissed. I reached down and felt a hard slippery stub.

"You got my spur on fire."

Her "spur" protruded about three quarters of an inch like a little pink hard on. I, having no clue what a clitoris was at the time, rubbed it with my index, and she swooned and twisted. I didn't want to betray it was my first time by not finding her "right" opening, so I requested her hand.

"Guide me in."

So, this is pussy? Yes! My other tongue had finally plunged inside the tongueless mouth it had craved. I had no experience humping. I was used to choking the chicken, but it was pretty much self-explanatory. Just stay in the pocket, Luna boy. Bebop-bebop-bebop-bebop. She let out a series of escalating moans. Her vulva quivered. Not long after that, I lost mine quietly, still shy and concerned about doing it right.

"I *knew* you could turn me on from the first time I saw you."

I smiled, not knowing what to say. I was acting like a real farmer or maybe not. I don't know how farmers fuck. I got up to piss, angling my hips toward the front door as I walked so she couldn't see my erection. It was very difficult to urinate through the hard-on that wouldn't leave. I finally managed to get it out in dribbly streams. Still rock hard and not going down, I stayed in the bathroom for a while. It didn't help. I opened the faucet and poured a little cold water on it. Nothing. Frustrated, I grabbed a towel and made believe I was drying my hands, letting the towel hang over *Smilo* as I walked. It would keep popping through. When it did, I'd rotate my pelvis away from her sight. She had left her night lamp on, and you could see. She caught on my shyness.

"It's okay. You don't have to be embarrassed."

Of course, that made me more self-conscious. Quickening my stride, I jumped back in bed.

"I think it's beautiful. Don't be embarrassed, baby. I love the way it looks. You have such a pretty one!"

She grazed the brim of Smilo's helmet lightly with her middle finger. I rubbed her spur-like clit again. I loved touching it. It felt just as stiff as me. We both gasped, and I was on her again. Four times that night. I wasn't so much enjoying fucking, which was hellacious, as much as the fact that I was *finally* fucking. I wish I would have told her how great I thought she was, how considerate for my feelings, and especially that it was my first time. But I didn't have the balls to tell her. I don't think I had to. She probably knew. She made me feel like I was the best, the most delicious thing, she had ever had. A toast to you, Sally. You made me a man. The man only La Venus could.

After we made it for the last time, we embraced for a long time, and I nodded out. When I awoke, she was looking at me. She winked and gave me a quenched lover's smile.

"I got to go home."

"You can stay if you'd like."

Oh, but I didn't want to stay. It was ten-thirty p.m., and I was hoping that at least one of my bros at the Beach Maisonettes across the street was up so I could go and brag that I had just gotten laid. I couldn't completely enjoy it until I told at least one of my buddies. Yeah, I know that was *tres* moron*ique*. Luckily, I outgrew that in a year or two. Some guys never outgrow that. They figure that makes them a real swinging dick. And nine times out of ten, they're swinging a bag of bullshit. I sat on the side of the bed, getting dressed.

"Well, I'm going to sleep. Good tonight. I'll hit Wally's by seven a.m., shuffling placemats like a card dealer. Good night, Luna, you little lover you."

We kissed goodnight, and I left. On the way down the elevator, I noticed a wax-like stain on my pant—the dry seminal fluid from earlier by the beach mats. Not real fashionable. I spit on my finger to dissolve it. It didn't work.

Once in the lobby, I walked out to the small pool, got some water, and rubbed it away. Of course, now it looked like I had pissed on myself, but somehow, I could live with that.

I ate up the sidewalk in titanic bliss. Boys, I finally got laid! Of course, I couldn't really share the full front headlines with them. In their edition, "finally" would be left out. I wouldn't be secure enough to tell anybody until I was in my twenties.

I don't think anybody admitted they were virgins. I was seventeen, and I made sure it was taken for granted that I had been getting laid *for years*. It would be more like, "Guess what little number I balled tonight while you punks were finishing your algebra homework."

No dice, though. Lights out at both of their places. I wasn't going to wake up their parents. I would have to wait until the next day to consummate my saga.

They say youth is wasted on the young. Nothing could be a more regrettable truth. I didn't realize for a long time just how unique Sally's pussy had really been. We never made it again after that time. I got sidetracked by appearances, something I could hang off my arm, show off to the other guys, which amounted mostly to a bunch of slim beach tarts. Sally had been a *woman*. It would have taken a riper spirit than I back then to recognize it. Face to face with a totem pussy and a warm big heart. One of those once-in-a-lifetime-if-you're-lucky rare finds indeed. Today, I would've declared myself her pussy vassal. After building a golden bench altar, which she could straddle and display her gifted mound, I would've lit votive candles before Her Clitness every evening, licking it several hundred times, and making my offerings before it: eternal loyalty, tomes of *vers libre*, exclusive bespoke lingerie, designer couture, late model luxury cars, seaside villas, animal sacrifices, Gwatever...The one thing I would never entertain is—tell a living soul about La Venus de Wally's.

Contrary Warrior
or Chicken Wheezing

And it's one, two, three, what are we fighting for?
Don"t ask me 'cause I don't give a damn,
Next stop is Vietnam.

–Country Joe and the Fish

It was midnight. Through the half-open door of the poolside cabana, the moon rose burnt-gold and fat out of the sea and scattered its light beyond the gentle breakers. It looked like the beginning or the end of some tropical romance.

Three of us had already burned half an ounce of choice Jamaican buds in a kuchie pipe, when I began my attempt to finish a carton of cigarettes before sunrise.

"Good luck, bro. Hope you beat 'em."

"Yeah, man. Cough yourself into a frenzy and spin on the floor like one of the Stooges screaming, 'I'm a fag, I'm a fag, Mee-mee-mee-mee-mee!'"

The guy who suggested the Stooge approach, though not gay, had gotten caught one afternoon a block away in his family's's living room, shorts by his ankles, getting a blow- job from the newspaper boy—not a minor. And though the reverse would have been considerably more compromising, he was still firing from a glass house. I was too distracted by my project and the Ganja for retorts.

They left. I lay on one of the lounges facing the sea, with a galvanized trash can lid for an ashtray, opened a pack, and lit the first Pall Mall. Given my history of asthma, I would wheeze for two weeks.

It was 1969, and the draft was glaring at me from its dank, dead-end corridor. Frankly, I was not in a hurry to descend from my drug-induced enlightenment and picaresque life around the pool decks of Miami Beach, unto a Vietnamese rainforest bristling with shit-stained bamboo spike traps and desperate men ready to gut their own mothers if it prevented my kind from treading on them.

Dig your head, make love and not war, flower power…Turn on, tune in, drop out…*Yeah!*

But after the rebellion, the renunciation, and the end of hypocrisy, there was no plan B for surviving The Establishment in case it didn't yield or you didn't die as some of the rock prophets. The Establishment would prove quite the hostile nanny when weaning the children of the Summer of Love. For some, there would always be the rural or urban commune. But one refrigerator and fourteen losers always implied discord to me.

Unbeknownst to Luna, in Miami as elsewhere, the "long-hair brotherhood" of Woodstock recent would mostly be replaced by legions of chimps still in gestation, dressed in platform shoes, gold chains, and sports cars, dancing to disco and wallowing in their new currency.

"You want a hit, baby? The first line is free. The second one starts at the head of my cock." Funny how some people would fall right in and not miss a step. *Burn, Baby Burn, Disco Inferno…!*

So, where did *one* go in this world after rejecting dehumanizing jobs, political and religious deceit, fiscal ambition, and the duty to kill *one's* fellow man for the State? Where did *one* go when the "Revolution" one had been living was dissipating into a stoned-out monumental hand-job?

Well, after chain-smoking six packs of Pall Mall by the sea shore, nearly throwing up before sunrise, and the respiratory doctor only finding a slight anomaly in *one's* lung capacity—nothing to keep *one* out of the draft—*one* moved back to *one's* mother's house, found *one*self a job parking cars, and called to enroll oneself in a crash and burn high school degree program. The motto de jour for one was becoming: Every Man for Himself.

The principal of the school got on the phone.

"Have you done any high school?"

"I went to Miami Beach High halfway through eleventh grade."

"Oh! You must know me. I'm Stan Levy, I had a candy store—"

"I'm afraid my memory fails me, Stan."

"Luna! You have acquired quite a command of the English language. Remember, I was next to—"

"Oh yeah…You have a child, right?"

"That's right. Rebecca. She's four now. We used to take her to the candy shop with us. Why are you wheezing?"

"I have a slight cold."

"Oh, that's nothing. A guy like you will lick that in a heartbeat. Listen, come by, and I hope we can welcome you aboard. As far as the tuition, a check or a money order is fine."

Now I remembered him. I would buy my Milky Ways there, in lieu of the beyond-my-lunch-allowance but delicious Ollie Burger two doors down. He wore eyeglasses with thick black frames, which made his gaff nose appear attached to them. I always felt sorry for their baby daughter, who had a purple growth on her cheek the size of a bottle cap. I had news for him too. My "memory failing" had less to do with command of the language and much more with still-unfurling psychedelics.

Stan, the principal, my ticket to student deferment, was decked out in a loud orange and black plaid sports coat and the same trick house black frame glasses that made his hooknose appear false. I had to give him credit, though. He'd conned himself into a principal's job.

But naturally, the other side of that was, what kind of school would have Stan for a principal?

"I'm afraid I can't give you credit for any of your eleventh grade because you got expelled mid-year."

"I got accused for something that I wasn't—"

"Look, it's none of my business. What happened before is past. I'm just telling you what the rules are. But the good side is, you'll be out of here in nine months if you follow the program. You pay your two hundred dollars, and before you know it, you're a high school grad."

The absolute truth was in the "before you know it" part of the pitch because I certainly was out of there before I "knew" a damn thing. How they remained a state accredited institution was anyone's guess. One's job for the degree? Outline the textbooks in a notebook, take an oral exam, and Sayonara Buckaroo. Then again, I hadn't learned much at Miami Beach High, for all its social and scholastic structure.

So I preferred it this way. Luna begins his *Etudes*.

During a break from my study table, I looked out the second-story window, and directly below, through the front windshield of a parked car, I saw a skinny arm glowing in a chunk of white-hot sunlight. The boy pierced his vein and drained a syringe. The rest of him was concealed by the car roof shadow. In a few minutes, a now more sedated member of our charming student body exited the car, waltzed up the fire stairs, and eased himself into a chair. He opened a world history book and nodded for a couple of hours, occasionally startling himself almost to the here and now when his fingers, enfeebled by the opiate, dropped the fat paperback on the table with a bang. Junk: a supreme but pricey sanctuary.

I mostly kept to myself. Uncle Sam was at my heels. I wanted to finish and get into college. I had an appointment with the friendly draft board Wednesday. That was in two days. The fact that I sat at a table by myself, away from the other bozos, caught the eye of a very attractive girl.

"Hi, I'm Tanya."

I was ambushed by her gaze. A crippling dose of beauty.

"Hi."

"How come you sit here by yourself? Are you anti-social or just shy?"

"I'm just shy of being anti-social."

"Funnyman? Hmmm."

"I hope the draft board doesn't think I'm a comedian when I try to get a college deferment."

Her feral cheekbones were accentuated by jet-black, straight hair and sky-blue eyes.

"My brother took off to Canada. We're a fourth Apache on my mother's side. Not enough to keep him from selective service, but he told the draft board that his people had fought and were still fighting a war of survival against the U.S. Government and refused to register."

"I just don't feel right about it in my guts. It's the…You know, they come and tell you what you should die for…I don't feel any hatred toward those people, much less consider them a threat to America."

"Why are you wheezing?"

I hesitated before telling her. Maybe being Apache and all, she might have thought I was yellow.

"You might think I'm yellow, and I don't know exactly why I did it, but a few nights ago, I sat up all night and chain-smoked half a carton of Pall Malls to try a get a physical deferment."

"You don't look Chinese, and anyway, you'll probably die of lung cancer before you step through the physical if you keep that up."

"I didn't mean Charlie Chan yellow. I meant as in—"

"Coward?"

"Well…Not…Yes, coward."

"First of all, pale face, Charlie Chan wasn't Chinese. He was played by a white guy, but since you brought up the pansy factor, I come from a people who were very much individuals. They'd only follow a leader if they trusted him. He couldn't force them to obey orders. So, I'm either the wrong person to ask or the right person to ask."

"I think you're the right person to ask. Can we do something sometime?"

"Anytime, but right now, I'm late. Pleasure to meet you, Two Lungs Wheezing."

"Likewise, Blue Eyes Fencing."

En garde, she thrust her imaginary saber, winked, and left.

*Hmmm…*Luscious possibilities of mind and hind. I pondered serenely with a slight wheeze. A cherished lull, out of harm's way. Any day, I might be marching to a different drummer. Marching at all was not a welcome predicament. Marching into the theatre of the My Lai Massacre was tragic indeed, especially for a politically naive acidhead who, convinced of a new way, had raised high the peace banner of his generation. Real *high.*

…'cause I'm a million miles away and right here in your picture frame… I'm a Voodoo Child…

On Wednesday, I realized I had made a scheduling error. The appointment for my physical had been for the day before. I called to report my oversight, thinking I'd just go the next day, but an assembly-line voice clarified, "That's not how it works, sir. You'll be receiving a new appointment in the mail." The new date would not be for several weeks. Stay of execution. And all those cigarettes! I wasn't going do *that* ever again. The God-awful taste and wheezing humiliated me for days, reminding me of the smoke rings I was jumping through for the prospect of a medical deferment. I felt my inbred sense of chivalry and honor, worshipped above all else by both of my grandfathers, dismantled by my evasion of duty. But something in my guts told me—along with the overall feeling of foreboding common to pending combat—that this was not my fight.

I didn't know then that the Tonkin Gulf Resolution had been a farce. U.S. ships had not been attacked. But that farce would put me, along with many draft-age slobs, in President Johnson's traveling fish barrel. After a "retaliatory" bombing of North Vietnam, the relishing honcho was overheard in the White House, "I didn't just screw Ho Chi Minh. I cut his pecker off." Except in the aftermath, Ho had a bigger *wang* than Big Tex imagined. And if inducted, they'd be flying me ass-first into it.

Half a million protested in Washington against the Vietnam War. But still, I felt a sense of guilt, a sense of flawed manhood, of stealthy freeloading for coveting deferment.

On another front, was Cuba any more *my* fight? Some *compatriotas* would impale me just for asking. But who *was* responsible for *El Caballisimo?* Who, through their own indifference, intolerance, and greed, had helped ripen the island and eventually lose it to the Olympic orator and Machiavellian tyrant?

And stateside, if I was to risk my "stoney" ass to help combat "the expansion of international communism," didn't it make more sense to do it in Cuba—not only the coveted destination for Soviet cruise missiles and only ninety miles away, but also the former home to several thousand willing national combatants? Would I fight in Cuba *si nos dejan?* No. My heart was not in it. Did that make me unprincipled, a pariah, a *pendejo?*

Oh! That ole nocturnal soul searching sho' took its toll on you, little doggie. And, in the end, made Luna intensely ravenous for crazy, heart-pounding, passion-swollen, trigger-happy, out of control, torrential, and in this case, Chiricahua pussy.

I awoke at 10 a.m., with the DNA message meant for Tanya glazing the inside of my Fruit of the Looms, the war far, far away…

My mother had left me three *pastelitos de guayaba* for breakfast. After hitting the shower, I inhaled the Cuban pastries with two *cafe con leches* and was out the door.

On my way to the bus stop, I cut a flawless pink rosebud from a neighbor's yard. A ladybug fluttered off the stem, scattering its polka-dotted good fortune hither and yonder.

Upon exiting the bus at the school stop, I concealed the rose under my notebook. I didn't want any wisecracks from the potheads, junkies, and backdoor flotsam who routinely loitered at the bottom of the fire stairs.

Nobody was there. I climbed the metal steps.

The backdoor opened with the vacuum seal sigh of a preserve jar and out stepped its freshest pulp.

"Hey, G.I., when you leave?

Tanya put on her best mock Asian accent and squinted her eyes.

"I don't know yet. I made a mistake with the appointment. They said they'd notify me."

I took the few steps to the top platform as an operatic paramour.

"But still, I risked my life today. Just for you."

I pulled out the rose.

"You might think this is an ordinary flower. But I cut it from the garden of a doctor who, according to my neighbor, fed his wife some brew that made her gradually sicker until she croaked. It seems he knew his shit because they never found a trace. I could be his next victim if he saw me pilfering."

I gave her the rose.

"I got news for the doc. He's gonna have to wait in line, sweet buns, 'cause you're *my* victim first."

She leaned into me, opened her mouth, and slowly closed it, grazing my lips and leaving a trace of moisture.

My sack quivered like a rattler tail as I entered crotch consciousness.

"Thanks for the rose, Luna. I have to hurry home. I'm waiting for a long distance call from my mother. I'm free this weekend. Call me, and we'll get together if you want."

"I want."

She gave me her number, and I watched her walk away, her earthy fragrance still inside of me. A yearned woman's phone number could always brighten my bleakest fortune.

At the study table, I wasn't much good concentrating on my American history for long. Today's chapter, *Conflicting Claims for the Oregon Country*: the U.S, Russia, Great Britain, and Spain were vying for an area rich, among other things, in the valuable trade of beaver pelts. I had a lead pipe for a peepee and was unequivocal about whose beaver I wanted to claim.

I went to the men's room and released my burden, whispering Tanya's name at the end just a fraction of a second before the janitor slammed the door open with his cart and began stocking paper towels, liquid soap, and perfuming the air with fresh urinal-puck pungency.

That evening, I called her from a lobby payphone in the Condo building where I parked cars. She told me about her ancestors, the Bedonkohe tribe of Apaches. Geronimo's tribe. "Geronimo was my great, great, uncle." I was duly impressed.

"How'd you end up in Miami?"

"Incest."

"Wait? You…"

"I am not the offspring of incest. If that's what you're thinking? I warned my mother that if my honkey father tried to get in my pants one more time, it would either be him or me. He tried, my mom didn't throw him out, so I caught the first Greyhound out of town, which was heading east and then south. I got out at the station on U.S. 1 and called my aunt."

I told Tanya I was sorry about her predicament, and she said, "Unfortunately, the one that should be sorry ain't, and that's why I'm down here."

I asked her where she was from, but she never said. Instead, she got into telling me about the Apaches. I interrupted, telling her I had liked Indians since I was a kid and how I had inadvertently shot my childhood friend on the forehead with a toy arrow—rubber tip removed of course.

"I would hang around in my Indian moccasins and makeshift loincloth after school many times in my backyard. And when we had to leave Havana, I packed the mocs twice in a suitcase, but they never made it. And I'm sure I packed them. It's a major mystery in my life."

But even though I had said "major mystery" in jest, she assured me with a shamanic tone that, "Some day, somehow, I have a feeling you and your childhood moccasins will have a reunion." I told her that if she believed she could foretell the future, then, "Let's go to Vegas."

"The Power is not to be ridiculed. I just have a feeling. Take it or leave it, cowboy."

"I was just joking."

"That's just it. You don't do that, because if the Power jokes back, you won't be laughing."

I didn't want to get into the fact that I was a skeptic about "the Power," or any other hocus-pocus, because frankly, what I wanted to get into was her loin shorts. Talk about *The Power*. Li'l Smilo, always the *a priori* diplomat, was keeping any impulse to be confrontational or derisive well in check. Tanya went on to tell me about her great-great-grandmother, and I forgot all about the fact I had neglected the condo's front door and parking ramp.

She said that her great-great-grandmother was captured by Mexicans and caged with webbed ropes in a "damn ox cart" with other Apache women, then guarded by a bad dog all the way to Santa Fe where they were sold as slaves. She was bought by some wealthy Mexican family, but she had paid attention to the landmarks all along the way. So, when she had a chance, she escaped. She said she had survived for days on nuts and berries, *walking* most of the 250 miles back. Then, she stole a horse and rode in to her camp in the mountains. Years later, I would actually read about her ancestor in Angie Debo's, *Geronimo*.

"My great-great-grandma was one heroic badass Indian bitch."

Naturally, after that story, I felt kind of stupid about my little bow and arrow mischief. But I did manage to invite her to the "love-in" the next day. She agreed.

Woo-woo-woo-woo.

I looked at my watch, and it was eleven p.m. Shit! I had left the ramp unattended for nearly an hour. I said my goodbyes and hung up the payphone on its cradle with an unintentional bang, spooking a Jewish retiree who, exiting the men's room, responded with a classic *Oy ve* while adjusting his Sansabelt shorts.

On the way out, I glimpsed a reproduction of a signed Neiman, *Tennis Players*, hanging above a lime-green sofa. Was *this* the end result and privilege of Indian removal? Hanging spurious impressionist drivel aside phony tiffany lamps in a condominium lobby? I undid my ponytail and let my hair hang down over my collar as a gesture of Indian support. Unfortunately, all the scalping had already been done by the artist.

"Your hair looks nice like that. Here, I didn't know where you were, and there were a lot of cars out there, so I gave them claim tickets and showed the people where to park."

"Thanks."

Wendy Weinstein handed me a little stack of three-part numbered parking garage claims with only one part left.

"The keys are lined up in numerical order on top of your desktop."

She was an eighteen-year-old red-haired ectomorph of considerable affluence who wore quirky though flattering 60's accessories. A music major at the University of Miami and a gifted concert violinist—passionate for Hendrix, Cream, Dylan, and the counter culture. She had gone to Woodstock and worried her parents half to death, what with all the LSD and the kid run over by the tractor. For her master's thesis, she would do her own arrangement of Spirit's "Fresh Garbage": two cellos, kettledrums, a tambourine, and timpani. Topless, with a makeshift long skirt of Romaine lettuce leaves, she blazed a fervent violin lead. Her boyfriend, unseen, manned the inside of a giant pink paper mache human ass, emerging from an American flag skirt which dispelled fake hundred dollar bills, small plastic guns, bombs, model Cadillacs, cheeseburgers, and sundry industrial and cultural excreta on a globe of the Earth until it buried it. She would make it to *The Miami News'* arts section, much to the unsavory regret of her socialite parents.

When I got outside ,I saw, to my horror, that she had instructed the guests to park their cars at right angles in the street itself. And though there was no danger, because the side street was wide and not too traveled at this time, all ten cars had received $25.00 hazardous parking tickets. A *lot* of money back in '69. I removed all the tickets and put them in my back pocket.

On the walk home, I smoked a joint, pulled out the stack of traffic tickets, ripped them up, and flung them in the air with renegade delight, dramatizing the showering bits of beige cardboard by belting out what I envisioned to be an Apache war cry, which only succeeded in waking up several dogs and some homeowner who threatened to call the police.

I sprinted off through a golf course, and in a THC-induced adventure, I imagined myself an escapee Apache finding *my* way "back home." But when I got home, I still audibly remained just *Two Lungs Wheezing.*

* * *

This late Sunday morning, our planned destination would be East Greynolds Park off US 1 for live music and trippy hippies. Occasionally, The Blues Image, before their national hit, "Ride Captain Ride," would make an appearance with lead guitarist Mike Pinera. Local boy made good. He later joined the Iron Butterfly but for some reason burned out.

193

Probably the same reason most rockers burn out: drugs, women, and alcohol. And frankly, if you gotta go…

We picked Tanya up at her aunt's house in the early afternoon. There was no room in the front seat of my friend's converted camper, so Tanya and I went around the back. I opened a small jalousie door to a wood-paneled cubicle and a wall-to-wall paisley fabric-covered mattress. My friend had to lock an improvised hasp on the outside, or the door wouldn't stay closed. A sweet north light spilled from a frosted-glass window. Tanya lay back on a big homemade cushion. The Chiricahua Maja.

"Cozy," she said.

The truck took off. I prayed for lock malfunction.

We lay on our backs on plump, well-worn cushions. Her lushness pulled me like a full moon tide. Our shoulders touched and sparked. I leaned over and trailed my lips along her velvet cheekbone.

She turned and convicted me with her tongue of perdition. I slipped her shirt down her smooth creamy shoulder, which glowed in the chapel light entering the single jalousie window above us on the plywood wall. I pushed the bra down slowly with my thumb, revealing a nipple the shade of copper and the rosebud I had given her. I drifted toward it slowly, hardly breathing, subservient to its Oedipal voltage and sensing the fabled "Power" in all its grandeur.

Thud! Thud! Thud! Thud…

Her breast jabbed me several times on the lips. The van pulled to the side of the road and stopped. I heard the driver walking around. Tanya pulled the bra over her breasts and drew her blouse together.

"Are you decent, little piggies? I'll huff and I'll puff…"

That was Mike, the driver. He jostled the lock. I pulled my T-shirt over my swollen crotch. Had the tires been as hard, we could have driven on a sea of five-inch nails.

"Sorry to break up your inspiration, bro' , but you lovebirds are nesting on the spare."

"You underestimate our inspiration. You're fired, James. Luna, you know any other chauffeurs?"

After an inquiring gaze, Tanya sat up, buttoning her blouse. Mike's hawk eye caught a lion's share of her smooth and noble tit. He raised his brows and pursed his lip, angling his chin upward in a silent wolfish A-ooooooh! Had she seen him, she would have thrashed the brazen cur.

We were on US 1, a block away from the entrance to East Greynolds. I pulled out the tire and tools from the compartment under the mattress, leaned the tire against the camper's rear right fender, then Tanya and I headed toward the love-in. "Love-in" was a term that, even back then, I considered on the edge of daffy.

Glancing back, I saw Mike gesturing to our other buddy about Tanya's proportioned endowment.

I had to agree. It *was* a snuggly conversation item.

"Hey, Luna, want to go for a whirl?"

Typical Willy the Gimp greeting. The boys and I had scored some turbo-charged acid from him two weeks before, when Jimi Hendrix had played at the Jai Lai Fronton. Willy was a well-connected paraplegic. Some said he was a chemist who learned his trade from the famous Owsley. The Gimp would keep hip locals, as well as visiting rock and roll talent, in psychedelics. On Sundays, he would open the "soup line" at the park. He gadded about in his wheelchair with a needleless syringe and squirted a hit in your mouth upon request—free dose. Except you never knew how much you were ingesting. You could be gone fishing for the next twelve to eighteen hours. I declined. A band was playing the last few bars of Santana's "Black Magic Woman". Tanya, who had been self-engrossed, finally spoke...

"My mom didn't call me, and nobody answers at her house. My father walked out on her about three weeks ago. I'm beginning to worry that something happened. I tried the restaurant where she works as a waitress, and they told me she had called in sick."

"Is there anything I can do?"

"I don't know *what* there is to do."

She grabbed my hand.

We went to the woods. I was in a swoon. I wanted to touch her, feel her against me. A flower girl fantasy? We found a clearing and lay down in the pines, watching the clouds scudding.

"Sometimes, I wish I could take my mom and my brother, get on one of those clouds, and sail away until I figured out where to land."

"I'm not invited?"

"Luna, you'd be on a cloud of your own. We'd only slow you down."

"No, you wouldn't. I think we'd get along."

She didn't answer. Being more mature, she could see the X at whose axis we were at the moment. Very soon, our paths would diverge. I was going east, she was going west, and that was okay with her. But there was no sense in talking shit. In truth, it was probably Li'l Smilo, still fired up from the camper ride, instigating the "we'd get along" optimism, knocking on any door that might get him housed.

She gazed silently at the sky, her aquamarine eyes turning gray with the darkening clouds. The incoming weather seemed to mirror the state of her soul. Unfortunately, the phenomena had been beat to death by filmmakers as a cinematic ploy. It smelled of ozone, and the breeze made the pine needles whistle.

"I said, I think we'd get along."

"That's what your ancestors told my ancestors before killing our warriors and enslaving and screwing many of our women."

"My ancestors? I'm not American, yet."

"It was the Mexicans."

"I ain't Mexican either."

"Okay, the Spaniards started it, and that's where the Mexicans, Cubans, and Puerto Ricans come from, is it not?"

"As far as I know, my ancestors were journalists. I don't know jack beyond that. And anyway, what the hell are we talking about? Shit, let's take it back to the War of the Trilobites."

In the distance, the band had gotten into Iron Butterfly's satanic-sounding love ballad "Innagoddadavida."

I continued. "Cause I'm not gonna sit here, bummed out, and break into a guilt trip about ancestors who I don't even know, killing the Indians. All I know is, I've always liked Indians."

"Everybody likes the Indians, but nobody understands them. The white settlers *liked* to see us all dead. We were 'pesky redskins,' and now to the hippies, we're some kind of Rousseauist saints whose shit don't stink!"

I said nothing. The cozy feeling was all shot to shit. The worst thing was that for the most part, she was right. What the hell did I know about the Apaches or any Indians besides what I had seen on T.V. or on the movie screen? Pretty much zilch. I just sided with them. I knew that in my guts. But she didn't have to attack *me*. I hadn't meant any harm. And what the fuck was a *roo sawiss* saint? Hell if I was going to ask. I just lay, face-up, looking at the approaching cumulus grayness, quiet as a paperweight.

"Hey, Luna, anyone in there?"

I felt hurt. So, I remained quiet. She moved on top of me and gave me a dose of her eyes head-on.

"Two Lungs Wheezing, I didn't mean to offend you personally by it. And hell, if it wasn't for some Mexican screwing my grandmother, you wouldn't have met yours truly, the mestizo delicacy, Blue Eyes Fencing.

She kissed me. I smiled, even though I was still pissed. A puzzling sensation. But her eyes…straight razors couldn't cut them. Not for their hardness. There was just no way to cut the sky or the sea. How would you go about cleaving mystery?

We kissed deeply, but not the kind that leads to foreplay. It seemed like a sisterly kiss, if there can be such a French kiss. That didn't stop li'l bro' Smilo from roiling in my pants and leading my hand to her mound. She pulled my hand gently away.

"Not here, not now. You've touched my heart. I don't want to cheapen it with a quick fuck in the woods to take me out of my worries and you out of yours."

What do you say to that? How about a slow one in the canal? Trying to fuck her after that would be as gratifying as trying to sell her a pyramid scheme. I loved fucking like the best of them, but I'd never let it turn me into the Carpetbagger of Love.

"Only if your heart's in it."

"It's not that my heart is not in it. I'm the one that's not in my heart. I just wouldn't be *there* for you at this point, Luna."

Her eyes saddened and watered. I tried to lighten the scene.

"Well, let's go listen to some music, then, 'cause if we stay here, I'm going to dry-hump myself clear through to Ho Chi Minh City.

She smiled, offered a short giggle, and weaved her way down to my zipper. Incidentally, that was the closest any girl's face had ever been to it.

"You're a good sport."

She *kissed,* then addressed Li'l Smilo.

"Next time we meet, dude, I'm going to make your master catatonic."

We got up and made our way to the makeshift stage in the clearing. She told me that Mr. Clay, one of the teachers, had made it with her. She had started to fall for him, but he wasn't going to leave his wife and daughter for her. The only reason he kept dating her was because he was afraid she might say something and jeopardize his job.

"I approached you in class just to make him jealous but ended up really liking you."

It began to rain. Not a heavy dramatic rain, but an annoying random drizzle. The second band didn't show. We felt a bit chilly in our wet clothes. Mike had just returned from dropping his friend home for a grass deal, and he was ready to leave. Back inside the camper, Tanya was distraught. Didn't feel like talking. The ride back was fraught with a sense of unarticulated doom, which naturally ended up depressing me. I began to think of the draft, of Vietnam, of having to kill people I didn't know, who I didn't hate, but would soon have to learn to out of sheer necessity. Survival. Not to mention the prospect of losing a leg or worse, my nuts, from a Bouncing Betty. Who the fuck knew? I hoped I could beat it. They can call me a coward. Was I? Who the fuck knew? It's hard to risk your life for something you don't believe in. If fighting the Commies was so important, then why was it allowed to persist in Cuba only ninety miles away? Again, who the fuck knew what all these motherfuckers at the top were ever up to? Tell you what, I'd rather die fighting the bastard that's out to tell me where, what, and when I have to die. Just before we reached her house, she rolled over to me, cradled my troubled heart in her eyes, and crucified me with her tongue.

"Just because we didn't make it doesn't mean I want you to forget me."

Mike let us out.

"We've decided to retain you. I trust you'll be less forgetful with the tires in the future." She put out her hand out for Mike to kiss obligingly. He did.

"Oh, forgive my oversight, Your Grace. I remain your Steel Belted Knight…and Day."

She embraced me and walked toward the wood-slat house. I stood by the camper until she opened the door. I shouted my goodbye, a bit unnerved.

"I'll see you in school tomorrow."

She waved and walked inside. Mike was under her spell.

"How is she, *mareecown*? Let me sniff your fingers."

"Oh men, you're all pigs!"

We got in the van. Once on US 1, a squall dropped on us like a B-52 payload. The old wiper blades just gave short glimpses of clarity in the diluvial meltdown of cars and traffic lights. Mike slowed our pace and took out a joint with a smile.

"So, is she hot or what?" He lit it and passed it to me.

"To tell you the truth, she's troubled."

Withholding the treasured *fumée*, Mike delivered the next line from the back of his throat, "Who isn't?" then exhaled in my face, trying to lighten the scene.

The next day, Tanya didn't show up at school. I called her aunt's, and nobody answered. I went to work in the afternoon and called her house after every four or five cars I parked. When I got home at one in the morning, I called her house. Lying in bed, trying to sleep, I would at first muse about her Indian riffs and her wit, the way her eyes flared when she argued. Then, her tongue would work its way into the scenario. Her nipples where not far behind, until I lost myself in Handjobville. Shortly after, I'd plummet into nasty visions of death, destruction, and blown-off limbs. I went on like that for weeks, hoping she'd be in school or answer the phone the next day. She could have at least called, left a message at the school, written a damn note. At last, her aunt finally answered the phone.

"No, she's not here."

"Where is she? Is she all right?"

"She's fine. But I don't know exactly where she's at."

"Is she coming back?"

"I don't know, but I have a letter here for you. I'll leave it in the mailbox if I go out."

I caught a cab with my meager savings of $20.00, went to her house, and inhaled the letter out of the mailbox. I opened it, walking back to the bus stop. There was a little leather pouch inside with a leather strip attached, like something you would wear around your neck.

Luna,

I'm sorry I couldn't call you—had to leave in a hurry. My brother, the one in Canada, came into town for his birthday, went out with his friends, got drunk, stole a car, and got arrested. The law found out he was a "draft dodger," and they will most likely send him to prison. My mother, who hadn't touched a drop in two years, hit the bottle like a train and then lost her job. I put her in a de-tox clinic a few days. I'm going to have to try to finish school up here, work, and keep my eye on her until this blows over. I'll try to call you. Take care, sweet dog.

A hot kiss always

Tanya (Blue Eyes Fencing)

P.S.

I have sent you some Apache "good medicine." Some hoddentin (corn pollen) and bit of my hair and a tiny bit of old cloth from a robe—my great-grandmother's side of the family (we are both survivors.) Anyway, just wear it. What do you have to lose? I think it will protect you against the (Great) White Chief: Nixon and his madness. Keep it with you at all times if you go to 'Nam. Can't hurt. At the very least, something to remember me by. I still got your rose.

No return address. No stamp. It must have been sent inside another envelope. Classic Apache disappearing act. *Sfumato* into the mountains. No trace. And also, very motherfucking frustrating. I wanted to get to know this woman, I really did. Maybe she was ashamed of her family. I didn't care, for Christ's sake! A wino trailer park would look like El Dorado with her in it. Not to mention, a decent hideout for a potential draft dodger. Shit-Shit-Shit. *Mierda.* I called her Aunt from work, and the phone had been disconnected. On top of that, I had to go for the physical again tomorrow. My *g*wish come true: let's go play war *en el Culo del Mundo!*.

President Nixon had what seemed to me an awfully slow hand if indeed he was intent on his campaign to end the war. The short and not too sweet of it was that a mortar round didn't know about no "Vietnamization." If I were in its way, the price of peace and stemming the spread of Communism would just go up one more body. One psychedelic Cuban refugee carcass. A very sustainable loss stateside, and politically speaking, not much of an incentive to hustle the peace quills.

Things got frisky at work that night. An older sugar daddy came out with his bodaciously endowed arm piece. But you could tell from the next galaxy that she was a razor in a mini-skirt. He asked for his XKE Jag. When I brought up the convertible, he gave me a quarter. I showed him the coin in my palm while stealing glimpses of the trollop's manslaughter thighs and random flashes of lacy crotch as she settled herself into the leather passenger seat.

"What is this?"

"That's a quarter. Did you just get off the banana boat, *Julio.*"

I threw it in his lap.

"Then why don't you stuff it "a quarter" of the way up your colon."

"You can't talk to me like that!"

He was ready to scuffle. His girlfriend intervened before he got out of the vehicle. And a good thing too. He was a burly bastard.

"Milt, if you hit him, he'll own you."

He peeled rubber out of the covered ramp, sounding like a twelve hundred pound pig getting stabbed. The head parking attendant, a middle-eastern immigrant, walked toward me.

"Loona, I kanatt permeetchu to tok likkathees to kests."

"Sal, a freaking quarter! Driving a new XKE with tramp deluxe and probably dropping C-notes like pigeon shit upstairs."

In the end, I couldn't argue with Sal. I was pissing in his rice bowl. There was a convention coming in, and he'd need all the runners he could get, so my job was safe, at least for the next week. I spent the rest of the night without incident, and Salman, seeing that I was a bit morose and the night being slow, let me go home early.

"Yoo go home andresst. We haffalon week."

It was about eleven o'clock when I reached the door to my mother's house. I heard the phone ringing through the window of my room, which faced the front yard. *Yes Tanya!* I dug into the pocket of my black trousers. Shit! Where are my keys? The phone rang again. I checked again. No keys. *Ring!* I was ready to bust up the window, when my hand groped again in my back pocket and there they were.

Ri_____ng

In four leaps, I was through the living room, hallway, and in my bed with the phone off the cradle and in my hand.

"I've missed the hell out of you."

"Is this the home of Mr. Yena?"

"Yes, I'm Mr. Yena."

"Well, sir, due to the death of President Johnson, the selective service offices will be closed tomorrow. A Moratorium has been declared. We'll mail you another appointment. Goodnight."

"Goodnight."

Damn right, it was a *good* night. I took the lucky charm, put it around my neck, and pressed the pouch against my heart.

Tanya, my Apache shaman, where are you? You're fencing the shit out of them pale faces.

My selective service lottery number was 235, which was like saying ten because unless you got from about 300 and up, you were basically frontline feed. What seemed like several weeks flew by and no word from Tanya. But the night before my new scheduled appointment, the phone rang at about eleven o'clock again.

"This is the selective service board. We are calling you to let you know that President Nixon has ended the draft, so you won't have to come in tomorrow or until further notice."

Woo Woo Woo Woo Woo Woo!

I slapped my fingers fast against my lips in your classic Hollywood Indian war cry, doing my own version of some shaman circle dance. Had the amulet helped? I didn't know, but I wasn't going to ridicule, "*The Power,*" until I was way beyond draft age.

Had Luna been a Contrary Warrior or Wheezing Chicken? Only the future would tell. Unlike others, I could never boast 'my country, wrong or right.' Was an administration a country? Did it merit martyrdom, right or wrong? Many questions would keep my adolescent soul awake at night, even after I was home free, but tonight, I reached for an old Zenith short wave radio my Dad had given me long ago. I kept it on a local AM station. Canned Heat came on. I cruised gently to Sleepland in the aura of Blue Eyes Fencing and the medicine pouch firmly in my grasp.

I'm going , I'm going where the water tastes like wine
I'm going were the water tastes like wine
We can jump in the water and stay drunk all the time
Tooroo-teee-teee, Toorooteh Toorooteh...

Circle of Confusion

The girl was nude, attached to a ball and chain, reclining inside a wooden box in the college library. Before her stood a chrome snare drum on a stand with a vibrating flesh-colored dildo spinning aimlessly, a prurient compass buzzing a drum roll introduction. Atop her "booth" lay a stuffed clown, with a long red-tipped nose face-up and tucked in tight, "tent-poling" the bed sheet above his groin. This portable harlot, a paid model and aspiring veterinarian, I might add, enticed people by undulating her oil-misted body while summoning them inside with her index finger. A paper cartoon bubble above her head read, "I'll ply wif yer deiick fir muney."

Luna Makes Art World Debut with *Port a' Tart!* A work inspired by streetwalkers and adult bookstores springing up in the neighborhood. I was a long way from the geeks and junkies at the crash-and-burn high school program and the stress of being drafted to Vietnam looming over my green Dadaist soul.

Port a' Tart, or portable tart, was my entry for the 1972 student art show at the junior college. The director of our art department, along with some professors, had gotten cold feet at the eleventh hour. But the man judging the exhibition, art director at the University of Miami, had approved it. When I attempted to show the film of the opening night to my philosophy class, under the theme of social commentary in contemporary art, Mrs. Prigsworth, the teacher, yanked the plug on the projector complaining, "Luna you've tricked us. This isn't art, it's por*na__h*graphy!"

When I assured her that, in fact, I had not tricked her, that my film was a chronicle of my entry for the Student Art Show endorsed by her peerage and, incidentally at this very moment, sitting in the college library, she became obsessed with *Port a' Tart's* immediate removal. Failing in her crusade to have the Art Department can my exhibit, which now was simply a record of the event—just a *photograph* of the nude girl, the empty booth with clown on top, and the formerly mentioned "items"— this puckery Savonarola resigned in protest.

Oh, yes! Luna had been hopelessly lur*ed* (French *r*) by the Avant-Garde. Marcel Duchamp had blasted the cage open in 1913 with his porcelain urinal, *Fountain*: the birth of the Ready-made. On the scat side, I related to Piero Manzoni's anti-establishment tuna cans of *Merde de Artiste*. Joseph Beuy's *live-in* with a coyote for a week in a New York gallery had piqued my spirit enough to experiment with performance, but never carried it as far as Burton—hiring a marksman to graze his arm with a .22 rifle. The extreme of that trail blazed by German artist Rudolf Schwertzkogler who, combining the ascetic's *via negativa* and Van Gogh's artist as martyr approach, severed chunks of his penis with a razor to crown, or in this case de-crown, his motif.

There was no upping the *ante,* after this manifesto of dubious sanity, short of killing yourself as performance. Although in my opinion, living dickless was not necessarily bested by suicide. Hey, at those prices, Rudy could remain Performance Art Kaiser.

But to continue with the story, *mein* disquiet was of considerably simpler and more mundane variety in the winter of '72. My two years were up at Miami Dade Community College, and soon, I'd have no venue for my work. I did not have the patience for and despised all manner of gallery fauna, foreplay, and toadyism required to get a show. Executing work became unaffordable and storing it tedious. I was still at my mother's in a twelve-by-twelve foot bedroom. In a word, I had gotten *fed up* with both art and art types, the likes of which would invade the avenues of South Miami Beach decades later with their insufferable posturing.

Documenting my installations and happenings had led to photography. Photography and the prospect of a *real* career led the way out of Miami.

I left for Rochester, New York in my '69 VW with one big $100.00 bill only two days before school started. After rolling out of the driveway, still within sight of my mother waving at the front door reflected in my water-stained rearview mirror, I inexplicably began to cry. O' human heart, cache of eternal riddles.

Somewhere past Orlando, I stopped at Stuckey's, palace of roadside swill, where during an after-lunch dump, I overheard some corporate malcontent at the urinal bust a salvo of atonal, *pizzicato* farts and grumble the following to his colleague as they pissed.

"Jake's been there only six months, and they already made him department supervisor. You know, it wouldn't bug me half so much if… Hell! That boy can't pull a greasy string out of his ass without calling me."

Later that night in Jacksonville, I asked a cop where I could buy the best steak in town. I went through more bridges than a Medicare dentist. Great looking bridges, I should point out. I finally found the place and was quickly stripped of twenty dollars—sixteen for the filet mignon, and a bombastic four-dollar tip on my part for a waitress with murderous lips, who in my mind had hinted at fun and games when she had wistfully delivered, "Luna, I love your ponytail. You just driving through, huh?"

That was all it took to renew my membership, vengefully, in the Rutting Chimp Society. I ordered several coffees, waiting for the manager to be out of earshot to ask what she was doing later. At my third cup, her freckled-faced husband walks in with their freckled-faced twin boys, who got into a burping contest that was swiftly checked by Daddy's skillful backhand-forehand combination, apparently the result of daily practice.

Wired from coffee and the prospect of hit and run love, I resolved to drive straight on through to Rochester, an ambition soon quenched by fatigue. "What the fuck is she doing! I slammed on my brakes, just short of mangling an old lady hobbling with a cane across 17 in the middle of nowhere! An imposing hallucination. Sensing I was deeply lacking non-stop driving genes, I opted to check into a motel outside of Savannah, further taxing my quickly ebbing stash.

That night, I had a formidable wet dream where I hiked the waitress's short white dress up her smooth and sturdy thighs while she leaned against a weathered pole supporting a tin roof over a picnic table. While she sighed in surrender, breathing white hot in my ear, I noticed the spilled box of chessmen, whose portly king, the only one left standing and glowing in the moonlight, gave me a whispered, "By Jove, Jim!" and nodde toward the prize so I might notice what he saw from his angle: a dizzyingly wet, shaved, and swollen vulva. Shaved! A rare delicacy back then. Garden of Eden denizen. As I'm about to enter His Majesty's vision—pants by my ankles—I spotted a Pomeranian who stared at me momentarily and appeared quite rational, as if about to say something. It suddenly rolled his eyes *a la* Satchmo' and leaped pell-mell, clamping on to my hamstring just below the left gluteus and dangerously close to my, by this time, rattled chestnuts. I woke up in a cold sweat, near the end of *Hounds of the Baskerville* flickering on the cheap black and white set, with a sparkly bead of seminal fluid festooning the tip of my unsaddled chub.

After a breakfast of ham, eggs, and hominy grits, I started the last leg to Rochester with the strength of twenty men. Somewhere around the Pennsylvania Turnpike, however, my Bug began running out of gas, and maybe I had fifty cents left. I had naively thought that a hundred dollars would last till the foothills of Forever. Once I got to Rochester, I had eighteen hundred dollars in a government student loan—large money—but I had to get there. Filling a VW Bug then was around seven bucks, so I attempted to drain the tank as close to empty without running out, in case I had to give up my mother's fifty dollar Sony radio for a fill up. I'd at least get as near a full tank as I could. Among other knick-knacks, I could hope to barter for gasoline—depending on the "background" of the grease monkeys—was a photograph of a breast on a dinner plate. I remembered foraging the halls in the art department, approaching girls and asking them what kind of nipples they had, and all this with a straight face. The first girl I had photographed had a wonderfully firm breast, but after going through the hole in the table and the plate, hardly looked like a breast. I finally found a girl whose breast had been slightly droopy on her chest but sat on the plate like a sunny-side up egg. Magnificent! It was so perfect, in fact, that one of my artist friends walking into the studio, and not thinking it real, just about poked it with the fork that was part of the dinner setting props. I remember rushing up, lifting the four by eight sheet of plywood, and showing him there was a *real girl* lying under the table. The guys at the glass shop, who ruined their blade cutting a hole into the porcelain plate, got a real kick when I explained what the hole in the plate was for. The manager's words to the cutter, "This is a fastidious gentleman. He likes his titties served on a plate!"

After passing many exits, precariously squeezing the reserve tank, I pulled off somewhere in southern Pennsylvania. Luckily, there were some long-hairs working there. I explained my situation. They loved the photo but pragmatically opted for the radio.

None-the-less, they filled my tank and gave me fifteen bucks and a joint. Yeah.

I continued for another ten hours, some of it at night behind a six-teen-wheeler, in a diluvial downpour through part of the Appalachian Mountains between Scranton, Pennsylvania, and Binghamton, New York. The back spray versus my junior wipers had the effect of driving by Braille. In my frustration, I attempted to pass the truck around a bend and nearly produced a head on collision with a lunging mad sea serpent of a tour bus. I swung violently back in behind the truck, narrowly missing the rocky mountainside in my headlights before straightening out. Heart thumping, I began the first evening of the rest of my life a model of tem-perance, following at a safe distance until we fed into a straightaway. I still trailed the truck for nearly an hour on a deserted four-lane highway before I realized it was now okay to pass. On the way down, I mused on the punch line of the bug-hitting-the-windshield joke, where the first thing to go through its mind at impact is its asshole.

At four a.m., I pulled into a truck stop west of Syracuse on the New York Thruway and slept in the parking lot. Woke up at six a.m., inhaled some coffee, and arrived at Rochester Institute of Technology about five minutes into my first class with Professor Leslie Stroble, author of *View Camera Techniques*, indisputable master of his craft.

His monotone British accent and technical gospels laid me out like a Seconal overdose. I excused myself, complaining of gastric problems, went to my dorm room, and crash-landed on a bare mattress. In the wee hours, however, I was awakened by deep eerie bellowing coming from the dorm room next door. Like some kind of mortally wounded half-human, half-water buffalo.

"Aannn aonnnoohooo! Aaaaaaah! Uuuuunh!"

I lay there in the dark, truly spooked and disoriented, going through a mental catalog of my stuff for something that could be used as a cudgel or stave of some type. I grabbed the Tiltall tripod from the corner of my room and felt the spikes, which still protruded from the rubber pads at the ends of the black legs, sharp as cat claws. It had been my only weapon when I slept at truck stops on the way up. In retrospect, chances were, the would-be assailant would've died of laughter at first sight of the pod, though if well-placed, even the Belzebub wouldn't want a face full of this. Finally, I heard one last discordant wail, then abrupt silence, a few sighs, and someone turning on a shower. Rochester Institute of Technology was also the National Institute for the Deaf. Since my neighbors couldn't hear themselves every time they did the nasty, it was a primal and uninhibited hoot. After a night's rest, I took a more anthropological stance. But soon I'd be ditching pith helmet and notebook for a branch and a banana. Pressure-drop in Eastman Kodak Town.

Now, after three photo-science-packed weeks attending R.I.T., the *non plus ultra* of photography programs, I wondered if I had made the right career choice. A blemished complexion later, I was halfway through a summer workshop where you were expected to assimilate in one day

210

what was normally taught in one week during the regular semester. At that pace, I had regressed to adolescence, and though I was twenty-four, I started to break out, in addition to jerking off almost every night. This wasn't too bad compared to the tragic reaction of students with a less absurdist sensibility.

Thus spake gossipthustra:

One jumped off the fourth floor through the interior fire stairs, allegedly the reason why now the center shaft of the emergency stairs had a metal grill barrier at each floor. His mangled body was found with a camera around his neck. Apparently, he had attempted to take a picture of himself on the way down. When the pictures were developed, they only revealed a series of mid-air, under-exposed, low-angle and blurred stair railings, with a receding hairline at the bottom of the frame.

The other casualty of note was a student under even more pressure to achieve. His father had been an internationally acclaimed local-boy-made-good photographer of Ansel Adams caliber who was the *stupor mundis* in residence at R.I.T. When junior received two consecutive semesters of C's, he, according to alumni lore, tried to slit his shooting eye with a razor—by happy chance caught in the act and taken to the infirmary. All in all, you can see that my zits and nightly chicken-choking bouts were minor league hormonal deviations.

Fortunately, the drab and soon frigid town of Rochester, New York, where already I was beginning a fourth week, had taken a turn toward worldly solace. It was still mid-July, summer of '74, and the breeze skimming south over Lake Ontario refreshed the evening. My good cheer, however, was not owed to the gentle weather, but chiefly to the ever-dazzling hand of Eros who had simmered the mojo.

Tonight, Melinda was coming to my dorm room. She was from the Midwest. On our second date—our first was spent in her dorm with her roommates—we had dined on hamburgers at a local bar and grill where a country band played Hank Williams' "I'm So Lonesome I Could Cry," one of the few country songs I liked.

As we completed one slow spin on the dance floor, a paunchy guy with one un-zipped black bootie half protruding from a pair of gray chinos and a T-shirt showing a live cat stuffed in a glass jug titled *Happiness is a Tight Pussy*, approached the rather gaunt singer, beaming in a silver satin pearl-button cowboy shirt, and asked, "You singin' this sowng fir Lila, ain'tcha ?"

Not waiting for an answer, he wrested the microphone from him and whacked him, splitting the skin above his eye with an amplified thump. That clamor was topped by the bass player, when he swung the neck of his electric bass vigorously into the guy's jaw, knocking him out cold and providing a cavernous feedback as he collapsed. The police showed up as we left. Destiny was not eagerly lifting the ramparts on the way to Poon Tang Hill. Or was it?

We had returned to the Institute and, not yet sleepy, lay beside each other on a grassy knoll inside the dormitory courtyard—a canyon of triangular red brick buildings whose edges were sharp as tomahawk blades. I pointed to the North Star, relating how it had been used throughout the ages as a point of orientation, ye olde *axis mundis*.

"I know you Latins. Your hormones are working all the time, even though we're just sitting here, talking about the stars."

Without responding verbally, I placed the open palm of my hand flatly on her breast. She flinched. I removed it just as mechanically as I had placed it.

"See? That doesn't mean anything unless I have some feeling behind it."

She had told me that I was "queer," that nobody had ever done that to her, but that somehow, she wasn't mad. The next evening, she had come up to my dorm room, and though she had a boyfriend back in Indiana, we feely-pooed. She capped the evening with a hellacious hand job, confessing, visibly delighted, that she liked to watch, a detail no doubt responsible for my evacuating every bit of seminal fluid this side of fatal dehydration. But that had been a long, *long* two days ago. Tonight, she was coming up for some wine.

The fare was a bottle of '62 Rioja white I brought from Miami and had kept in my friends' refrigerator for just this kind of occasion. I had the no-fridge economy dorm room—a tiny cell with two bunks and an air conditioner between them. But the good news was, no roommates.

My cheap drafting table sat below a window facing a courtyard with another brick dormitory across the way. I placed a candle there for ambience. After retrieving the bottle from my buddy's fridge, I cut an ice bucket from a plastic gallon container with his matte knife and emptied an ice tray in it. My buddy jibed me with a fake British accent, mocking our view camera teacher.

"I say! Are you pursuing coitus, you incorrigible lech?"

"I do aim to lay some pipe, Governor!"

"Well, away! You lucky beast!"

He hadn't had much luck in the lady department either, so it was all esprit de corps. I, of course, was *tres* hyped. Melinda was a lovely little Viking flower. She wasn't beautiful by runway standards, but she was sensuous and tight and smelled like a sweet potato pie. In the shower, I popped a boner, thinking how she had touched me and how great it would feel to be inside of her. I turned the cold water on myself, an Arctic bloody stream up here, I might add, and got out of the shower before I gave myself one for the road. I looked out the window several times, but I couldn't spot Melinda below. Just then, there was a knock on the door.

"Hi, Val."

"My name is not Val."

She did not hide her displeasure at my apparent *slip*.

"No, you are Val. As in Valkerie."

"Who's Valkerie?"

I gave her a glass of the chilled '62 Rioja *blanco* and let her into my candle-lit shoebox.

"Valkeries were daughters of Odin, a Norse god. And they would take the fallen Viking heroes into Valhalla, a sort of eternal…party house."

"The only thing I see 'falling' is your drool, you little Latin wolf. Look at this, candles and everything. Cheers!"

Mr. Smooth goes to Rochester. We clicked goblets, which I had picked up for fifty cents apiece in a thrift shop, and watched our shadows flicker on the wall. She sat on my bed. She was dressed in sky blue gym shorts, a tight white T-shirt, and white slip-on Keds. Her legs were tan. She looked delicious.

She picked up one of my technical photo assignments I had forgotten on the bed. A tabletop black and white photograph of an apple, perfectly exposed, perfectly lit, perfectly developed, perfectly printed, then torn to a dozen pieces and mounted perfectly on a piece of cardboard.

"What happened to this?"

"A victim in the battle against structuralism."

"What does that mean?"

"Hell if I know."

"Don't be a wise ass, buster."

Her eyes were hot brandy.

"Well, the photo-class is devoid of any place for self-expression. Ju know Arrrt, so it was my way of saying 'here's the assignment, but kiss my ass.'"

"Why are you so angry?"

"I not angry! I hangry! Arrrrrgh!"

I leaned into her, growling and biting lightly across the top of her shoulder and the back of her neck, which smelled of a soothingly fragrant soap. She put her goblet down.

"Now you're getting me hot and bothered, Picasso."

"Is it…morrre…hot…or morrre…bothered?" I asked in a cheesy sigh.

She laughed.

I came around her ear and pecked my way softly to her mouth. She released her tongue, putting some serious r.p.m.'s on the erector set. I removed her T-shirt, and her breasts, seeking their own level, bounced gently into place in front of me. We lay down. I kissed her delicately down her belly, up to the gym shorts' elastic, and pulled them down and out her ankles slowly, kissing my way up again and beginning ever so slightly to tug down on her panties. She dug her fingers in my hair. The top edge of her soft little fur grazed my chin, Eros' own shoreline. I could almost taste that musky little fruit. My "wolf" drool was in full effect now, little piggies.

Buzzzzzzzzzzzzzzzz!

I reached for my alarm clock. It was off. She pulled her panties up.

"Saved by the bell!" she chimed.

I heard people moving out of their rooms and into the hallway, then someone approached the door and knocked.

"Anybody in there? We are evacuating the building!"

Buzzzzzzzzzzzzzzzz!

"Let's just stay here. It's a drill. It's not real. They'll be back shortly." She was already getting dressed.

"No, we have to go. We can't stay here. What if it's a real fire!"

"C'mon, you're not serious!"

"Yeah, we got to go!"

The only damn fire was in my shorts, and it was quickly engulfing my composure.

"Okay, fine."

I jammed my pants on with marked annoyance, then took a long and inelegant swig from the bottle.

She went out first, and I followed down the empty hallway. When I passed the fire alarm unit, which was deafeningly loud, I took my belt off and swung the square brass buckle at the buzzer fiercely.

She looked back once with the eyes of a tourist beholding a voodoo ceremony gone awry, turned, and walked away. I believe she had made up her mind to take a different tack home. Luna the Mocked Zombie followed.

Once outside, the multitude stood at a distance from the building. I walked up to her.

"See, there is no fire! We could have stayed in there fine, instead of listening to these assholes and joining their drill lemmings!"

"You better take it easy, Luna!"

I looked at the two patrol-boy types who were guiding people and keeping them away from the building.

I walked over and leaned on the corner of the building.

One of them raced up. "Would you please go stand away from the building with the rest of the students?"

"No, I won't. This ain't a real fire, and you've ruined my evening, so I am gonna piss all over your little maneuvers."

"Would you pleeeease stand over there!"

"Make me, fuckface!"

Another group leader came up behind me. "Don't bother with him, Tom. Can't you see he's sick?"

"You don't know how sick I am, you civic-minded little farts. Sick of you, sick of this red-bricked rat lab…Of all the nights to play fire-engine-motherfucking-Fido!"

They walked away. I leaned against the corner of the building, attempting to get my normal breath rate back. Shortly, everyone was allowed in the building. I looked back, and Melinda had gone. Going up the fire stairs, I flashed back on the portentous little Pomeranian of my coitus interuptus dream.

Back in my room, as I finished the bottle of wine, I seriously entertained the idea of really setting fire to the building. Luckily, I nodded off to sleep. I don't think I would have really done it. Too many innocents might die. The enduring problem of sorting culprits from corporations, governments or institutions, thus everybody is innocent or everybody is guilty. So, either you become a Zen master or a mass murderer. Most of us take the easy way out and live as neurotics.

I never saw Melinda again. Her boyfriend came to visit for a week, and she didn't even look my way when I passed her. Back to photo science boot camp: *sensitometry, densitometry, circle of confusion*. This last term I could relate to personally. I did attempt one last time to read my Science of Photography book with gems like the *Bunsen-Roscoe Law of Photochemical Equivalence*. Try this sampler, the *Herschel Effect*, from the Chapter on Reciprocity Failure:

"Moreover, if the surface latent image is destroyed …by an oxidizing agent, and the material with its residualinternal latent image then exposed to red light, redistribution again takes place and surface latent image is formed at the expense of the internal image."

After several paragraphs like that, you can see where sexual fantasy could be a treasured option. And it was. I daydreamed myself cross-eyed about Melinda's *perfumed garden*. Eventually, I quit the Photo Science class before my face turned into an acne- ridden rasp or I blew my nuts out my pee-hole, like ten-gauge single slugs from back to back hand-jobs. The last two weeks, I watched movies in the film library. I would show up every morning to the projectionist, his worst nightmare, with a two-foot pile of 16 mill reels. I sampled sundry animations, short subjects, documentaries, and computer films—late 60's inspired shit like spinning mandalas of geometric shapes with mantra soundtracks.

Also, the standard fare, D.W. Griffith's *Intolerance*, Welles's *Citizen Kane*, Eisenstein's *The Battleship Potamkin*, Pudovkin's, *Storm Over Asia*, of which I only remember a band of terrifying Mongol horsemen galloping over a tundra. One which particularly intrigued me was Bunuel and Dali's *Un Chien Andalou*, not so much for its unbridled surrealism as the possibility that the tormented bastard who had allegedly tried to slit his eye in my dorm building got the idea from this movie, perhaps even sitting right where I was. Not a comforting thought. My anxiety was eased, however, by the antics of master Esquimo survivalist, *Nanook of the North*.

Finally, school was over. I packed my Bug, took the $1400.00 I had left from my student loan, which I hid inside a little zippered slit on the side of the passenger seat, and hi-tailed it out of town forever. The whole way back, I would stop at Howard Johnson's and order club sandwiches, French fries, and double chocolate milkshakes, a diet that allowed my stopping briefly at rest stops for cat naps but mostly laying tracks. The car was loaded to the ceiling with trash I had accumulated. It boxed me in with just enough room to steer and shift, proving fatal to a possum that stumbled into my right front tire. I hated that here-this-second-gone-the-next thump. It always sent a chill up my spine. On these highways, nocturnal critters were just mangled meat waiting for a place to squash. I felt bad. Just then, I remembered that possums were marsupials. I stopped, backed up in the emergency lane, and got out to check. I turned it over with my foot. But this one was not playing dead.

Its jaw was crushed. I felt the pouch with my *foot.* I was no freaking naturalist, so thank God the pouch was empty of young ones because I wouldn't know what the hell I would do with infant possums at five a.m. on the Sunshine State Parkway. I pushed it with my foot behind a roadside clump of grass, then turned it on its stomach to hide the awfully tragic and bloody snarl away from view.

"Sorry, old gal, I didn't see you."

I felt a bit moronic after saying that, but anyhow, after my condolences, I drove off.

I remembered a friend of mine, George el Picaro, a true road kill devotee. Not only deer—venison, understandably was his vice--but possum, raccoon, and not just his own. Any fresh roadkill. I was with him when he found a soft-shell turtle drowned inside a crab trap in a drainage canal just west of Everglades City on 41. He took it home and turned it into *asopao de jicotea,* then proceeded to spoon up the aromatic and nutritious stew to the last drop, absolutely unscathed. He'd always carry Lawry's salt, pepper, garlic powder, a bottle of wine vinegar, olive oil, a one ouncer jar of McCormick's ground cayenne, for variable voltage, and a roll of heavy-duty tin foil. He'd figured out thirty minutes per pound of roadkill in the engine compartment of his 1970 El Dorado would cook it pink. Oh yeah, I could see this on syndication: *On the Road with Chef Eldo.* Believe it or not, years later, I heard someone had published a book on road kill recipes.

Now, the next set of events would raise the aforementioned possum from just ordinary possum-ness to an omen of mythological proportions. I had hit this luckless sibyl of the Sunshine State Parkway somewhere around Ft. Pierce. About eight in the morning, I stopped for gas at the Pompano Beach rest stop, and I realized the tire that ran over the possum was almost flat! I called the attendant to check it while I had some coffee. No meek bartering this time. Now I *had* some crank, to the tune of fourteen Franklins. A veritable fortune then.

I sat down at the counter and ordered a ham and egg sandwich from the waitress. She brought me the coffee, and I started thinking there's some bad mojo in the air. The tire going flat…Maybe it was some Indian shaman's animal brother. Or *un brujo* in the shape of a possum had put the bad mojo on me for killing the Great White Possum. What would be next, waking up with a pencil dick and swollen nipples? Too much Cocoa and Java. Oh yeah, Dr. Milethus Hysterius could use some sleep.

"Luna, is that you?"

Chill up my spine. Past the glass doors at the end of the counter, by a basket of what looked to be fake Indian River oranges, stood a long-legged blond, a truly neck-turning vision in a pair of denim cut-offs, old work boots, and a faded *Resurrection of Pigboy Crabshaw* T-shirt, shrunk beyond her bellybutton. She looked very familiar. I waved and smiled as she walked up but still didn't place her. She said her name, noticing my confusion.

"Nancy…*Port a' Tart*?"

She was the nude model who had done my piece at the student art show.

"Nancy Moore, the veterinarian?"

We hugged and kissed cheeks.

"The very one, dogger. I thought you were in Rochester."

"It's a long sad tale."

"I have one of those too."

"You go first."

"Well, for starters, my ancient wagon, you know…the Valiant, is right out there with what seems like a transmission noise. I *was* on my way to camping around Hobe Sound."

"Okay…my car is also out there with a flat. Go on."

"I broke up with my boyfriend this week."

Oh! under my breath. "So, he came back from 'Nam?"

"Yeah…or I don't know if *he* came back. I mean, I don't know how much of him was him. *He* was pretty fucked up. *Beau coup* paranoia. He accused me of going out on him when he was away. One night, I came home, and he threatened that if I wouldn't tell him who the guy was, I would regret it. The next day, when I was in school he took my…"

Here, her voice quavered slightly. And I felt rather cheesy about my previous relish on her break-up.

"Dog and….threw it off…the balcony and broke its leg. You know… how I am about animals. I slept for three nights with a baseball bat and swore if he came back I'd beat him into a coma. But he didn't show, and I haven't seen him since. That motherfucker."

I didn't know what to say. Frankly, it kind of sounded like low-brow beat-to-the- ground made-for-TV melodrama, with the mentally fucked up, paranoid, socially maladjusted, war damaged 'Nam Vet coming home to roost. Thank God, that apparently the dog had healed and the sympathetic macho man cop/male interest was missing in this libretto, so far. Though there was no doubt that she was very *real*. And hurting.

"I'm sorry." I put my hand on her shoulder, very testosterone-lessly.

"It's okay, man…You know, it's over. And besides…I want to very much be there for the animals that I have yet to tend to."

At this point, the station attendant comes in to deliver the diagnosis.

"You're okay. I put your spare on. That flat tire was thin as Saran Wrap, and I wouldn't drive around much longer on the other front tire if I was you. Look here, did you run over some animal. Damn if these don't look like little fangs or teeth?"

I felt Nancy tighten up.

"I…ah…matter of fact, a possum ran out on the road, and I tried to swerve, but I couldn't. I did go back to see if there were any babies in the pouch. I…"

"Hell, I ain't any Humane Society, kid. Road kills are a dime a dozen out here. Don't lose any sleep over it. Here."

He handed me the sharp little fragments, which I quickly slipped in my pocket and out of sight.

"Miss, you need a universal joint. I called a yard in North Lauderdale, and he said he has one. It will be ready by this afternoon. You're lucky. That's one old car."

"Oldie but goodie."

"That's what my wife says about me."

He laughed and walked out. I recounted to Nancy the techno-night-mare R.I.T. had been. Naturally, omitting the fire drill ordeal—didn't want to gamble, although I would have raised the purse on the side of her enjoying the story. After a while, the attendant came back and said Nancy's wagon wouldn't be ready till the next day. She decided to call her mom to pick her up.

"Hell, my car works. Let's go camp and come back to pick it up tomorrow, or the next day? I can use a little open-space time."

"Are you sure?"

"I've seldom been surer."

"I think that's a grand idea, Luna. I see those techs at Eastman couldn't techno-cize all the nature out of you."

I got two new front tires, Mr. Moneybags now, and dumped the stuff from my passenger side into her wagon. She took her camping gear, and we were off.

We found a spot in the Australian pine thicket just north of some fancy condos. It was a gorgeous clear blue day. The sea was calm. I rushed into the sea in my underwear and pushed myself off the bottom, doing dolphin leaps out of the absolute joy of being out of that school and out of my VW. Snorkeling off shore, Nancy spotted some lobsters. I broke off a stout, thin pine branch, borrowed her snorkeling gear, and using a T-shirt for a glove, teased the four crustaceans out into my grip with the switch. I tailed them one at a time and stuffed them halfway down the elastic of my underwear serrated edge out. Later that evening, we lit the brickets after blocking her Hibachi out of sight with my car—it was not legal to camp there, north of *The Have's* Condominiums. Ironically, a malady endemic to many of the well-heeled was the stress over loosing their nut, or feeling threatened by whomever they perceived to be the desperado *du jour*. Namely, anyone whose demeanor was not blaring out conspicuous consumption. Namely us: The Camping Underground.

We grilled the tails with butter, lime, and a bit of crushed pepper. We also found an ancient miniature of Myers's Rum in the bottom of her knapsack. I poured a scooch into the melted butter to baste the corn on the cob. We washed them down with iced beer from her cooler.

When time came to turn in, there was only one sleeping bag. I spread a bed sheet I had swiped from the dorm over the pine needles. Around midnight, it got chilly, and I curled up into the fetal chimp mode. I was not going to try to slime into her sleeping bag after her ex-boyfriend and dog scenario.

I then heard Nancy whisper. "Luna…Luna?"

I turned toward her. "What?"

"Did you really go back to check the pouch on that possum?"

"Yes, I did. Why?"

"Come, punkin'. It's warm in here."

When I got inside the sleeping bag, Nancy was in her panties, topless. Fire drills be damned!

Cape Florida in the Golden Days of the Portable Luna

Upon parting the Dutch pantry door, from the inside of the pool "office," I see him. The pot-bellied bastard tossing aside the fresh yellow towel from the fiberglass recliner I had just set up, he lugs *her* lounge to the far end of the pool deck, wraps *his* towel on it and lays his fat ass down very *après moi, le déluge.* On the way to him, I saw that the towel he'd thrown had crushed the wild flowers I had handpicked and arranged in a Heineken bottle for Maxine, Poolside Nymph of Gender Discomforts. The gap he'd left in the row of white lounges resembled a missing front tooth in a smile, a condition befitting the self-entitled Clown at Rest.

"Sir, did you just move this lounge from over there to here?"

"No."

"You know you did."

"No, I didn't."

The perjurious vulture, *Wall Street Journal* on his belly, denied the fact with minimum lip motion and an air of annoyance.

"There's an easy way for me to find out because the backrest is faulty on this one."

I whisked the backrest away from the lounge in one motion. The newspaper and the pendulous flesh on his arms flapped as he tried to balance himself. I grabbed the shirt collar of his loud and matching cabana set, to prevent possible head injuries, just before he tumbled to the pavement.

The following I delivered in a patronizing tone as if addressing a toddler. "See? You wouldn't want somebody to take *your* lounge."

"You haven't heard the end of this, Mister. You're way out of place!"

"Just like the lounge chair you grabbed, sir."

He got up and stomped off to a section of lounges by the kiddy pool.

I carried the lounge to its original place and dressed it with the towel. Most of the Black-eyed Susans were not repairable, so I returned to the park next door to get some more.

Incidentally, I later found out from an old lady botanist whom I befriended that what I had called Black-eyed Susans, *Rudbeckia hirta*, were actually Beach Sunflowers, *Heliathus debilis*. So, all this time, I had been spreading my floral ignorance to sundry touristss, including Maxine.

The Towers were the last condominium property before Bill Baggs State Park, a woodsy stretch of Atlantic beachfront thick with Australian pine, coconut palms, sea grapes, and the nearly indestructible and invasive Brazilian Pepper tree. Hurricane Andrew seventeen years later would shear it to a stubbly beachhead. A mile or so down the road to the south, Key Biscayne ended on a point of land where the red brick Cape Florida Lighthouse stood.

I went down to the beach. Not too far south from here lay the dreaded reefs and Keys that a few centuries ago claimed many ships, souls, and gold from the avaricious Spanish Main. And later still, those reefs enriched a number of early Florida wreck rats.

Entering the pine thicket out of view of the building, I lit a joint. The *cannabis* spread through me like hot gravy on a tablecloth. As I picked flowers, I mused about the many Cape Florida follies of centuries past. The place had been previously named by Ponce de Leon, *Cabo de los Mártires*. I imagine, referring to his own countrymen as *los mártires*, even though every time he or his "martyrs," and later English pirates, landed, they did little else than murder and enslave and martyrize Tequesta and Calusa, who hitherto had mostly spent many a moonlit night spearing, then barbecuing the proceeds along the shores here. As usual in many of these feuds, some work-a-day Willie gets it in the keester. In the 1820's, the government built Cape Florida Light, but calamity was in the works for the lighthouse keeper. A couple of white men from Key West stole skins from a nearby Indian camp, after getting the owner drunk on their whisky and murdering him. Soon after, Indians attacked the lighthouse keeper, who as a last resort rushed to the top of the brick tower. The Indians then set fire to the door. The flames ravaged the door but also incinerated the stairs, cutting access to the singed pale face who, to combat the painful blaze and bursting glass, sat legs hanging down on the edge of an iron balcony about three stories up. The Indians, frustrated in their efforts to seize him, shot up his feet, looted the homestead, and sailed off with his sloop. The next morning, the feverish and bleeding keeper was rescued from the smoke-blackened tower by the crew of a passing ship.

Things had not been very smooth at The Towers Condominium either, whose previous manager I would very much like to see terrorized by a torch-wielding war party. Turns out, the guy who hired us was just a temporary manager who left when the last condo unit was sold. He had promised us a series of work-related benefits, which the new manager, Mr. Bouchette, had trouble selling to the board of directors, who in turn wanted to lower our salaries for starters. So, they were looking for reasons to fire my buddy, Fling the Pool Meister extraordinaire, holder of the pool operator's license and presently on a three-day out-of-state death-in-the-family leave. Naturally, I would be fired as well, since he brought me in. Earlier this week, the new manager had "surprised" me in the pool office, where I had sat practicing chords and scales on a cardboard keyboard, customarily propped above a real piano keyboard by beginners to identify the notes. Bouchette had appeared at the Dutch pantry door.

"Caught you sitting down!"

Bouchette delivered this in a singsong voice accompanied by a wry smile for that serio-comic effect.

"You didn't *catch me*, Mr. Bouchette. I already swept the deck, washed the towels, and now I'm waiting for them to dry, as you can hear for yourself. Would you like me to goose step in a circle until they're ready?"

"It's my job to check, Luna. No offense, but we all get paid to *do* something."

"No offense taken, and no offense intended on my part. Hail-fellow-well-met!" I tapped him on the shoulder with upbeat camaraderie, then continued. "We're just a bunch of inoffensive and happy cogs around here, Booch!"

Maybe not the way to endear you to the new boss, but today, the tune blowin' at poolside was, *No Time For Assholes, Come What May*. A few days later, he pulled the same crap. But this time, I was ready for him. For a few days, I had been collecting cigarette butts and cramming an old shoe box full in case he showed up to the window to repeat the dumb-assed line. Enter stage left.

"Caught you again!"

"No, sir. Again, I already swept the deck." I emptied the shoe box in the middle of the office, making a two-inch high pile of butts on the concrete floor. "Seeeee!"

"You certainly march to a different drummer, Luna."

He smiled, raising his eyebrows into a ridged forehead, and left in managerial puzzlement. He hadn't returned since. That was two days ago, and not necessarily a good sign.

I took a second toke of the joint, popping a seed that spiraled toward the pine needles by my feet trailing smoke like a tagged Japanese Zero in a WWII newsreel. I shoved it into the dirt with my toe, licked my palm, and snuffed what was left of the joint in it. I couldn't smoke as much as I used to in the Sixties. By myself, it could turn me into a self-chastising gargoyle of blunders past. In public, I became a semi-paranoid imbecile, and in bed, it flushed the hydraulics from Li'l Smilo, to engorge existential tirades, expressed in somewhat melancholic figure eights, discomfiting not only me but my philosophically ambushed lover as well.

With a fresh supply of flowers, I approached the edge of the thicket through a shaded tunnel of Brazilian Pepper. As I walked through this natural blind, the mottled sunlight strobed patterns on my feet and the blossoms carried in my hand. I parted a branch and beheld: The Towers of Key Biscayne.

Before exiting from the edge of his arboreal past, a barefoot and rather buzzed Luna, the Coastal Forager, interprets modern luxury condominium living. *"Look at that…That…bastion of…pirates-and-beggars-and…garish whores crawling all over each other up there like…crabs in a bucket.* Before I could take this weed-driven tangent to its nihilist finale, some kind of hellish bug, *Insectus d'Infernus,* Lunaeus, flew in my eye, stinging it like a cigarette ash. I rubbed it, but when retreating into the shielding bush, I dug my heel to the hilt on a jumbo-sized sticker, the spiked fruit of the Puncture Weed, *Tribulus cistoides.*

Hobbling pogo style on one leg and a tearing eye, I landed on my ass, breaking all the flower stems, a tremendous rendition of, I believe, Debussy's unfinished masterpiece, *La Danse de l'Aborigine Idiot.*

After pulling out the pesky thorn, I noticed that the "stickers" of this prostrate weed were blooming into bright yellow flowers, whose chivalric value had accrued appreciably since inflicting my wound. I also gathered a few strands of its deep green leaves for filler. That accomplished, I quickly abandoned my floral design craze lest I slip into fruitdom.

Walking back below the high-walled edge of the property, I could see the second-story window at the back of our pool office. In reality, the "pool office" was simply a room with a desk and a washer and dryer, where piles of towels, monogrammed with tenant surnames, were laundered, folded, and then stacked alphabetically on shelves lining the walls.

I searched the sandy weed-ridden area along the wall below the pool office window through which two weeks ago, at dusk, I had flung Maxine's tampon. No sign of it. Perhaps some scavenger had carried it off, mistaking it for some kind of New Age *morcilla.* Luckily, those were pre-AIDS days. Today, that could be considered an act of negligent homicide, with me as the surrogate forefather of a likely HIV-positive band of raccoon hostiles preying on unsuspecting beach goers.

On *la notte di amore,* I had locked the office door, spread a bunch of laundered towels on the floor, and lay next to my savory damsel. Upon discovering the little white cord, I tugged it lightly. Maxine responded in a mock talking-doll voice.

"Its-that-time-of-the-month-do-you-mind?"

"No, not I, said the Bear."

She had a shaved and truly adorable little hillock. While pulling out the stopper, which she had hardly stained, I popped a forefinger off the side of my mouth with my other hand, mimicking a champagne cork, and toasted.

"Here is to the cutest little poo in the world!"

I then flung it out the window. We made love on our homey pile of terrycloth. Here a Schwartz's monogram peeked out under her shoulder. There a "guez's," from The Rodriguez's supported my chin when I kissed her smooth and cleaved little peach. After our lovemaking, I grazed her silky olive shoulder with the tip of my nose as we lay on a myriad sur-names, resembling the list of benefactors on the back pages of symphony programs. Except here, they had unknowingly provided a fuzzy love hollow for the ruttish coolie and the wayward *femme-enfant.*

"I lied to you. I'm not eighteen. Not for ten more days. Are you mad?"

"Mad? I'd be *mad* if I *was* mad. But being that I am twenty-five, if you decided to kiss and tell, a judge would throw his whole law library at me."

"What do you mean?"

"The age of consent, you're not old enough to..."

"I'm legal in New Jersey, that's where I live,"

"We're not in Joyzee... Will the defendant please rise, you know"

"And rise you did, studley."

She giggled, biting the tip of her tongue with perfect incisors framed by pink-brown lips. They were swollen, the way women now try to make them through injections. Above them, a magnificent Roman nose ascended. A bit too long, perhaps, for those subjected daily to the mandates of Pop beauty. She glimpsed up with her permanently sad, amber eyes and confessed.

"I have something else to tell you. I'm bi-sexual."

Feigning indifference and strutting "a cool I had none of at the moment", I countered. "I also have a skeleton in my closet, o' little one…I'm a lesbian in a man's body."

She chortled, with a wonderful and raspy, *pícara* delight. Though was surprised that I, being Latin, wasn't put off by lesbianism. She wasn't far off the mark. For a standard issue Cuban, a *tortillera* was a freak to be avoided, except as an amusement, *pa' un cuadro*, and those menages for the most part were arranged with paid-for lipstick lezzies. As a teenager in the Sixties, I had always thought that lesbians were the butchy dykes of the wrestling canvas whom one might have to slap around in a challenge *a ver quien es el que mas mea*. But Maxine's young curves, crested by piquant roan-pink nipples, were to be found on no canvas except perhaps Botticelli's. She told me how her cousin had initiated her on an overnight stay at her aunt's. She had actually liked it more than with a man.

"Don't take it personal, Luna. You were wonderful, I like you a lot, but this will probably be my last time with men."

So long to future plans. I recalled, fraught with no disillusion, that age-old consumer warning against bunko artists, "If it seems too good to be true, it probably is", writhed in my head like a snake. Although there was a good side, for the kissing cousins at least, never a fear of inbred chillun' in the future. Maxine continued.

"With women, it feels like you're kissing a young boy, soft, tender—"

I interrupted. "I guess that's why I persisted in kissing women. Hey, maybe I'm a pederast lesbian in a man's body?"

"No, Luna, I'm serious. You know how I found out I had a strong tongue?"

"How?"

"When I licked my cousin and it made her squirt. I didn't know women came like that."

My feeble attempt at aloofness, through secondhand wit, was terminated decisively by her naiveté, like an ape's treetop antics are by a *curare*-tipped dart. Soon thereafter, I became harder than the Death of a Thousand Cuts. When she saw my state of potential suicide by self-abuse, Maxine capitulated.

"Okay, but this *is* my swan song, Luna, my swan song. I promised my lover."

"Oh, thank you, Goddess of the Merciful Pubis!"

'Nary a less cynical line would I ever utter.

Nine more days. Strange planet. I hoped Venus was in my corner.

Now, two weeks later, I winced slightly, climbing the stairs leading to the pool deck with my third handful of flowers. My knees were still registering a sort of ghost soreness from Maxine's Swansong on the concrete floor.

She was visiting her mom for the weekend. Maxine resided in Cherry Hill, New Jersey with her dad. Nothing wrong with celebrating a *friend's* return with flowers, right? Who had to know that I fervently prayed for recidivism, or at least Swan Song II?

When I bent over her lounge to fetch the water-filled Heineken bottle, my periphery darkened. I felt a bowling ball roll on the interior curve of my forehead. I held on to the lounge, invoking all deities I to keep me from fainting. After taking a slow deep breath, consciousness returned, along with the general din: high end squeals from the kiddy pool, lounges re-arranged on the deck, newspapers rustled, generic murmurs, etc. I took another breath. I made it to the water fountain and sucked at the ice-cold stream, then filling my cupped hand, rinsed my eye where the bug had landed. Luna, the Coastal Forager, was glad to be in the shade and standing on a thorn-less deck.

Once in my "pool office" cubicle, I placed the flowers and bottle on the desktop, still way too buzzed. I had taken one too many pulls from that Thai-stick weed, which in addition to the heat was fingering my synapses like double-time castanets. Reaching behind the washer, I found the pint of Dewar's kept there for those after-hour laundering duties. I sat, took a good swig, then poured a little on the tiny thorn hole in my foot, figuring I'd disinfect it from both ends. A truly dazzling bacteriological theory, Dr. Hoochenstein. Taking another swig, only to assure it would not fall short of its mark, I reclined in the chair, no longer so contrary to the whimsies of the Crab Bucket Dwellers. Perhaps I had spoken too soon.

On the elevated and landscaped gazebo directly across the pool office, members of The Towers' directorate appeared to play poker, but mostly they were surveying me out of the corner of their eyes. From that perch, they could easily assess the activities performed in the office. After arranging the flowers in the bottle with marked effeminate gestures, I skipped gleefully to the lounges, placed them by the one I had toweled for Max, then beholding the arrangement, clutched my chest with unchecked rapture. Stepping back inside the office, I yielded to anarchy with the following mental preamble: *Whereas you want something to look at? I'll give you withered nutsacks something to look at.*

Slipping a diving mask on, I approached a family of towels. "The Woodwards", singled one out and vociferated my reproach.

"Mr. Woodward, I folded you three times today, and look at you!"

Fairly certain of having attracted the attention of the Board of Directors, I proceeded to pounce on Mr. Woodward's towel with a vengeance.

Bam! Bam! Bam!

"I'm not gonna put up with this! I warned you."

A few more straight lefts. *Bam! Bam! Bam!*

I looked out of the corner of my eye, and the directors were definitely engaged. So now Luna became the *de facto* Prince of the Beholden. I then noticed a towel monogrammed "The Murrays" had been placed after "The Myers" on the shelf. I persecuted the alphabetical error with unmeasured zealotry.

"Now, Mister Myer, I'm getting *damn* well tired of you not getting the picture. Mis-ter Mur-ray comes *first!* M-U, then M-Y.

I yanked Myer out and shoved him below Murray with a murderous right, burying it deep inside the stack and delivering the next line through clenched teeth.

"Now, you stubborn toilet stain, you're gonna stay there, knotted up, until *I* feel like it."

I put the snorkel in my mouth, turned my back on the stack of towels, and disappeared behind the wall, mumbling loudly through the tube and trying to control the laughter. When I peered back at the poker table, they were no longer at their perch.

I removed the snorkeling gear, sat at the cardboard keyboard on the desk, and began fingering a minor seventh blues progression in C, which was all I was gonna ever learn before quitting the piano. Someone showed up at the pantry door. It was Mr. Bouchette. The axe had arrived as I fingered the blues.

"Luna, can I talk to you for a minute?"

I went up to Bouchette, who already had one elbow propped on the countertop of the door.

"Listen, it's not *you*, but I have some pressures from above…"

I looked quizzically above his head for the pressures.

"Above what?"

"It's the board of directors. They feel like things aren't being done the way they—"

"Don't soften the blow, Mr. Bouchette. Are we getting canned? Is that it?"

"Well, it's not you so much, but your partner—there are a lot of things that aren't being done."

"Like what? Show me one thing? I'll tell *you* one thing that is not being done. We were promised a raise after sixty days. It's been ninety days? And another thing is, my partner was promised a concession for tanning products and sailboat rentals and zilch. Obviously, a verdict has been reached…from above."

I pointed up with my forefinger.

"Listen, they're willing to give you guys two more weeks so you can try to get other employment."

Bouchette waited to be thanked or acknowledged for this tidbit of largesse. When I gave him nothing, he left. I went back to the cardboard piano. Within minutes, he was back at the counter, my own interactive little stage.

"You wanted me to show you something? Come with me. Let me show you."

I walked with him to the upper deck, where some people read the paper and others lay back on their lounges. He bent over behind a lounge and pointed his index at a cigarette butt as if identifying a murder suspect. I could sense it was high time to gig this toad.

"Look, this is one of the reasons!" said Mr. Bouchette.

"Mr. Bouchette, first of all, I'm not some kind of retriever sitting in my office, ready to pounce on the slightest litter that drops on the deck. Second, and most important, you're pointing at this cigarette butt like you were the untiring champion of *their* well-being, but you don't fool *them*."

Here, I waved my outstretched arm over the sun worshippers, like some messiah spreading the mantle of enlightenment over a people heretofore vexed by a false prophet. Meanwhile, "ye faithful" lay in a semi-circle of lounges, feeling a bit self-conscious, twitching and cringing and burrowing a little deeper into their sundry reading material, feigning self-absorption or *siesta,* when in fact they were listening to every word and very much wanting to remain exempt from the gladiatorial scat. I advanced effortlessly and lanced the vexing little upstart.

"Oh no. You don't fool them, Mr. Bouchette. They all know you're an undiluted asshole."

Bouchard tightened his lips and threatened in froth. "I'm gonna call Metro police and have you arrested!"

"For what, Mr. Bouchette? For calling you an asshole? They'll probably tell you you're an asshole for calling them."

He stormed off. And just before he opened the glass door leading to the lobby, I fired off one more round from across the deck to drive home his retreat.

"And take that gray suit off. You look like an undertaker!"

I walked back to the office and gathered my belongings, which amounted to the folding cardboard keyboard, the *Easy* Chord Picture Chart by Jack Morris, Rabelais' *Gargantuan and Pantagruel,* a home-made jazz cassette of *Coltrane* containing two of my "desert-island" must-have songs, "Out of This World" and "Soul Eyes," and lastly, almost a pint of Dewar's. Those were the Golden Days of the Portable Luna. Only one catch: now it would be back to the want ads, the pavement-pounding, and the form-filling job hunt. Possibly my least favorite of tasks "under the benign indifference of the universe."

"Luna, I came to escort you to your car."

It was the young Jewish body builder who was assistant manager.

"What do you mean, Jack? Escort me!"

He braced, expecting escalation.

"You ain't built right to be my escort, Thzailor. What the hell do you think I'm gonna do, rip out the plumbing and set fire to the pool? Spare me the melodrama, okay?"

"Employees *have* been known to get back at their employers when they're fired."

"Huh? Rule #2 from the Condo management manual? You've been brushing up, slick."

"Let's not make it hard on ourselves. I'm just doing what I was told."

Most zombies do, I thought, controlling the urge to vent on Sluggo, lest we scuffled and Metro took me downtown.

Begrudgingly, I picked up Maxine's bottle of flowers, which now had become a whole other program. Walking through the deck toward the garage, I felt the subtle gaze of my sunbathing tenants, though none had offered a trace of succor. Why should they? Bouchette was just doing their dirty work. In the end, it was they who didn't want to pay what had been previously negotiated. I walked by the insentient jury, opened Rabelais, and asked Sluggo if he cared for a poem.

"Did you ever hear the poem that the child Gargantua dedicated to the toilet?"

Foreseeing reproach, Sluggo attempted to stem the flow of verse. "I think you should read it to yourself."

"Okay, here's what the Toilet said to the Shitters."

Sluggo stiffened at the motif.

"Shittard, Skittard, Turdous,

Thy bung has flung some dung on us,

234

Filthard, Cackard, Stinkard…"

When we turned the corner, he opened the fire door and entered the covered parking. The door closed behind us.

"Okay, you've had your little day in the sun. Now get your ass in gear and leave the premises, wise ass." Out of condo-owner earshot, Jack channeled, "Street."

"Wise Arse indeed. They don't make them like they used to, Jack," I continued as I headed for my '72 yellow Bug, my back to him and my voice echoing in a mellifluous soprano throughout the cavernous parking facility as I read the last line. "May you burn with St. Anthony's fire, if your Arseholes are ill-wiped ere you retire…" Then, turning toward him, feigning interest in his literary opinion, "the rhythm…Uh…is a bit awkward, when you go from French to English. Don't you think, Jack?"

As I reached my car, Sluggo approached me, intent I believe on manhandling me, or at the very least shoving me into the car. I gripped the Heineken bottleneck with the flowers, hoping not to have to defend myself. A car turns the corner. It's Maxine on the passenger side of her mom's brand new white '75 Wagoneer Woodie, smiling.

I waved and raised the flowers. They pulled up, and she opened the window, disarming Sluggo where he stood. He waved hello to Maxine's mom.

"For me?"

"*Para tí.*"

Maxine blew me a kiss when I gave them to her. "You are not leaving, are you?"

"Actually, I just resigned. I'm sure going to miss this place…Jack here was opening the door for me and everything. But I got a project coming up."

Sluggo stood awkwardly.

"I was *just* telling my mom about what a great photographer you were, and she wants you to photograph her paintings. But she wants to know how much you'll charge her?"

"I'll have to take a look and see how many, how big you want the enlargements, or is it just slides?"

"Why don't you come up for a beer and take a look?" offered her mom.

"Okay. I'll go around the front to valet park since I'm no longer an employee. It's just a formality, but these poor guys get a lot of pressure from *above*, right, Jack?"

Sluggo excused himself and walked away at a quick pace. I'm sure on his way to bring home the news to Bouchette. Maxine wanted the real dope.

"What happened?"

"Nothing."

"Okay."

Maxine's "okay" sounded more like "fat chance". Mom pushed her eyebrows and upper lip upward but did not pursue it. They drove off to park the car. I throttled my loud little German four banger around to the front entrance and had it valet parked as a *guest* of Maxine's mom.

Her mother's paintings were late Sixties' Palm Beach drek. "Idyllic" beaches with seaside shacks, executed in a generous *impasto* of flake white and pastels, which when minced by the green coastal grasses turned into some kind of chives dip. The sea, an aqua and ultramarine remoulade, kept the land apart from the sky, also knifed into shingles of baby blue with gobs of meringue clouds. You would need a bottle of Pepto Bismol after one of her shows.

"So, what do you think?"

Her mother awaited my opinion.

"Yeah, I think I can photograph them."

"No, what do you think of the paintings?"

"Oh…Yeah…I like them. I love the pastel colors. It gives you a sense of serenity…but at the same time, your use of the palette knife makes it unpredictable, like…like the elements themselves."

If I had been Pinocchio, my nose would have shot out like a surface-to-air missile and impaled her seascape. I stood, scanning my face for any twitching that might betray the monumental whopper I had just laid on her.

"So, how much would it be? I have about ten paintings."

"About a hundred and forty bucks for slides."

She agreed. I went home, got my beloved Nikon F Photonic and two 500 watt scoops, which I hadn't taken out of the bag since my rendezvous at Rochester Institute of Technology two years back.

I photographed half of them, drinking wine with Max while she played Bach on her flute and fancifully broke off into some ballsy licks *a la* Jethro Tull. She had *duende*, soul, raison d'être, presence. O' that delectable Sappho-struck little piper. How easily she could bum rush my pitiful attempt at the Middle Way of the sages.

"I want to get some sun."

"Your lounge is still there. I had put those wild flowers by it this morning."

She came up to my ear and whispered. "If you had a pussy, I'd be at odds."

"Chile', I'm ready to re-incarnate or get a sex change," said Luna, the duly bum rushed, teetering for a foothold.

She kissed me on the cheek and grabbed the flowers, and we took the elevator to the lower lobby. Thank God she was leaving day after tomorrow because I couldn't take much more without involuntary dry humps on her leg.

Some of the same sun monkeys were still out by the pool. She placed the flowers where I originally had them and smiled, pleased at the results. I took the lounge next to hers and helped myself to Mom's towel in the office. Max undressed to a scanty, finely threaded, macramé-like bikini, which maddeningly defined her cleft pubis. A few of the old goats peered covertly over their *Wall Street Journals* and best-seller espionage or detective hardcovers. Not for you, Play-doh dicks! She took out one of those eye protectors that by now must have been classics—the ones that looked like double-ended spoons—lay down, and placed them in her eyes. My tainted mind thought of what other double-ended items the kissing cuzzins might engage on their journey through the land of Lesbos. I never got the nerve to ask her to let me watch which was just as well, for most certainly I would have turned into a howling glazed donut within the first two frenzied minutes. Luna, the Epileptic Roué of Cherry Hill.

But just at the moment the scenario began rustling *Li'l Smilo*, I saw Bouchette in the distance, emerging from the lower lobby door. He walked toward our direction. I turned my head, making believe I hadn't seen him.

"Could I have a cigarette?"

"Help yourself. They're in my purse."

I heard Bouchette climbing the wooden steps to the gazebo a few yards behind my lounge, where the board of directors had a few hours ago *dealt the cards*. He was well within earshot, and I could picture his jowly face peering through the palmetto palm fans. I lit a cigarette by the filter.

"They taste awful like this." I flicked it behind me and heard it strike one of the palm fans, like it had struck a drumhead in the near vicinity of Bouchette.

"You can have another one. I'm trying to quit."

I lit another one, inhaled, lay back, and blew the smoke in a long exhalation.

"You know, there's nothing worse than bottled-up emotions. But I guess it's better than selling out."

"I'm not repressed. I just need lungs for my flute."

"Oh, I didn't mean *you*. I don't think I need these smokes either. I had asthma as kid." I put it out on the deck. "Remind me to take this butt. I wouldn't want these assholes berating the new pool boy right out the gate."

"What are you talking about?"

"Just shop talk."

I heard Bouchette go down the steps and walk away. What a way to make a living. I lay still for a little while, but as usual, got bored. Never knew how people lay there like casualties for hours. Some had laid their souls prone before the low road status quo in much the same way. *Profanum vulgus,* as they say in Pago Pago.

"Max, I'm gonna go up and finish shooting your mom's work. I'm not much for laying in the sun. I got to be doing something—surfing, fishing, boating—I just can't lay here."

Maxine didn't answer. She was deep into wine and sun languor. I opened the umbrella next to her lounge and watched her curl up in her sleep, slightly goose-bumped as she felt the shade. What a sweet sister she was. What the fuck would I not give to be dyke for a day and die.

As I walked toward the elevator, I saw Bouchette exit the sundry shop and walk toward me. I pushed the UP button. He approached now with a runt-of-the-litter demeanor and delivered his hackneyed wisdom.

"Luna, remember, those we meet *on the way up*, we will probably meet on the way down."

I entered the elevator. "Who's climbing? Anyway, I think this planet is big enough to crash-land my rocket well out of your vicinity…By the way, Booch, you should alert Sluggo. I believe I heard stalkers out there in the bushes."

The elevator doors closed, slowly screening out Bouchette's flushing jowls. Some people just made way too much out of this "going up" business. Hell, even the Baker Acted could tell you that the trick to arriving lay not in one's ability to go up, but to *go off*.

Aspecto Femenino

The Little Samoans, a pair of barrel-chested wrestling twins, climbed into the ring. On their first set of frenzied acrobatics, highlighted by fluttering native-print loincloths and untamed Afros, I let go a howl that struck my broken ribs like a trident, cutting short my glee and turning me into a whining cur. In the adjacent bed, under the scant privacy of a white sheet, a Smithsonian-approved Tibetan Holy Man tried to piss in a bedpan. The trauma and the opiates made pissing an odyssey. I could relate. I was already sporting a catheter, and my left leg had been in traction for thirteen days and counting at George Washington Hospital to set a dislocated hip. Add to that a flaming torn pectoral, a slightly fractured nose, and a seventeen-stitch cut nagging my chin to condiment my immobility. I begged my buddy Luis to turn off the TV set before the Samoans mauled me any further. Shortly thereafter, he left to study for his final law exams. The "feminine aspect of matadors" had long ago ceased to be fighting words. As the Tibetan fell asleep, my silver '79 Firebird, now a gruesome wreck, accumulated storage fees and rust in some Bethesda junkyard. At dusk, a light snow fell. My future was uncertain, but for the moment at least, my heart no longer pined for Dolores. Then again, I was likely to not have to park another car. But what truly waited in the wings, at the very last loop of this seemingly blessed then cursed journey for the soon to be crutch-toting ex-car valet and former *artiste*, was truly worthy of Verdi's title, *La Forza del Destino*, in spades. And as Socrates would confirm, it all started with a question.

"Can you come up for an interview?"

"Are you pretty sure about the job? The ticket is two hundred dollars. I mean, it's not like it's my *last* two hundred dollars, but I'd like to know if it's fairly certain?"

It was my-last-and-only-in-the-past-sixty-days-of-hard-savings, two hundred dollars.

"Oh, we're pretty sure. There are two positions for vacation relief, and you are one of the ones we are strongly considering for the opening. When can we expect you here?"

"A week from this Monday?"

I needed a week to go over the gear I had never *used.*

"That's fine. By the way, the head of production really liked your resume reel."

My resume reel! That snook had inhaled that plug like a live ladyfish. A "world record" hooked on handheld sewing thread. *I had never shot news in my life.* Could I let a minor detail like that forestall my destiny?

As I had told my friend, "I'm not gonna park one more friggin' car."

Note the use of the word "friggin'" as opposed to fuckin', already an attempt to embellish my social skills for the interview. I had received *the call* from Washington D.C., where I now lay convalescing, in May of 1979. I was twenty-seven and desperate to establish myself. Primarily, in the pursuit of an older woman's love. I had always subscribed to romance as a core motivator and believed there wasn't much redemption forthcoming without the love of a woman.

Naive perhaps, but in the scheme of metaphysics, a world above existential embitterment, fundamentalism, or ripping chicken heads to Afro-Cuban incantations.

I had been working one day a week as a *studio* cameraman at a local station in Miami, thanks to the kind reference of a good friend in the business. Otherwise, I parked cars, *again*, to make the rent while hoping for a permanent five-day-a-week opening. And even though studio cameraman was quite the upgrade from parking ramp chimp, I found it a debilitating routine. The director telling me where to move on the studio floor through the headphones, and me, essentially, aping the same moves every time. The act for the six o'clock news consisted of pointing the camera at the anchorman, then panning to the *weatherman*, back to the anchor, then dolly back and boom-up during the commercial for a high angle, wide shot close and credit roll.

The weatherman, whose successors, for all their future gussying up with superior technical fripperies behind them, would still remain, with few exceptions, mostly dull witted and effete vulgarians. Fuckin' idiots in short—with the obligatory exceptions.

(A brief tangent, *if you will*. This weatherman's M.O. was the by-product of people who "think" they are funny. Standing before a blue chroma key wall, he would appear to the viewer and himself, by the grace of electronic TV wizardry, to tower over the republic, surrounded by cartoon-like puffy gray clouds, lighting bolts, golden rays on a smiling sun, or giant snowflakes for the northern end of the continent. From this absurdist domain, he'd song and dance, according to local weather conditions. Generally, sunny days turned these guys into elated jesters mincing their predictions with "charming" buffooneries. Foul weather changed them into groveling lapdogs of apology. As if bad weather wasn't in the universal scheme, especially on weekends. They lamented those rainy forecasts like mourners for hire at funerals of the well-to-do, a role played with relish by these climate Punchinellos and garnished with all-in-good-fun chiding from the news anchors. Maybe that's why these guys, at least the ones I met back then, were all rummies. Someday, we would boast of *weatherettes*—high-kickin', low roadsters and very distant descendants of the essential and entrancing, Salome Sisterhood of the Piquant *Duende*. Sheathed in chimp-kryptonite provocative-*erie*, these TV Tart versions would sashay about forecasting, while trolling for couch barney ratings, making our simple meats croon Frankie Zappa's "Let me be your G-spot tornado.")

I lusted for news camera on the street. Birddoggin' action. But in the street, you had to make decisions for yourself in the heat of the fight. Excuses for missing the pictures were for the most part non-existent. Job openings for the inexperienced were scant as well. Short of begging on my knees and offering to submit to unnatural acts, I had run the gauntlet of *cul de sac* interviews in Miami.

"I have the eye. I know I can do it. Just give me a chance!"

"I'm sorry. We can't take that chance. *Especially* when there are experienced applicants for the position."

"I'll work for half their pay?"

"You have the spirit, Luna. Can I call you Luna? I wish I could give you the opportunity. But really, I couldn't justify it, not with experienced applicants available."

"Can I intern for free?"

"Our intern program is for senior journalism majors. According to this application, you majored in art and…uh, still-photography? And you're…I mean, not *really* student age anymore. That doesn't mean you're over the hill, but…Did you try the Miami Herald? Perhaps they need a still-photog. Maybe you can come to television through the back door."

The only "back door" evidenced here was my Poop Chute in Fingerland. What exactly was "student age"?

So, when I finally boarded the not-yet-defunct Eastern Airlines jet to D.C. for *the* interview, sporting an itchy three piece, wide lapel, brown plaid Yves St. Laurent wool suit, I was not throttling up my expectations. Miami from the air looked like a giant computer chip. But in the light of my day-to-day life, it had shorted itself into a barren loop. In the aft station, I asked the stewardess for another coffee. I wanted to be fully awake for the fifteen rounder with Mr. Mittelman, Head of Electronic News Gathering.

"Cream and sugar?"

"Put in everything you got, baby. This bad boy's gonna hit D.C. like a hijacker on angel dust."

"That's not funny, Sir."

"Oh, don't be afraid. I'm just your everyday job applicant, jockeying for position. No need for the Sky Marshall here, Alarmée!

"The name is Aimée, Sir."

She handed me the coffee, turned sternly, and left without comment, as to not draw further exchanges. With a name like "beloved", *très* continental to be sure, I wondered who her fan club could possibly be? Ah, what the hell. We had all been adorable babies once.

When we flew over Lake Okeechobee, a thick flock of ibis flew with their matching black shadows on the scalloped water. I remembered the grisly scene of late nineteenth century bird slaughter in Marjory Stoneman Douglas's *The Everglades*. Egrets by the thousands, scalped for *fin de siècle* fashions. But that had been long ago. Now, Okeechobee was the homestead of sugar and cattle barons whose cavalier use of water and dispersal of pesticide, if unchecked, would soon turn the Glades into tainted beef jerky. A little further, the pilot did the Disney Shuffle on the P.A.

"Folks, we're now over the Magic Kingdom, home to Mickey, Minnie, Goofy, and so many other of our childhood friends…Kids, if you look to your left, you might even spot Tinkerbell."

Disney, in a swingy little free-form way, would somehow become a permanent part of my matrix, a rather sobering matter if you referenced it in terms of Disney being the cartoon version of the Jesuits.

Goofy had been the name of Dolores's dog, a cross between a beagle and a Great Dane and the grand court jester of the canine world, hands down. None of us knew which of the parents was the female, in short who mounted who, but either way, a Beagle-Dane coupling must have made one gravity-defying marvel. Dolores eventually had to put Goofy to sleep, due to painful spinal arthritis which degenerated into his near immobility. A pitiful occasion for her, the kids, and needless to say, Goofy, whose mournful eyes seemed to foretell his one-way trip when he glanced up from the prone position next to an untouched bowl of day-glo yellow Cheese Doodles in the back of Dolores' station wagon—a sun-faded ultramarine '75 Ford Country Squire with a 454 eight-banger and soft as toffee shocks. I had volunteered to chauffeur to the veterinarian so the family could surrender freely to the vagaries of emotion. Puzzled at Goofy's lack of interest in his favorite snack, whose bowl she had lovingly inscribed with, "*We'll see you in Heaven, Goof*," in multi-colored Crayola, the eight-year-old daughter, Kali, released the following question in a heart-rending crescendo, followed by a chest-heaving and tearful wail that tied my throat into a monkey's fist.

"Mommy, why won't Goofy eat his Cheeeeese Dooooodles?"

I knew melancholic review was inimical to the bullshit juice needed for the job interview ahead, an event that customarily demanded a vast measure of conspicuous "good cheer" about life in general, not to mention the dick-suck euphoria I should display at the mere likelihood of becoming one of their employees. My soul lapsed, putting me on my own perverse rendering of that old TV show, *This is Your Life!*

The announcer in my head continued, "*Then Luna, after a routine evening at your parking job, you visited your ex-lover's home, uninvited, and…*"

The uncensored scene I had witnessed through Dolores's window at the eleventh hour looked like this: her head was on his arm in post-coital snooze. Further down, a limp and gratified dick lay at rest on his slightly protruding lower belly.

I had cautioned myself from the get-go against stopping when I'd spotted his classic Porsche in front of her apartment building. Granted, I hadn't anticipated this scenario when passing her place in *my* German ride, a '62 VW with a rag sunroof, no passenger seat, but snappily carpeted with lime green shag, including the dashboard, also a classic—a backwater Hialeah Renaissance chariot I had bought for five-hundred dollars from a Cuban mechanic at a gas station across the Okeechobee Canal.

I had met up with Dolores again three years after she had been my teacher at a junior college. A custody battle for her two kids frayed her emotions on a daily basis. Long legs, deep soul, short fuse in the sack, sanctuary eyes, and the hands of perdition, I came over one night and had stayed for a year, never making it my "official" residence for obvious legal entanglements on her end. At that time, I had gone back to work as pool boy, so financially, I had been very day to day. Out of a sixty-dollar grocery bill, which I helped consume, I could perhaps offer a fiver. Yesiree, that gal had found herself a real *breadwinner!* She never asked me for money, but still, I felt like buzzard vomit. The last days had been painful for the now-parking attendant and the painting professor.

"You have places to go, Luna. The children and I would eventually become a burden. You'd resent it, trust me."

"But I want you there with me."

"That's what you say now, but I'm older than you by almost ten years, which might not matter now, sugar, but things change. Our needs change. In another ten years, maybe you'll want to be chasing young tail. I'm a little stronger now...I don't want to fall in love with you. If you left me years from now, it would destroy me, baby. We need to do what we need to do. Just remember, Mama loves you. I'll always love you."

Sometimes after these talks, Dolores wouldn't make love but go down on me like a head-on collision. I would later leave for my parking job, absolutely mystified."

When I had found out Dolores's new *beau* was an older local newspaper reporter, I didn't know what to do to become established. So, I agonized at the parking ramp in between cars, looking at my watch, thinking, *It's 8:05, and I'm still not established.*

Then *8:06, 8:07, 8:08*, and still not established, *8:09, 8:10*...All the way to eleven p.m. I couldn't wait till the next day, to see what I could do to get on the road to career ascendancy.

It was the late Seventies, and the ultra money-talks-bullshit-walks brutality of the 80's could already be heard whistling down from the skies like a payload of turd cluster bombs. I didn't see a way to break out of the bonds of minimum wage. The next day, more-of-the-same, with no immediate solution. And "immediate" was nothing short of *now. What the fuck was Luna the Art Major going to do?*

When I had stopped and bolted to the back window of Dolores's place, I had expected to maybe find the new-some two-some at a candlelight dinner, or perhaps sipping a cocktail? Luckily, I was spared them dining on each other. But the nude snooze had made me take off, spiked heart lodged in my throat, at sixty five miles an hour—a suicidal speed in that ancient VW—down a very residential area of Alton Road, running several red lights before a cop stopped me.

"Give me what tickets you want. I just found my girlfriend in bed with another guy, and I just want to get the hell home."

"Where does she live?"

"*Excuse* me, *fuckhead?*"

Fortunately, *that* question never left my lips. But had he tried me just a smidgen further, it surely would have, and a grizzly death, his or mine, would have transpired. When he witnessed my state of distraction, eyes focused tacitly on the ground, breathing deeply, he got the picture that I was already a man kicked, and he showed hitherto uncommon cop empathy.

"Listen, bud, take it easy. I'm not going give you a ticket, but do yourself a favor. Drive straight home. *Slowly.*"

Once home, I tore out murderous burning slivers from my heart for hours by sleepless hours, one by one and minute by minute. No end in sight. For months, I would do time in the Dungeon of Love. For me, Dolores had been, as also for many other male students, my college teacher fantasy, an extremely potent persona to shake in and of itself. But it had been precisely that spiked blow to the inner sanctum when it ended that had put me on this jet plane. To continue parking cars would have been impossible without a double lobotomy and an IV of lithium on a wheeled stand. I had sat too many nights at the ramp, slitting my wrists with unanswerable *whys*.

"*You have such a pretty cock.*"

Even now at 22,000 feet, a *year* later, *en route* to D.C., recalling one of her whispered observations doomed me to wonder if she was telling newspaper boy the same thing. But I caught myself at the very first curve of the caustic downward spiral.

Man, man, man! That ain't the way to get over. You're gonna go down. The *job*, man, the job is ev-ri-thing. You can't go back to her, you can't go back empty handed, you can't go back at all. Yeah, well, fuck her! Hey, hey, easy there, *Inamorato*. Don't pull out the heart spikes and fill the holes with shit. You'll rot, man, and the world will smell you coming.

Dolores, whether I would or could admit it, besides schooling me on how to lick a woman like I was playing a Stradivarius—no small gift, Cadets—had been a major help getting me here from poolside coolie, where I had taken refuge after another dead-end stab at a B.F.A., this time in Canada.

"Luna, your work is better than most of the scholarship applicants this year. You have a good chance. Get off your duff. You don't belong in this two-bit pool-boy job, baby. You're no punk, unless you want to be."

After culling my art portfolio, she had helped me receive a full art scholarship at the U, where I made it to the Dean's list a few semesters but unfortunately never graduated. I had a run-in with the teacher who pre-sided over a 100 level design course required to graduate. The Canadian credits had not converted evenly.

"The projects you did work on, you didn't complete adequately, and you never showed involvement in the other students' work."

"Then why didn't you…What kind of involvement? And Mr. Wretcharton, it wasn't 'several projects.' It was *two*, so why didn't you give me an Incomplete instead of a D?"

"I guess it was both our faults. We should have talked."

"Yeah, maybe so, but I'm paying a hundred percent of the conse-quences. *and* I owe ten G's in student loans from the other schools."

"You can always take the course again."

"I think it would be easier for you to change the letter grade to Incomplete, then I could just finish the two projects"

"No, I can't do that. I've already sent it in. I don't change grades."

"Even when *you* make a mistake?"

"Whether *I* made the mistake is arguable. You have the option of taking the course again. What is non-negotiable is a grade change. I can't."

"Believe me, I understand about can't because I can't take another semester of a 100 level shit-sack-fossil design course like yours."

"Don't burn your bridges ,Luna.

"Mr. Wretcherton, somebody needs to torch your calcified lard ass, never mind about bridges."

I never went back to school, except for what was to be my last visit to Dolores's office, which incidentally was adjacent to Professor Wretcherton's painting studio. There, while I heard Professor Wretcherton assigning homework for the summer course I never signed up for, she regaled me with a last Dear-John cardiac-arrest blow job. *Ho ho ho, fuck you and the sophomoric tempera jar you rode in on, Mr. Wretcherton.*

"We will be landing in the nation's capital in approximately twenty-five minutes."

Oh yeah! Exorcising demons left and right, five miles high over Land-of-the-Free Headquarters—Washington D.C., where rags-to-riches were both dream and reality. Either way, a thrilling enclave of sex, violence, and the pursuit of alcoholic beverages whence to greet *Terra 2000*.

Hey *Play-Doh*, you're not applying for philosopher king. Keep your mind on the gig, ten-four? Still seat belted in my seat, my mind doing figure eight tangents, I quizzed myself on the equipment I had "used" in Miami.

Camera? *RCA TK 76.*

Recorder? *Sony BVU 3800.*

Mikes? *Sennheiser 416, Ecm 50's* and a *635 Electro Voice.*

I went through the warning lights, filters, and white balance—things that I had learned about professional video cameras only the week before on a crash course with the night crew. It had not been easy to line-up the sights on this interview. After I had sent my paper resume, Mr. Mittelman, the head of E.N.G., had made other requests by phone.

"Please send us a resume reel."

"I don't have a resume reel. We mostly do live-shots, and I haven't kept stories."

The latter an astonishing hill of Lunar shit, ladies and gentlemen.

"I'm sorry, but without a reel, we don't hire anyone."

"Okay, I'll dig one up one up for you."

Dig one up, *literally.* I didn't have one. Never shot news. Never held a news camera on my shoulder etc. So afterhours, I went into the news file library, grabbed some file footage, and took it to one of the editing rooms, on the lookout so nobody would catch me. Although, if someone barged in, "I'm using the stories to practice editing."

Dig?

I dubbed me four stories me thinks were good and show variety, then made two copies. One I kept to study, and the other one I mailed up to Mittelman, in whose hometown I was about to presently land. The pilot put on his tour guide hat once more.

"In the distance to our left, you can see the White House, home to the Commander in Chief."

A portly fellow in the seat in front of me, wearing suspenders, a Stetson above a sweaty neck, and three-pound double chin, who had been tipping Jim Beams since Pompano Beach, quipped his observations on the Commander in Chief to his lady companion over the pilot's announcement.

"And self-professed lusty-hahted peehnut fahmeh. Laydis, keep yo fannies to the fuselage wall. Or Jimm"ll dew dee yew wud hee's dewin' to the owal endistree."

A few chuckles, then some heads turned toward Tex from seats in front of him. Some smiled. Some frowned. Oh yeah, we had arrived in the land of *which side are you on?*

My cab rounded DuPont Circle—at this time of year, accented by multicolored tulips in full bloom. A soothing effect. I loved those flowers. They reminded me of old *National Geographic* pictures of beautiful, full-lipped Dutch girls in blonde pigtails. If you stood by the tulips, you could just about hit Luis' sister's brownstone with a rock, which was where I would be staying tonight, in the very heart of our capitol's opulent hearth.

A few miles ahead, the cab pulled into the parking lot of a fairly run-down strip mall off western Connecticut Avenue where the station was located. My heart raced. I paid the cabbie, took some deep breaths, and entered the station.

I walked down a long hallway whose walls were lined with giant photographic portraits of the station's local Broadcast Gods *de jour*, a risky Olympus where a few negative rating points could result in the twilight of their reign. I approached the receptionist.

"Hi, I'm here to see Mr. Mittelman."

She pecked the intercom code, smooth as a concert pianist.

"Mr. Mittleman, your *first* summer relief interview has arrived."

She seemed to have a slight smirk after she said, "your *first*," like I was only one in a long line of hungry lampreys.

"Please have a seat. He'll be right with you. You can help yourself to some coffee, if you'd like."

She delivered that line with the emotion of a rubber stamp and then marked off what I imagined to be my name from a small list with an impeccably manicured hand. I had to piss.

"Thank you. I already had some. Where is the restroom?"

"You don't seem too observant for a news cameraman."

"What d-do you mean?"

My voice quaking. The adrenalin made me frisky. My hands had already been clammy.

"Oh, I'm just joking. You passed the restrooms on the way in on your right."

I turned and walked toward the men's room, controlling an impulse to piss on her desk. Like I needed her dumb, stupid, un-*fucking*-solicited secretarial shit-assed jokes... *Take it easy, Goddamn it.* In the bathroom, I focused on the stream bouncing off the fresh urinal puck, which helped to transcend the vexing. Luna, the Urine Roshi. I breathed deeply and tried to relax while re-playing in my head the individual stories on the resume reel I had sent: a fire, a press conference, a feature on a legless guy who pushed himself around with his hands while sitting on a skateboard. *Smell the fire...Feel the guy's pain...RCA TK76, Sony BVU 3800...Uh...! Sony 200 Editing console...Relax.*

When I returned, Marty Mittelman, the rodent-esque head of E.N.G., was waiting for me. After the hellos, we walked in his office, where a soft-spoken black man was introduced to me as Cedric. They went to town on my paper resume. I did the *Truth or Consequences Shuffle*.

"So, where did you go to school. I see here you have a BFA?"

"I took my first TV courses at the community college, then I went to Rochester Institute of Technology, where I received a scholarship for photography and film making, but I found the course a bit dry, so I decided to come back to Miami, and after a few months, I received a full scholarship for photography to the U, so I went and graduated there."

(The real deal wuz: in college, I had majored in art, took one (1) studio TV course, found the class and the people homicidally retrograde, and quit in two weeks to do the nude girl in the box, Port a' Tart—my entry into the student art show. Got a scholarship to RIT, where I was pummeled by photo science courses, little of which I retained except for a treasured hand job provided by Melinda, a photo business major. God bless her Midwestern little heart with sundry celestial merits. RE: At the U, I did receive a full scholarship <u>and</u> a Fear O' God B.J., gents, but never a BFA.)

As I answered each of Mr. Mittleman's questions, I had to simultaneously slay all the real content, from my answers appearing in my head, which darted to and fro after every question like spooked truth dragons, singeing my continuity with their fiery and italicized snorts and chortles. Cedric, the gentle-spoken black man, just watched me. Mittleman resumed the questionnaire.

"Tell me a little about your professional life, you know, the work at the different stations, the commercials that you shot?"

"There's not *that* much to tell. I worked the studio at Channel 23, the Spanish network affiliate, and when needed, I would go into the street. I liked it, and they liked what I shot, so when the opportunity came up to shoot some in house and location commercials for a food manufacturer and a jewelry shop, they asked me to do them."

(I had never *gone into the street. I had been lucky to get a studio camera job at Channel 23, since I had bullshitted my way in then, as I was trying to do now, attempting to overcome the barriers to employment due my shortcomings, like having no experience, and hopefully thwart off what most likely would end up in terminal job desperation hell. The "commercials" were, one, a plate of black beans and rice on a table surrounded by the canned brand name shot overhead from the roof of a house in Hialeah, very near where I had purchased my iniquitous, though utilitarian, VW Ship of Love. The other commercial: a "journalist" from the Spanish station stood in front of a Cuban jewelry shop, Joyeria "El Trompón", and displayed various bracelets and rings on himself. For the ending, I zoomed into a close-up of an oversized,*

gold Saint Lazarus hanging from a half-inch thick chain, encircled by the standard number of the folkloric Saint's wound-licking dogs. All this nestled in a veritable rainforest of the reporter's very own thick, black chest hair. Oh Yeah! Real Mahdisong-avenue, Tigre!)

"Why did you leave? Where did you go after Channel 23?"

"There were no permanent positions for news camera at 23, so I applied at…"

(At Ch.23, I had been fired for saying out loud exactly how I felt about their programming. Evil tongues bearing me ill will took it to management. Synopsis: One day, just to fight boredom during the inspirational message, "con el Padre Elixe," the TV pastor, I side lit the crucifix, and it cast a long German expressionist shadow across the background. Miguel, a studio cameraman with a formidable paunch, who wasn't even taping the show, comes up and says, "Luna, you and your Existentialist lighting techniques. Just light it like always. This is Catolicismo Romano, no Existencialismo." Incidentally, every time some well-endowed female guest would happen on the set, this dogmatic imbecile would verbalize his erotic fantasies to me, which customarily involved lapping Cuban food from their erogenous parts.

"Pa' echarle un arroz con frijoles por las tetas!"

To his rebuke on my "existential lighting," I had answered, "No te tires los pedos mas altos que el culo Miguel" (a Cuban expression regarding farts intended to deflate delusions of grandeur), then proceeded to explain that "the only reason the station stays on the air and you have a job, is largely owed to the 'nivel cultural' of the majority of the non-English speaking Cuban audience who has remained culturally rural. And besides all that, this is the only Spanish speaking 'gasolinera' in town, so everyone is gonna fill up here. It had all been down hill after that. Miguel was the news director's ass-lick yes-man. On the day I got fired, I went into Miguel's locker and twisted a pair of 14 kt. gold frame prescription Ray Ban sunglasses into a figure eight, then hung them on the air conditioner vents horizontally, echoing the symbol for Infinity, a terminal while infinite gesture. Luna, Master of the Koan Riposte.)

"So, it was a hard job to leave. I had made a lot of lasting friendships at Channel 23, but for the sake of my career, I had to move on to where I am now."

"What kind of equipment are you familiar with?"

"*RCA TK76* camera, *Sony 3800* recorder, and the *Sony 200* editing console, where I cut pieces for the 11 o'clock news."

(I had only looked through the camera once—when one of the guys let me peer through the viewfinder before a press conference. I had carried the recorder from the truck to the conference and watched the soundman ride the audio levels, pointing out to me where the needles should range. Then, I would bring them coffee. The editing console? I knew just enough of the right buttons to push to dub someone else's stories—with which I presently scammed.)

Cedric, the black guy who up to now had just been listening, threw in a wicked curve.

"Why did you roll *out of focus* on the legless man story?"

My head took the hairpin turn at a hundred and fifty mph. But I had done my homework. I knew the shot he was talking about, so luckily, I didn't lock the brakes.

"Well, I try to be artistic when I can. It was a…a transition. When I have time, I like doing that, a bit off the beaten path for 'news,' but when it won't mess up the deadline, uh…but for that guy, it was worth it. Man, that guy had more spirit than all of us with legs, so naturally, I wanted to go the extra mile."

"No pun intended, right!" Brother Cedric said.

Mittleman chuckled. My heart sighed with relief. Thank you, Brother Cedric. Mittelman looked at his watch. I side glanced at mine. It had been a forty-five minute ass-drenching bout.

"Well, I think it's time for lunch. What do you say, Cedric?

Mittelman wanted to wrap it up. Cedric extended the invitation to me. My Bro…

The three of us walked down the Corridor of TV Idols, past the receptionist, who now wasn't taking so many liberties. She sat typing and glanced at me, trying to salvage a stitch of her bulwark authority. She knew after someone got hired, the gate keeping party was over with that individual.

We crossed the street to a pub decorated in that spurious hearth ambience that a lot of white-collar alkies are fond of for lunch. You know, red brick walls, brass details at the bar, potato skin side dishes, nacho chips, and $1.50 Margaritas at Friday happy hours. I went to take another piss. The bathroom was wallpapered with sepia prints of "old" barbershop ads claiming five cent shaves, and the rest of that *fin de siècle* drek. But I am ashamed to admit that at this point, I wanted to be part of all this, mostly the paycheck, of course. I visualized myself coming to lunch here, working news, having a modest apartment nearby. Hey, life wouldn't be so bad for the ex-parking attendant art major.

Back at the table, I ordered a Bass ale and a cheeseburger. Mittelman ate a Caesar salad. He had quite the spare tire to police. Cedric ordered some soft-shell crabs, straight out of the Chesapeake. He was a jazz fan, so we talked about 'Trane, of course, and one of my favorite tunes was also Cedric's, "Out of This World"…and Roland Kirk and Monk. Here Mittelman's white ass was left out, so I went into a fishing tableau, which he loved, although I suspected he wasn't all that at the pole.

"When I was thirteen, my Dad took me to Bimini."

"Bimini?"

"Yeah, this little Bahamian island surrounded by some of the clearest water in the world."

"What a great name."

Mittelman, now enchanted, took a good pull of the martini, ready to head to the tropics. Apparently, he wasn't about to submit to the salad Calvary without some kind of distilled redemption.

"It was the cleanest turquoise water I'd seen since leaving Cuba. When we arrived at the dock on our first afternoon there, I saw a three- to four-hundred pound black fin tuna that had a bite mark the size of a small truck-tire missing from its side."

"What the hell was it?"

"The dock master said it was a big mako shark."

"Wow! That's fishing, man! I'm gonna have to see when I can break away from here to get some of that action. I've never done any saltwater fishing!" Mittelman drew closer to me. "And make sure I have enough cash, too, so I can leave the little woman shopping in Miami."

"If you hook up to a black fin tuna, you won't forget it. They can sprint fifty miles an hour. You better eat your Wheaties."

"What a bear!"

Mittelman drained the martini and started on his rabbit food. I turned to Cedric, who was just finishing the last piece of crab.

"What's a good jazz club here? Maybe I'll go with my buddy tonight."

Cedric told me about a club whose name I forgot three minutes after he told me. Presently, my whole existence awaited the *Yey* or *Nay*. We stepped outside, and Mittleman got all business-like after he paid for the bill.

"So, Luna, we'll let you know within the next week if you got the job. We have two more interviews today, and—"

"Mr. Mittelman, I'd like to know tomorrow because I have an interview in New York, and I'd rather not spend the money, and I don't think it's fair to the other employers, you know, for me to fly there and offer something that might not happen because I think I would prefer to work in this town."

"Okay, I'll see what I can do."

After they left, I went back inside the bar and had another ale. Mr. Mittelman had swum off without feeling me set the hook. Apparently, I was getting more accustomed to dancing on the plank. I took the bus to Georgetown, went around the back of Luis's townhouse, found the key under the plant pot where he had said it would be, and I let myself in. It was warm and humid. I switched on the central air, got down to my underwear, pulled a beer out of the fridge, and crashed on the plaid couch after I drank it. An hour and a half later, I woke up to Luis opening the front door.

"Make yourself at home…How did it go?"

"I feel like I just ran up here from Miami. I feel slow, I had an ale with lunch, and the beer here kicked my ass."

"I got some Cuban coffee if you want to make some."

"Yeah!"

I walked to the kitchen and packed the coffee maker with the main bean.

"They took me to lunch. I seemed to get along with both of them. They said they'd let me know in a week, but I said I wanted to know tomorrow."

As we finished our coffees, the phone rang. Luis picked it up.

"It's for you?"

I grabbed it.

"Luna, it's Mittleman. Congratulations, you got the job."

"Great! Mr.Mittleman, thank you very much…Two weeks, okay? Thanks, again. I'll be here!"

I hung up the phone.

"Yes! Yes! Yes! Fuck parking another car! Fuck paperboy paramour. Fuck the woooooorld!"

"Hey, keep it down. The neighbors will have a shit fit. Remember, this is my brother-in-law's place."

"Fuck him! C'mon, I'm gonna take you to eat somewhere, pop a beer. Let's toast this muthafuckaaah!"

"Luna, stop yelling, man."

Luis, a handsome ectomorph with hazel eyes and a concave chest, was looking full on law student with his wire rim glasses and tapered khaki chinos.

The cuban coffee kicked in and we power-walked we power-walked to M Street in Georgetown, where I noticed the inordinate number of women to guys. "Eight to one," my friend told me. And most of the "ones" these girls had to choose from were government geeks in a wardrobe of conservative suits and low paychecks. After eating and drinking like pigs, apropos for the *Pie de Cochon* Restaurant, I spent the last of my savings. Two hundred had gone for plane fare, thirty to taxis, and now the last sixty for two onion soups, veal Francaise, my friend's beef tournedos, a bottle of burgundy, several Courvoisier VSOPs, two espressos, and a couple of Royal Jamaicans (still made in Jamaica) for the walk home on Q street. Luna, Cuban Carnegie Lite for a Night.

Ah yes, the feeling of employment! I marveled at all these fine solid red brick northern homes, with maples, oaks, and wrought iron fences, bay windows glowing golden in the night, and at a stone's throw, panda bears in the zoo. I drew in a rich pull from the Royal Jamaican Gold Parklane. And for an instant, the demons dozed. But it was the promise of a real job, not this manicured and coveted enclave, that seemed to lift years of parking ramp excreta off my heart while I toured this *Nirvana Patriciana*.

Back at the townhouse, Luis pulled out the sleeper-couch. He was not allowed to sleep in the master bedroom since the maid had come and prepared the bed for his sister and brother-in-law due in the next day. He threw a pillow on the carpet for me. I perused the liquor cabinet, found half a bottle of Cardenal Mendoza, and poured us a nightcap—quite an improvement over the V.S.O.P. for my taste at this hour. I lay down on the carpet, and we reminisced about Cuba. Somehow, we got into the subject of childhood outfits. I told him about my Indian outfit and the Indian moccasin story. He told me about his army green *miliciano* get-up and a *matador* outfit he had owned. I told him that I had read somewhere that the bull fighter was the *aspecto femenino* of the bull/man duet, what with the frills, the lace, the grace...

"Hey, Luna, I ain't no faggot! Fuck all that Freudian baggage."

Had I inadvertently tapped into a homophobic streak at 2:00 a.m.?

"That's not what I meant. I meant compared to the bull, you know, brute force, raw emotion, and then the bullfighter, the cape, the stockings, the moves, the finesse demanded, the elegance. It's definitely the feminine aspect of the pair."

"Hey, fuck you, man. You're the faggot! If you don't like that, we'll step out in the patio! I'm not gonna stand here and allow you to sully my character."

Sully his character? Drunk fucking law student *speak,* completely insufferable, especially at this hour and stage of the game.

"Listen, Luis, bro. I just got *the* job. I'm feeling *a*-typically on top, and that's the way I want to go to sleep. I promise you that if you still take umbrage in the morning, I'll provide you satisfaction, after coffee, Sir Barrister."

"No, man, that's bullshit. Just because I had a bullfighter outfit when I was young, *ahora soy maricón?* All this noveau analysis can get pissed on. It was probably a faggot that came up with that. They think because *they're* fags, *every*body is a fag. The new Annotated *Fag* History of the World..."

After a few more disgruntled passages, Luis fell asleep.

The next morning, potential duel forgotten by both parties, he made breakfast, *huevos rancheros,* and he took me to the airport. He apologized. I guess Luis had been a little rattled. What with the long, boring and *tang-less* study and research hours at the law library, the short cash flow, and helping his younger brother get through a nasty barbiturate addiction back in Miami, he had a full house. And *shit* did have a habit of piling up right at the crusty and permanently frayed contacts of the tolerance capacitor.

I would return within two weeks in mid-April to triumph over my first Career Dragon through the summer and fall to a background of Donna Summer's "Badgirl," the Commodores's "Brick House," and myriad Twilight-of-Disco favorites. But one evening, two weeks before Christmas, nearly at the end of my first TV job tour, I hit an oak tree doing forty-five on an icy stretch of Rock Creek Parkway *en route* to cover the return of the beaten Redskins at Dulles Airport for the ABC affiliate I was working for. But just to prove that not all that had been stuffed in my stocking fell from the hand of Calamity at the end, a fresh dusting of snow would blanch the streets, cars, and trees below my hospital window. It was Christmas Day, and now even the garbage cans had a halo.

I still lay with my leg in traction, convalescing from a dislocated hip, torn pectoral muscle, and a nearly healed fractured nose. I had told Dolores that my underwear had been cut off in the emergency room, so she had sent me a little bottle of baby powder and a neatly folded new pair, tied with a ribbon. "For your cutest of butts. Get well soon, baby cakes. Merry Xmas, Mama Dolores." After opening a few more greeting cards, I opened an envelope containing my pink slip from the station, announcing that regretfully, they could not hire me full time. It was postdated two days before Christmas!

And so dragons begot other dragons. All you could do was to keep your lance sharp, your aim true, and if possible, your ass talcum-ed. Riots, war, and *force majeur* calamities simmered over the horizon. Soon, my leg would be good enough to mount the indomitable Steed of the Fates again. Luna, the Errant Knight of Gimpville. I tried to humor myself, though in all honesty, the future seemed rather bleak and the ending anti-climactic.

But early in the morning, two days after New Year's, a petit doe-eyed Filipino nurse, with a Hindu goddess hinny, came in to help me dress on the day I was dismissed. She leaned a pair of wooden crutches against one of the closet doors. I sat on the side of the bed, still in my gown.

"Where do you keep your underwear?"

I pointed to the night table.

"Oh, I'm sorry. I don't do baby powder," she smirked. "Hmm! Someone tied your skivvies with a ribbon?"

"A gift from an old flame."

She handed me the crutches. I felt dizzy sitting up. She untied the ribbon, got down on one knee, slipped first one of my legs, then the other through the underwear, and pulled them up toward my hips.

"I imagine the more you lied, the more she loved you."

I had never unwrapped Dolores's tissue-wrapped undies. Pinocchio's face was printed on the front, but from my vantage point I couldn't make out the title below it.

"The Nose Grows," she clarified, giggling and shaking her head, Heaven and Hell in her slightly Asian eyes, and pinching the tip of her rose-colored tongue between her teeth, that last move dispatching an immediate nut buzz despite my atrophied state…

* * *

Luna, indisputable Rabbit's Foot Incarnate and temporarily crippled Network News hopeful, hobbling down the snow-laden sidewalk toward the Eastern Airlines counter, still smarting a bit after a lovesome three night stand at the nurses' cottage, could attest that his heart was still hot and humming the latest arrangements of that duplicitous god called life.

www.ingramcontent.com/pod-product-compliance
Lightning Source LLC
LaVergne TN
LVHW011415080426
835512LV00005B/74